The Politics
of Consumer
Protection

The Bobbs-Merrill Policy Analysis Series

The Politics
of Consumer
Protection

Mark V. Nadel

Bobbs-Merrill Educational Publishing
Indianapolis

James A. Robinson
CONSULTING EDITOR IN POLITICAL SCIENCE

Thomas R. Dye
GENERAL EDITOR, *The Bobbs-Merrill Policy Analysis Series*

Copyright © 1971 by The Bobbs-Merrill Company, Inc.
Printed in the United States of America

The Bobbs-Merrill Company, Inc.
4300 West 62nd Street
Indianapolis, Indiana 46268

Library of Congress Catalog Card Number: 78–170712
ISBN–0-672-61223-2 (pbk)
ISBN–0-672-51415-X

Fifth Printing—1978

For Beverly: a frequent consumer

Foreword

The aim of the Policy Analysis Series is the systematic explanation of the content of public policy. The focus of the Series is on public policy choices of national, state, and local governments, and the forces which operate to shape policy decisions.

Books in the Policy Analysis Series are not concerned with what policies governments *ought* to pursue, but rather with *why* governments pursue the policies that they do. Public policies are not debated or argued in these volumes, rather they are assembled, described, and explained in a systematic fashion.

Each volume deals with an important area of public policy—education, taxation, economic opportunity, agriculture, urban problems, military affairs. Each volume treats public policy as an output of political systems, and endeavors to explain policy outputs with reference to historical, environmental, political, and cultural forces which generate demands upon political systems. Each volume attempts to employ systematic comparative analysis in the explanation of public policy. This involves the comparison of policies past and present; the comparison of policies generated by national, state and local political systems; and the comparison of the effects of political, environmental, and cultural forces in the shaping of public policy. Each volume strives for improved theoretical statements about public-policy determination.

Thomas R. Dye

Preface

A few years ago it was commonplace to lament the fate of the consumer in the policy process. Consumers were unorganized, amorphous, and generally voiceless in the nation's important political arenas. While all citizens are consumers, their role as consumers was not believed to be as important to them as their role as producers. Producer interests were considered to be only really influential actors in the policy process.

Yet today consumer politics is popular with the news media, the rhetoric of consumer protection echos from the White House to Capitol Hill, Ralph Nader has become a household word, and Congress has acted in several key areas—automobile safety, truth-in-lending, and drug safety—to protect the consumer.

What accounts for the increased popularity of consumer politics? How do consumer interests become political issues? Does consumer protection differ significantly from other policy areas? Is a crisis or scandal essential for the passage of consumer legislation? What is the role of the publicists—the Ralph Nader types—in consumer policy? Exactly who are the important participants in consumer politics and how do they act to achieve their goals? Have executive agencies been responsive to the interests of consumers or have they been immobilized by pressure from producers? Is it essential that a consumer protection policy coincide with the interests of a particular producer before it can pass Congress? What other factors affect the outcome of battles over consumer policy?

These are a few of the questions dealt with by Professor Mark V. Nadel in *The Politics of Consumer Protection*. This volume provides a concise history of consumer protection policy, a description of the development of current interest in consumer issues, a critical analysis of the role of Congress and executive agencies in consumer protection, and an examination of the role of the press and the new consumer advocates in the policy process. These discussions are enriched with specific case studies of the Pure Food and Drug Act Amendments of 1962, the Consumer Credit Protection Act (truth-in-lending), and the National Traffic and Motor Vehicle Safety Act. Finally, the author provides interesting beneficial discussions of the allocation of costs and benefits in consumer policy, and the problems of representing an unorganized public interest in the policy process.

Thomas R. Dye

Acknowledgments

The research for this book was originally done while I held a Brookings Institution Research Fellowship, and I am greatly indebted to The Brookings Institution for providing financial support, facilities, and a most stimulating year. I particularly wish to thank Gilbert Steiner, director of governmental studies at Brookings, for his comments and aid throughout various stages of this project. Additional financial assistance was provided by the Meigs Fund at Cornell University.

This book would have been impossible without the cooperation of more than seventy interview respondents. For their generous assistance beyond the call of duty for interviewees, I appreciate the help of Michael Pertschuk, general counsel of the Senate Committee on Commerce; former Commissioner James Nicholson of the Federal Trade Commission; Erma Angevine of the Consumer Federation of America; and Evelyn Dubrow of the AFL-CIO.

Two of my former teachers at Johns Hopkins University, Francis E. Rourke and Milton C. Cummings, gave me an extraordinary amount of assistance in writing an earlier version of this manuscript. I always profited from their advice even though I was not always wise enough to heed it. I am also grateful to three colleagues at Cornell, David Danelski, Barbara Hinckley, and Robert Weissberg, who read parts of a later draft of this manuscript. They spared my readers (and myself) from much confusion and unnecessary verbiage.

Three research assistants worked at various stages of the research and manuscript preparation. Eric Freedman and Debra Levin performed a variety of research tasks and were a constant and delightful reminder of the interests of undergraduates. Gary Reichard greatly aided in the research on the history of consumer protection.

While I gladly give credit for improvements in this book to my earlier critics, the responsibility for any of its faults of course belongs to my wife, Beverly, without whom this book probably never would have been written.

Ithaca, N.Y.   Mark V. Nadel
March 1971

Contents

Tables

Introduction

Consumers, by definition, include us all. They are the largest economic group in the economy, affecting and affected by almost every public and private economic decision. Two-thirds of all spending in the economy is by consumers. But they are the only important group in the economy who are not effectively organized, whose views are often not heard.

—President John F. Kennedy
Special Message on Protecting
The Consumer Interest
March 15, 1962

When President Kennedy sent his first consumer message to Congress in 1962, no one could seriously dispute his statement that consumers were not "effectively organized" and their views were "often not heard." The power of consumers in the economy was a subject of contention, but the lack of consumer pressure in government was universally acknowledged. Yet, only eight years later, consumer protection controversies regularly surfaced in the news, a Republican President had a special assistant for consumer affairs, and Ralph Nader had become a household word. Consumers today may or may not be organized, but it can no longer be said that their views are not heard.

Vexing questions remain, however. The prevailing conceptual framework in which politics is studied provides both theory and data on the activities of pressure groups pursuing their own narrow and particular interests. Although all such groups regularly equate their own interest with the widest possible consumer interest, this is generally regarded as mere window dressing designed to advance their special claims. The manner in which a truly wide interest is pursued is not so well known and is little studied. Consumer legislation has been passed. Consumer protection policy is carried out within the Executive Branch. Who has been responsible for pursuing the consumer interest? What are the techniques utilized in this activity? Is the policy process in consumer protection different from that in other areas? These particular questions revolve around the central concern of this book—the role of consumers in the policy process. Specifically, this study presents an analysis of the formation of consumer protection policy in the federal government with emphasis on the manner in which participants claiming to represent such an amorphous and all-inclusive group as consumers mobilize their resources and pursue their goals.

Before proceeding further, a few words of definition are in order. As it is sometimes used, the term, *consumer* is so broad as to be meaningless. All business firms are consumers as much as they are producers. Moreover, a variety of things are consumed that we do not ordinarily think of as products, such as air and water. To refine and limit the notion of consumer, that term will be applied here only to the ultimate retail noncommercial consumer. Rather arbitrarily, this rules out such issues as conservation where no voluntary purchase is made.

Furthermore, since this study is concerned with the consumer interest as a universal interest, we are examining only those consumer protection issues which affect goods and services normally purchased by nearly all family units in the United States or which can reasonably be considered to have that potential. Thus, such important issue areas as the regulation of the securities market and the sale of cigarettes are not covered. This limited definition is in keeping with the common understanding of the term *consumer protection* by the press, the public, and politicians.

Since the basic thrust of this volume is to examine the way in which a particular type of interest is articulated and represented in the policy process, it is important to note two major characteristics of consumer interests which both round out the previous definition and which provide the rationale for this study. First, the consumer interest is a collective or a public interest. Since every person is a consumer, policy which benefits the consumption pattern of citizens and protects them from untoward effects of their consumption is a policy which benefits all citizens. Given this benefit, it is a policy in which all citizens—the public—have an interest. It is therefore a public interest or part of the larger public interest. Secondly, the consumer interest is an interest of relatively low intensity and salience. That is, while all citizens are consumers, their role as consumers is not nearly as important to them as their role as producers in the one field in which all their income is received.

In having these characteristics, the consumer protection issue is similar to other issues such as pollution and taxation which affect all citizens but which normally, and over a long period of time, are not the key motivating factors behind the polictiial activity of the citizenry. Although it is not precise, the term *unorganized interests* can be used as a shorthand reference to this type of interest.

In the pages that follow, the fate of the consumer interest in the policy process will be examined. Chapter 1 traces the history of consumer protection politics and policy in the United States and provides a basis for historical comparison while Chapter 2 brings the issue up to the present time and discusses the factors associated with the emergence of consumer protection as a current political issue. Chapters 3, 4, and 5 analyze the activities of various types of consumer activists— those whose efforts are directed toward the implementation of consumer protection policy. The analysis centers on selected participants in the Executive Branch, the Congress, and nongovernmental groups, including the press. Although certain questions vary with the group under discussion, basically the discussion of the participants proceeds in pursuit of the following questions: Who are the relevant participants? How are their goals articulated? How do they proceed to achieve those goals? With whom do they interact? What are their resources and liabilities? How successful are they, and what accounts for that success?

Chapters 6 and 7 will be an overview of consumer protection policy that results from the activities examined in the preceding chapters. The output of policy will be gauged against the original intent of the consumer activists. Finally, the study will conclude by hazarding generalizations applicable to the articulation and representation of a public interest.

The Politics
of Consumer
Protection

chapter 1

Consumer Protection in History

The Early Antecedents

While consumer protection sprang up as a newly discovered issue in the 1960s, its apparent novelty was deceptive. Rather than being a new issue, it was one which was dormant for almost thirty years. In its broad form, consumer protection has been a governmental responsibility and a subject of intermittent public concern since the earliest years of the Republic.

In taking this brief look backward, it is profitable to consider consumer protection policy in the context of the general pattern of government intervention in the economy since consumer protection is ultimately one form of government regulation of economic activities. In spite of the growth of the doctrine of laissez-faire in the late nineteenth century, state and federal governmental concern with the economy extends back at least to the very first years of the Republic. Indeed, some historians—most notably Charles Beard[1]—contend that the Constitution was designed to give positive government protection to the economic interests of the men who drafted it. One need not enter that hoary argument, however, to note that there are several traditional

[1] *An Economic Interpretation of the Constitution of The United States* (New York: Macmillan, 1913).

governmental functions related to the economy. Emmette Redford has
labeled these as the "core of government" functions which are to maintain order; administer justice; provide a money system; provide a postal
system; provide certain facilities of commerce such as patents, copyrights, and uniform weights and measures; protect the home market
and promote foreign trade; and provide internal aids to commerce such
as building roads.[2]

In the federal government the controversies surrounding such
early economic issues as tariffs, internal improvements, and the Bank
of the United States are well known and need no recounting here.
Suffice it to note that the Constitution, particularly article I, section 8,
makes ample provision for Congress to intervene positively in national
economic life and that the history of United States governmental regulation of economic activity extends at least as far back as the third
clause of that section empowering the Congress "To regulate Commerce with foreign Nations, and among the several States, and with
the Indian Tribes."

It was in the states that the greatest measure of government participation in the economy took place. Studies by Oscar and Mary
Handlin, Louis Hartz, and others make it clear that from the Revolution
to the Civil War the states were extremely active in the promotion and
regulation of commerce. Indeed, Hartz concludes that in its efforts to
encourage economic development, the state of Pennsylvania's economic
objectives "ramified into virtually every phase of business activity, were
the constant preoccupations of politicians and entrepreneurs, and they
evoked interest struggles of the first magnitude."[3]

In this early period, governmental participation was not for the
purpose of protecting consumers except as such policy was purportedly
designed to aid a general public interest which included consumers.
Nonetheless, like later regulatory legislation, a variety of state and
national policies coincided with a broad consumer interest and most

[2] *American Government and the Economy* (New York: Macmillan Co., 1965),
pp. 7–9.

[3] Oscar and Mary Handlin, *Commonwealth: A Study of the Role of Government in the American Economy: Massachusetts, 1774–1861* (New York: New
York University Press, 1947); Louis Hartz, *Economic Policy and Democratic
Thought: Pennsylvania 1776–1860* (Cambridge: Harvard University Press,
1948), p. 289.

economic issues involved costs or benefits for consumers. We can return to the Constitution again for an illustration of this phenomenon. Among the enumerated powers of Congress is the power to "fix the Standard of Weights and Measures." While this authority is clearly designed to aid in the orderly flow of commerce, it incidently provides protection and convenience for individual consumers who then had a uniform basis of comparison in their shopping.

In the states, there were more overt manifestations of government services for consumers. Thus, Pennsylvania had an extensive amount of regulatory activity in the early nineteenth century including the inspection of various foodstuffs, leather, tobacco, lumber, liquor, and gunpowder.

While such activity benefited consumers, that was not its primary purpose any more than that benefit was the purpose of the commerce clause. Rather, it was a manifestation of the belief in the orderly development of commerce as a positive good and as a common good. The benefits that accrued to consumers were incidental to the prime purposes of the legislation.

While there was no overt articulation of a general consumer interest in the period under consideration, the crucial issue of tariffs brought forth a long series of legislative struggles involving an important component of that interest. Being an exporter of raw materials and an importer of manufactured goods, the South naturally fought (unsuccessfully) the tariff bills of the Northern manufacturing states. Switching the perspective from negative to positive, the Southern congressional leaders can be seen as fighting for lower cost manufactured goods and thus actively pursuing the consumer interests of their constituents. Of course sectionalism per se was an important factor in the tariff controversies and consumer protection was not the prime consideration behind the efforts of John C. Calhoun and other Southern leaders. However, like state regulatory provisions, the consumer interest was carried under the umbrella of other interests and purposes.

In general then, in the early nineteenth century consumer protection was not an explicit concept, but rather a governmental function which occurred incidental to other aspects of governmental intervention in the economy. A more explicit form of consumer protection began after the Civil War and it is at that time that familiar and recurring political patterns emerged.

The original thrust for post–Civil War regulatory activity came from farmers, particularly the Grange organizations. The initial governmental concern with the railroads in the early nineteenth century was directed toward providing for their development and expansion. State legislatures granted charters and franchises to railroad companies and subsidized them directly or indirectly. However, by the late 1840s the rose had lost its bloom. Railroads had been guilty of a number of abuses, most notably discriminatory pricing practices and exorbitant rates in some cases. Resentment against these practices boiled over into political action and the result was the passage of the "Granger laws" in Midwestern farm states in the 1870s and 1880s.

Even during the time of state regulatory activity, however, farmers and commercial interests were turning to Congress for federal regulation. Between 1868 and 1887, more than 150 bills for railroad regulation were introduced in Congress. In 1886, the need for congressional action became apparent as a result of the Supreme Court's decision in the Wabash case. The Court held that the states could not regulate interstate railroad traffic within their own borders, even in the absence of congressional regulation.[4]

At that time, there already were separate bills passed by the House and Senate which were apparently deadlocked in conference committee. The Wabash case added a sense of urgency and a greater incentive to compromise. Both chambers made concessions and on December 15, 1886, the conference committee reported out the bill which became the Interstate Commerce Act of 1887. The act forbade certain railroad practices such as rate discriminations. Secondly, it set up a regulatory commission to administer the act.

The passage of the Interstate Commerce Act is significant in the development of consumer protection for two reasons. First it was a landmark bill being the first comprehensive regulation of a particular industry. Second, it established the Interstate Commerce Commission and established the precedent of the independent regulatory commission. This development was by no means the intention of all those who favored regulation. There was considerable argument about the relative

4 *Wabash, St. Louis and Pacific Railroad Co.* v. *Illinois,* 118 U.S. 557 (1886). This was a serious retreat from the Court's earlier position in *Munn* v. *Illinois* and the other *Granger* cases that the states had limited authority to regulate interstate commerce. 94 U.S. 113 (1877).

merits of various enforcement schemes, and it was not until later that the independent commission caught the fancy of Progressives as a mechanism to insulate regulation from "politics." Nonetheless, the form had been set and it proved to be a momentous precedent in its implications for later enforcement of the law.[5]

The Twentieth Century: Food and Drugs

In considering the major episodes of consumer protection activity in the twentieth century, we are for the most part considering a different type of policy. Where the drives for regulatory and antitrust policy were in response to perceived economic abuses, the emerging modern packaged goods economy of an increasingly specialized society allowed new abuses of a different sort. These involved the safety and wholesomeness of foods and medicines produced in bulk and sold in an increasingly urban society in which most citizens no longer raised their own foodstuffs. In short, the two most extensive and heated periods of consumer protection activism prior to the 1960s involved the attempts of the federal government to protect consumers' physical safety as well as their economic well-being in their purchases of foods and drugs in an impersonal market. While the regulatory drive discussed above formed the institutional patterns of present consumer protection policy, the food and drug controversies discussed below established political patterns of policy formation as well as institutional forms whose parallels were seen in the later periods of consumer activism.

The first major federal legislation in this area was the Pure Food and Drug Act of 1906. Before examining the legislative history immediately preceding passage, it is useful to review some of that legislation's precedents which reveal early patterns of policy formation. In the late nineteenth century two types of policy developed with respect to foods. The first arose in response to adulterated and synthetic food products—products which either deceived the consumer who unknow-

---

[5] For a complete examination of the commission form of regulation see Robert E. Cushman, *The Independent Regulatory Commissions* (New York: Oxford University Press, 1941), and Marver Bernstein, *Regulating Business by Independent Commission* (Princeton: Princeton University Press, 1955).

ingly paid real food prices for imitation products or dealt a competitive disadvantage to farmers and others dealing in original or unadulterated products. The form of governmental response to these problems was primarily based on the taxing power. In 1895 and 1896, the federal government levied taxes on mixed flour, filled cheese, oleomargarine, and renovated and adulterated butter. Needless to point out, the impetus behind these measures come not from consumers, whose interests would have been protected by merely requiring truthful labeling rather than by raising prices. Rather it came from farmers whose markets were being invaded by the cheaper substitutes. Indeed, restrictions on margarine exist in the major dairy states even to this day.

The second type of policy, a direct antecedent of the Pure Food and Drug Act and its amendments, was inspection—mainly meat inspection which, with the exception of banking regulation and railroad regulation, is the oldest of American regulatory systems. In 1865, Congress passed a law preventing the importing of diseased cattle and swine. In 1887, agents of the commissioner of agriculture began the surveillance of animal disease. In 1884, a Bureau of Animal Industry was established in the Department of Agriculture to control the health standards of cattle exports and, in 1890, all exported meat was inspected. In 1891, this inspection was extended to cover live animals at the time of slaughter and included most of the cattle designated for domestic interstate shipment. In 1895, the enforcement provisions of the meat inspection laws were strengthened.

While the various meat inspection provisions up to and including the Meat Inspection Act of 1906 were consumer protection measures in the sense that at least some health standards were applied, there were also considerations of competitive advantage. The heavy emphasis in early legislation on meat standards for exports lends weight to Gabriel Kolko's emphasis on the role of the meat packers themselves in instigating early legislation out of a need to maintain their position in the world market.[6] Again, consumers were brought under the umbrella of some commercial interests although American consumers had to wait in line behind foreign consumers of American products.

Quite apart from developments which led to new forms of compe-

[6] Gabriel Kolko, *The Triumph of Conservatism: A Reinterpretation of American History,* 1900–1916 (New York: Free Press, 1963), pp. 98–100.

tition, the major developments of the food industry posed serious problems for consumers. The centralization of the industry, the development of refrigeration and the use of preservatives led for the first time to national distribution of products by individual firms. The most typical problems revolved around the use of chemicals to disguise otherwise stale or rancid foods. Because the centralization of the industry had nationalized problems, state regulation was inherently ineffective. Nonetheless, many state legislatures did pass laws dealing with adulteration. However, slack enforcement often made such laws ineffectual—a precursor of a recurring problem in consumer protection. Furthermore, just as in the field of state railroad regulation, the Supreme Court struck down such state regulations holding that goods shipped in their original packages in interstate commerce were exempt from state interference.[7] Once again, economic and technical growth created a new problem for consumers and the states were rendered powerless to take effective remedial action. Political pressure started to build.

The earliest pressure came from farmers. In order to protect their interests, farm organizations in states where they were politically strong brought about the creation of state departments of agriculture with the power to take action against the sellers of imitation or adulterated farm products.[8] As the need for a national law was increasingly perceived, the state agriculture department chemists organized themselves as the National Association of State Dairy and Food Departments and proceded to lobby vigorously for a national law to succeed state regulations.

The prime mover behind the Pure Food and Drug Act was clearly Dr. Harvey W. Wiley, then chief chemist for the United States Department of Agriculture. For several years preceding passage in 1906, he was the nation's leading crusader for a pure food and drug law. He carried his appeal before both Congress and the public, and the two forums frequently intertwined as they would for Ralph Nader sixty years later. To a large extent, Dr. Wiley's effectiveness lay in the publicity and even sensationalism he was able to mobilize for his cause.

---

[7] *Rhodes* v. *Iowa*, 170 U.S. 475 (1898) and *Leisy* v. *Harden*, 135 U.S. 100 (1890). This doctrine has been called the "original package" rule.

[8] Thomas A. Bailey, "Congressional Opposition to Pure Food Legislation, 1879–1906," *American Journal of Sociology* 36 (July, 1930): 44.

For example, Wiley testified before the Senate Committee on Manufacturers during the committee's investigation of food adulteration in
1899 and 1900. He was rather conservative throughout the investigation, and stated that while most foods had been subject to adulteration
at some time or another, the amount of debased goods on the market
was very small—in the range of five percent. However, either by
design or accident, newspapers quoted him as reporting that ninety
percent of the food on the American market was adulterated. Naturally,
public opinion became aroused and the problem generally began to be
conceived of in terms of the public welfare rather than as simply a
problem between competitors.[9]

Wiley's fame and publicity for his efforts especially increased as
a result of the "poison squad." Wiley had set out to investigate em-
pirically the effect of preservatives on humans. To accomplish this, he
had a group of volunteers, young men in the Bureau of Chemistry,
eat a strictly supervised diet with measured amounts of preservatives. These experiments caught the popular imagination more than
anything else the bureau had previously done. Although Wiley tried to
tone it down, the resultant publicity was flamboyant and some of it
tended to ridicule the project. Nonetheless, Wiley found that the experiments gave him a topic of wide appeal and they aided in awakening
the public to the problem.[10]

Citizens' groups were active in the struggle for legislation. The
joint effort of the Federated Women's Clubs of America and the Consumers League of America, a labor-oriented organization, was considered by Dr. Wiley to be the most forceful of the private lobbying
efforts.[11] Health organizations also added to the pressure for the bill
and several observers credited the American Medical Association with
playing an extremely important, even decisive, role.[12] Although the
AMA's role seems strange today in the context of its performance on
present public health questions, it should be pointed out that a major

[9] Oscar Anderson, *The Health of a Nation: Harvey W. Wiley and the Fight for
Pure Food* (Chicago: University of Chicago Press, 1958), pp. 130–131.

[10] Ibid., pp. 150–152.

[11] Harvey W. Wiley, *The History of a Crime Against the Food Law* (Washington: Harvey W. Wiley, 1929), p. 52.

[12] Bailey, "Congressional Opposition to Pure Food Legislation," p. 44.

target of the AMA's efforts were the patent medicine manufacturers who were important competitors for the consumer's health dollar at that time.

Prior to final success in 1906, the House had twice passed pure food legislation with no action taken by the Senate. In 1905, however, the campaign began in earnest and President Roosevelt delivered a message urging passage of pure food and drug legislation. Senator Heyburn who had sponsored earlier legislation reintroduced the legislation in December, 1905. As previously, the opposition was led by Senator Nelson Aldrich, a former wholesale grocer. However, by now the support for the bill was greater and there was a greater degree of public interest in the measure. In February, 1906, the American Medical Association put direct pressure on Aldrich and this pressure was apparently effective. Rather than holding fast against the entire omnibus bill, the opposition senators managed to remove one major provision which forbade false advertising of foods and drugs. Removal of this provision occurred along with several other weakening amendments and the opposition gave way allowing the bill to pass easily on February 20. This time, however, the House stalled the bill. With the end of the legislative session nearing, the situation looked bleak since, if the House failed to act, the bill would have to start from scratch during the next Congress.

Then Upton Sinclair's *The Jungle* was published. Revealing the filth in which the nation's meat packing supply was surrounded, it came as close as any book could have to horrifying the nation and intensifying the demand for legislation. While Sinclair meant his work as an attack on capitalism and not simply as an exposé of the meat packing industry, the effect was the same. President Roosevelt was shocked no less than other citizens, but he did not act until he received advance copies of three magazine articles based on an investigation of the meat packing industry by Sinclair's publisher which corroborated the conditions described in *The Jungle*. He appointed Charles P. Neill, the U.S. labor commissioner, and James B. Reynolds, a New York reformer, to make a thorough study.

The resulting report of Neill and Reynolds was a document which again validated the charges made by Upton Sinclair. Although the *Jungle* episode and its aftermath are popularly associated with the passage of the pure food and drug law, these events are more directly related to the Meat Inspection Act of 1906. However, President Roosevelt was able to use the scandal to good advantage in simultaneously pressing for passage of meat inspection and pure food and drug legislation. In May, 1906, Senator Alfred Beverage, with the blessing of President Roosevelt, drafted a meat inspection law and succeeded in attaching it as an amendment to the agricultural appropriation bill for that year. It passed the Senate but as it went to the House an effort was made by the House Agriculture Committee to emasculate the amendment. The President had not yet released the Neill-Reynolds report, realizing that the report was itself far more damaging to the meat packing industry than any legislation might be. Finally, when it appeared that the delay might be indefinite, President Roosevelt delivered the preliminary report to Congress and the Beveridge amendment was quickly adopted.

Although the meat packing scandal concerned matters most directly related to the Meat Inspection Act, the resulting political pressure was nonetheless also directed to the pure food and drug bill languishing in the House. According to Oscar Anderson, President Roosevelt "seemingly roused by the heat of battle" began to directly pressure House leaders, particularly Speaker Cannon, on behalf of the pure food bill.[13]

For purposes of the present study, the major question is why had the pure food bill finally passed. The efforts of the President, Dr. Wiley, and medical and women's groups have already been cited. Also, the publication of *The Jungle* and its aftermath seem to have provided a dramatic moving force behind passage and these circumstances yield a compelling parallel to the publication of Ralph Nader's *Unsafe at Any Speed* and the subsequent passage of automobile safety legislation in 1966. However, *The Jungle* was not the whole story, but rather a symbol and culmination of more basic forces behind the struggle for consumer protection legislation. These forces were public opinion aroused by muckraking journalists and the era of Progressivism.

Public opinion played a great role in the success of the legislation and muckrakers must be given prime credit for arousing that public opinion. As C. C. Regier pointed out, the prime cause of muckraking in the Progressive era was the rise of cheap mass market magazines

[13] Anderson, *The Health of a Nation*, p. 190.

which were made possible for the first time by developments in printing and paper production in the late nineteenth century. After initially attempting to compete by cutting prices, competition between the magazines centered on the content of copy.[14] The sensational exposures of the muckrakers became good copy and, after 1903, several popular magazines devoted themselves wholeheartedly to muckraking articles. In short, the very process of muckraking was fueled by the fact that it was in the commercial self-interest of the magazines to publish these materials and thus it became consistent with the self-interest of the writers to produce the stories.

Although other reform-minded articles had been appearing for the past few years, the muckraking era really began with the October, 1902, issue of *McClure's* which published "Tweed Days in St. Louis" by Lincoln Steffens and announced that in the next issue it would begin the serialization of Ida Tarbell's now-famous *History of the Standard Oil Company*.

Along with political corruption and general corporate abuses, the purity and safety of foods and drugs and frauds associated with foods and drugs were major themes of the muckrakers. The *Ladies' Home Journal* and *Colliers* became the leading magazines in the campaign against patent medicine fraud. In 1905, Samuel Hopkins Adams wrote a series of articles in *Colliers* entitled "The Great American Fraud" in which he graphically described the contents and costs of popular patent medicines. This series was widely read and, among other articles, is credited with being an important element in the campaign for legislation.[15]

In general, business bore the brunt of the muckrakers' attack. In words which sound disturbingly familiar today, Regier notes that:

> The muckrakers discovered that the great corporations were behind the corruption in municipal, state, and national politics, behind the suppression of liberal magazines, and the perversion of news, behind the pollution of foods and the misrepresentation of medicines. It was

---

[14] C. C. Regier, *The Era of the Muckrakers* (Chapel Hill: University of North Carolina Press, 1932), pp. 10–21. This is still one of the best accounts of the subject.

[15] Louis Filler, *The Muckrakers: Crusaders for American Liberalism* (Yellow Springs, Ohio: Antioch Press, 1939), pp. 152–153.

the opinion of most of the muckrakers that almost all the evils of American life were directly traceable to the aims and methods of industrialists and financiers, and it was in the hope of arousing public opinion and thus changing these aims and methods that they did their work.[16]

Progress and industrial development were increasingly perceived not as a blessing but as a threat. In a revolt against big business and its attendant corruption, intellectuals and political leaders turned to the government and to new political forms for protection. Muckraking was thus part of a larger social, intellectual, and political development—the Progressive movement. Indeed, Richard Hofstadter asserts that Progressivism largely rested on its journalism and that the crusading exposures of Progressive journalists were the "fundamental critical achievement" of American Progressivism. He credits muckraking for providing the information and exhortation which gave vague grievances specific objects and bringing the "diffuse malaise of the public into focus."[17] This journalistic linkage between information and political action is an important theme and one which recurs in consumer protection politics.

Just as muckraking was a central feature of Progressivism, so too was the cause of pure food and drugs championed by the muckrakers. Even among historians with different interpretations of the Progressive impulse, there is general agreement that the crusade for clean meat and pure food and drugs was an integral part of the spirit of Progressivism.[18] In its broadest form, the Progressive spirit was popularly seen as the struggle (or occasional triumph) of "the people" against the "special interests." Where earlier consumer protection measures were not instigated by consumers, but by competing interests, the Progressive crusades were generally perceived in terms of regulating industry for the common good. While some later historians interpreted the era as a "triumph of conservatism" with the same factors of competitive disadvantage still behind consumer legislation, nonetheless consumer

---

[16] Regier, *Era of the Muckrakers,* p. 201.

[17] Richard Hofstadter, *The Age of Reform* (New York: Random House, 1955), p. 186.

[18] See, for example, Kolko, *Triumph of Conservatism,* p. 98; Rexford G. Tugwell, *The Democratic Roosevelt* (Garden City, N.Y.: Doubleday, 1957), p. 464; and Hofstadter, *Age of Reform,* p. 172.

protection was then perceived as part of a general reform movement.[19]

At the end of the nineteenth century, consumers were not even recognized as a group with common interests. In 1897, when Louis Brandeis testified on behalf of consumers before the House Ways and Means Committee against the Dingley tariff he was met only with jeers. Although consumers still did not act with common economic purpose, by the time of the debate on the pure food and drug bill it was apparent that consumers were a legitimate political force of some importance. In the Progressive movement, consumer interests were important because, as Hofstadter notes, consumer consciousness was the lowest common denominator uniting different classes of people. Reformers began increasingly to talk about the "common man," the "taxpayer" and the "consumer" rather than just about the working class or the middle class. Emphasis on broad interests such as that of consumers increased the political appeal and force of Progressive leaders.[20] Therefore, the consumer protection issues at the beginning of the century were not in a vacuum. Rather, they were part of a broad reform movement which helped create consumer awareness and which capitalized on that awareness.

Although the period between the Progressive era and the New Deal was devoid of any major consumer protection crusades or legislation, changes in policy were attempted and some amendments were passed. In 1911, the Supreme Court emasculated the already modest labeling provision of the Pure Food and Drug Act by ruling that it did not prohibit false therapeutic claims. Urged on by President Taft, Congress responded with the Sherley amendment which explicitly prohibited "false and fraudulent" curative claims. Dr. Wiley, however, pressed for a much stiffer amendment, but met with no success. In 1927, the Food, Drug, and Insecticide Administration (later the Food and Drug Administration) was established to take over enforcement of the legislation from the Bureau of Chemistry.

The major campaign launched by advocates of expanded consumer protection in these years centered on standardization of containers and quality grading of food. In the years prior to World War I, several acts were passed regulating and standardizing the size of some containers. But containers were not the chief problem in the eyes of

---

[19] Kolko, *Triumph of Conservatism*, pp. 98–110.

[20] Hofstadter, *Age of Reform*, p. 172.

reformers, whose real aim was to establish national standards of quality for food. Though largely unsuccessful, they met partial success in the McNary-Napes amendment of 1930. The amendment empowered the secretary of agriculture to establish standards of quality, condition and fill for canned products below which they had to be labeled as substandard. However, this was a case where the consumer interest was somewhat coincident with the interests of industry—in this case large canners who sought protection against competition from the lowest quality canned goods.[21]

In general, vigorous consumer protection activity died with the Progressive movement and the onset of World War I. The business dominated spirit of the 1920s also effectively muted any articulation of consumer interests. It was not until the depression and the New Deal that the consumer interest again emerged as an important political factor and the paramount consumer legislative issue was again food and drugs. The crusade was led this time by Rexford G. Tugwell, a member of President Roosevelt's "Brain Trust," who was serving as assistant secretary of agriculture. Shortly after the onset of the new administration, Tugwell received authorization from Roosevelt to undertake a revision of the food and drug laws. The staff assembled under Tugwell quickly concluded that merely amending the 1906 law would be insufficient due to restrictive court decisions and problems arising in the interval since 1906. Tugwell solicited the opinion of trade groups and businessmen, but kept them in the dark as to the emerging provisions as the new bill was being drafted. This, plus perceptions of Tugwell as a wild socialist and ivory-tower professor, made industry instantly suspicious. Indeed, when the bill was revealed, the most troublesome factor in achieving any initial acceptance was that it had become known as the "Tugwell bill."[22]

There were additional problems in building support for legislation. Unlike the situation in 1906, there had not been a gradual buildup of support or a growing perception of a need for legislation. Indeed, there was a widespread belief that food and drug problems had been resolved with the 1906 act. Although there was a new brand of muckraker in

21 John M. Gaus and Leon O. Wolcott, *Public Administration and the United States Department of Agriculture* (Chicago: Public Administration Service, 1940), p. 176.

22 James Harvey Young, *The Medical Messiahs* (Princeton: Princeton University Press, 1967), p. 160.

the 1930s, they were confined to periodicals of limited circulation and books such as Ruth deForest Lamb's *American Chamber of Horrors*. Moreover, periodical and newspaper publishers' associations actively opposed the bill because of its regulation of advertising. There was even an almost total blackout of news about the emerging bill.[23] Thus, the potential for public pressure was greatly reduced. The most visible and strongly felt pressure relating to the bill was that of the opposition and Tugwell even had trouble securing a Senate sponsor. Finally, Senator Royal S. Copeland agreed to sponsor the legislation.

The original Tugwell bill went far beyond the existing legislation. It contained a much tighter definition of mislabeling, and labels would be required to state ingredients and whether the drug was habit forming. Many dangerous substances such as radium were to be banished. So-called medical devices came under the provisions of the bill. For the first time, the places of manufacture of proprietary medicines would be subject to inspection. The major change, and the one which was one of the key objects of political pressure was the prohibition of false advertising—a prohibition to be enforced by the Food and Drug Administration. The original bill held advertisements to the same standards as package labels.

Hearings were first held on the bill in 1933. The general posture of the drug industry on the bill can be summed up in the dire verdict of the general counsel of the Proprietary Association: "I have never in my life read a bill or heard of a bill so grotesque in its terms, evil in its purpose, and vicious in its possible consequences."[24] Copeland modified the bill in 1934, but industry opposition was not ameliorated.

Although there was less public enthusiasm for the new law than in 1906, the familiar pattern of support did emerge. One of the most effective tactics in arousing public and congressional interest was the "Chamber of Horrors" assembled by the Food and Drug Administration. This was a series of posters graphically demonstrating that self-medication still posed great hazards to Americans. Documented by bottles, advertising, labels and death certificates, the posters showed cases of horrible disfigurement, blindness, poisoning, and death caused by some unregulated drugs and cosmetics.

[23] Arthur M. Schlesinger, Jr., *The Age of Roosevelt: The Coming of the New Deal* (Boston: Houghton Mifflin Co., 1958), p. 359.

[24] Quoted in Young, *Medical Messiahs,* p. 167.

Women's organizations again played a leading role in lobbying for the Tugwell bill and the American Medical Association was also behind the bill. Although consumers were still not organized, Consumers Research had been formed and it was aggressive, even uncompromising, in support of reform. ·

But, in spite of the growing broad-based support, the Tugwell bill still could not pass. It was reintroduced in modified form in 1935. The proprietary manufacturers countered with a bill of their own and continued in opposition to Copeland's bill. This time, Consumers Research considered the modified bill a complete sellout and opposed it as worse than no legislation.

By 1935, there were two basic issues. The first was the multiple seizure power of the Food and Drug Administration to confiscate all retail supplies of drugs found to be in violation of the law. This issue was soon resolved largely in favor of the drug industry and the seizure power of the FDA was limited. The second issue was advertising. If there was to be any control over advertising, the industry preferred it to be lodged in the more lenient Federal Trade Commission rather than the Food and Drug Administration. Although a compromise on this issue was reached in the conference committee in 1936, the issue in the House was still posed in terms of making Rexford Tugwell "czar" of advertising and the bill went down to defeat 190–70.

In 1938, the way was finally paved for passage of the bill when the advertising issue was resolved. A separate measure, the Wheeler-Lea amendment to the Federal Trade Act, assigned responsibility for advertising to the Federal Trade Commission.

While a major roadblock was thus removed, a positive impetus toward final passage of legislation came with the elixer sulfanilamide tragedy. The "elixer" was a sulfa drug with diethylene glycol as a solvent. It was never tested for safety and it was not until after it was marketed that the manufacturer learned that the solvent was toxic. One hundred and seven persons died as a result of taking the drug. When it was learned that the FDA could act on this situation only after the fact and only because of a technicality (the only violation of federal law was that the drug was mislabeled as an "elixer"), a great deal of public pressure was generated.

The House and Senate again passed different bills, with the House bill considerably the weaker of the two. This time, in the wake of the elixer sulfanilamide episode, the conference committee version was more in line with the Senate bill and both houses accepted it. The President signed the Federal Food, Drug, and Cosmetic Act into law on June 25, 1938. The new law went considerably beyond the original act of 1906. Its scope was wider in that cosmetics and medical devices were included. The misbranding provisions were tightened and the government no longer had to prove fraudulent intent in cases of false therapeutic claims. Drugs which were dangerous even when taken as directed were prohibited, and appropriate warnings were required on all drugs. The common names of all substances in drugs were required on labels. New drugs could not be marketed until previously proved safe—the lack of such a provision allowed the elixer sulfanilamide tragedy to occur. The definition of food adulteration was expanded and all coal-tar dyes for foods had to be certified as safe. Finally, the FDA was given power to obtain injunctions against the sale of products it found hazardous.

Unlike the cheerful optimism accompanying the passage of legislation in 1906, there was considerable grumbling by consumer advocates over the compromises reached in the 1938 act. Tugwell, who had left the Agriculture Department prior to final passage, accused Congress of selling out to "every shabby interest that had appeared, shamelessly and openly." He concluded that "The Food, Drug and Cosmetic Bill as it passed in 1938 was a discredit to everyone concerned with it."[25] Nonetheless, many of the basic provisions of the original Tugwell bill had been preserved, and the bill in substance was an unquestioned improvement of the existing legislation. The weaknesses in the 1938 legislation became the subject of the controversy in the early 1960s when the safety of drugs again became a major congressional issue.

The New Deal

Although the 1938 legislation represented the only consumer protection action of Congress, there were also some attempts to protect the consumer interest in the expanded bureaucracy of the New Deal. While the Department of Agriculture's Bureau of Home Economics and the

[25] Tugwell, *The Democratic Roosevelt*, p. 464.

Labor Department's Bureau of Labor Statistics officially had the consumer interest as one of their concerns, the first explicit representation of consumer interests occurred in mechanisms attached to three New Deal agencies: the National Recovery Administration (NRA), the Agricultural Adjustment Administration (AAA), and the National Bituminous Coal Commission.

President Roosevelt created the Consumers' Advisory Board (CAB) of the NRA even though its establishment was opposed by the NRA administrator, General Hugh Johnson, who viewed it as "consumer interruption" of NRA code proceedings. Partly for this reason, the board had almost no influence in protecting consumer interests in the drafting and administering of NRA codes. But the more basic reason for the board's lack of influence was that while the NRA code-making process reflected largely the power of organized pressure groups channeled through the industry and labor advisory boards, the Consumers' Advisory Board had no such organized backing. Consumers had no articulate or organized group at that time. Effective organization was limited to a few women's groups, cooperatives and Consumers Research, Inc. However, their efforts were uncoordinated and had only limited objectives.[26]

The board tried to overcome its lack of an organized constituency by trying to establish a national network of countywide consumer councils to inform the public of NRA activities and to persuade them to assert the consumer interest in those activities. Professor (later Senator) Paul H. Douglas was brought in to head the project. However, although approximately 150 local groups were set up, they did not provide effective pressure and the project eventually fizzled out.

By 1935, the CAB achieved slightly more influence in hearings on code revisions, but after the Supreme Court declared the NRA to be unconstitutional in May, 1935, the CAB was dissolved. It was somewhat reconstituted as the Consumers Division of the remnants of the National Recovery Administration where its role changed from advocacy to study. However, it soon withered away.

The President also instituted consumer representation in the Agricultural Adjustment Administration over the objection of its admin-

26 Persia Campbell, *Consumer Representation in the New Deal* (New York: Columbia University Press, 1940), pp. 59–61.

istrator. Conflict was inevitable since a primary purpose of the AAA was to raise farm prices. The conflict usually pitted the consumer interest, represented by the Office of Consumer Counsel, against the better-organized interests of farmers and distributors, and adjustments were usually worked out between the latter two at the expense of consumers. The conflict was inherently insoluble and after its functions were gradually attenuated, the office devoted its attention to consumer education. In 1941, some of its functions were transferred to other agencies and, in 1945, the office was terminated.[27]

An Office of the Consumers Counsel was provided for in the Bituminous Coal Conservation Act of 1935 and in the substitute act of 1937. It was the only New Deal consumer representation agency that had been established by Congress. The counsel was to be appointed by the President and have an independent appropriation for his office. He was required to represent the consuming public in all commission proceedings and to carry out independent investigations. However, he had no voting power in the commission nor any direct decision-making power.

Like the other consumer representatives, the counsel was largely ineffective because of the hostility of the Coal Commission. The counsel succeeded in delaying some price-fixing agreements which he deemed detrimental to the consumer interest, but he was unable to stop most agreements to which he was opposed. He also attempted to arouse the concern of consumers by circulating a newsletter and by getting a variety of people to testify at commission proceedings. However, the response of consumers was apparently minimal. One observer attributed this largely to the complexity of fixing coal prices. Although this was an important subject for domestic consumers, there were other, easier to comprehend, matters which claimed public attention.[28]

The Coal Commission was abolished by President Roosevelt in 1939 and the Interior Department was made responsible for administration of the Coal Act. The independent status of consumer representation came to an end as the functions of the consumers counsel were assumed by the Solicitor's Office in the Interior Department.

[27] Consumer Advisory Council, *First Report, October, 1963* (Washington, D.C.: Government Printing Office, 1963), pp. 27–28.

[28] Campbell, *Consumer Representation,* p. 97.

In general, all the consumer boards and counsels were primarily interested in the economic aspects of consumer protection. They were concerned with the prices set in the various codes and agreements. They were largely ineffective as a result of the opposition of administrators reacting to pressures from industry and labor constituencies, even though they were established precisely to counter those pressures. In 1940, when the National Defense Advisory Commission was established, it included a consumer commissioner who was supposed to be equal in power to the commissioners for industry and labor. In fact, he also was overwhelmed, and the whole venture ended with the end of World War II. From then until 1962, the only formal representation was in the Council of Economic Advisors which sporadically had a Consumer Advisory Committee from its inception in 1947.

The Administration of Policy

Although the passage of legislation was once regarded as the end of the battle for the establishment of policy, that supposition has long since been discarded by scholars and practitioners alike. Thus a brief recounting of the history of the administration of consumer protection policy is particularly relevant here. As before, we will consider the Interstate Commerce Commission first since it was the first of the consumer protection bureaucracies and because both through legal precedent and bureaucratic tradition it typifies the other regulatory agencies.

In his classic study of the ICC, Samuel Huntington recounts a pattern of agency action and accommodation which has become common in regulatory agencies.[29] For the sake of convenience, I will follow Huntington's division of the agency's history into two periods. The first of these was from the agency's establishment in 1887 until the end of the first World War. During that period, political support came from the reform groups which had fought for the establishment of the agency, and opposition to the practices of the commission came from the railroads and the courts whose rulings frequently hampered the commission. As was the case previously, adverse court rulings led to de-

---

[29] Samuel Huntington, "The Marasmus of the ICC: The Commission, The Railroads, and the Public Interest," *Yale Law Journal* (1952): 467–509.

mands for further legislation. Under pressure from President Roosevelt and the consumers of railroad services, Congress expanded the commission's authority in 1906 with the Hepburn Act.

Although the commission was vigorous and even vigilant during its early years, even then the seeds of future trouble were being planted. The first chairman of the ICC was Judge Thomas Cooley who brought great prestige to the new agency. However, he continued to maintain a judicial orientation in his approach to the work of the commission. Although the regulatory commission concept was chosen for the ICC in order that it could avoid the inherent complexities and unwieldiness of direct legislative or judicial regulation, Judge Cooley from the start opted for a case-by-case approach to regulatory matters. Precedent, loosely interpreted, rather than rules was the guiding principle behind the commission. Thus, the regulatory policy of the commission was largely influenced by the individual composition of the commission rather than by any ongoing previously determined policy decisions. The ICC has continued in this mold and the other regulatory commissions have also followed the ICC practice.

It is unfortunate that the independent agencies developed as they did because this led them to fall far short of their potential to pursue novel or even rational policies. Furthermore, it was a decided step back from the ideal pursued by the original reformers. As Marver Bernstein noted, the ICC "regarded itself as a tribunal for the adjudication of disputes between private parties, rather than an aggressive promoter of the public interest in railroad transportation."[30]

This departure away from a self-conception as promoter or protector of the public interest is significant and its significance is seen in the second stage of the commission's history—1920 to the present. After the worst abuses of the railroad's had been corrected by the commission, there was less motivation for the continued existence of a reform coalition. Also, the period of the 1920s heralded a return to "normalcy." With regulatory fervor declining, the ICC turned to the railroads for support. In the lexicon of the classic syndrome, the ICC had been "captured" by the industry it had been charged with regulating. Whereas prior to the 1920s the railroads had opposed the commission at every turn, they now praised the commission, defended

---

[30] Bernstein, *Regulating Business by Independent Commission,* p. 29.

its independence, and supported expansions of the agency's power. This support was not motivated by any change of heart in the railroad men. Rather, it was a reaction to ICC policies which proved highly beneficial to the railroads. Samuel Huntington lists three major areas of ICC protection of the railroads. First, after 1920, the commission consistently granted fare and rate increases to the railroads which brought the ICC into conflict with shippers, price stabilization agencies, and state and local regulatory bodies. Secondly, the ICC has helped the railroads avoid the strictures of the antitrust laws by amplifying loopholes in the Interstate Commerce Act. Thirdly, the ICC has consistently promulgated regulations giving the railroads a competitive advantage over truck lines and water carriers.[31]

This brief account of the ICC is sufficient to emphasize the trend of regulatory agencies—they shift from regulator to partner of the regulated. With some variations, this trend can also be seen in the two agencies considered in greater detail in this study, the Food and Drug Administration and the Federal Trade Commission.

The pattern was slightly different in the case of the Food and Drug Administration which was more a case of regulatory weakness resulting from outside pressures rather than from a purely reciprocal relationship between agency and industry. The enforcement of the Pure Food and Drug Act was initially undermined by President Theodore Roosevelt himself. Angered at Dr. Harvey Wiley's statement that saccharin might be injurious to health (the President's doctor gave it to him every day), Roosevelt appointed a five-member board chaired by the president of Johns Hopkins University, Ira Remsen, to monitor and "review" the decisions of the Bureau of Chemistry (the predecessor agency to the FDA). Although such a board was not even provided for in the law, the secretary of agriculture followed the board's advice in almost all conflicts with the Bureau of Chemistry. In sum, two-thirds of the prosecutions recommended by Wiley were overturned by the Remsen board. Wiley resigned in protest in 1912.

The pattern of lenient enforcement was not the work of venal men deliberately undermining a congressional mandate. Rather, they viewed regulatory authority in a different light than did the Bureau of Chemistry. They were more willing to trust the good faith of the manu-

---

[31] Huntington, "Marasmus of the I.C.C."

facturers, and consequently they were inclined to place a greater burden of proof on the government. Thus, they frequently urged the overruling of Bureau of Chemistry decisions, which rested on what they considered an insufficient probability of danger of food additives. The issue of the sufficiency of proof and the degree of probable danger thus emerged early in the FDA's administrative history and has remained an issue ever since.

The belief in the good faith of industry translated into a doctrine of voluntary compliance held by a string of administrators who held sway at the FDA from 1926 through the 1960s.[32] Basically, the doctrine of voluntary compliance meant that the regulatory agency should not act as a police or enforcement agency, but should use a variety of techniques of cooperation, including compromise, to obtain compliance with the law. Persuasion rather than reliance on sanction becomes the basic orientation. While cooperation and voluntary methods are intuitively pleasing in the American ethic, it does seem somewhat strange that so great a portion of an agency's energies are devoted to persuading people to obey laws that they are obligated to obey anyway.

A second recurring theme in the FDA's administrative history is its lack of financial resources to execute its responsibilities adequately. Of course, small budgets are not independent of voluntary compliance. If an agency does not have the money to enforce the law, it has little choice but to hope that everyone will obey on good faith. The FDA, however, has considered this necessary evil a positive good.

Nevertheless, it is significant that the doctrine of voluntary compliance took hold in the 1920s during which time the agency's resources were increasingly inadequate to keep pace with the expansion in the food and drug industries. It has been estimated that when inflation is taken into account, the agency had a smaller budget at the end of the 1920s than it did in 1910.[33]

During the depression, the financial pinch on the FDA was even tighter and the inadequacy of its resources was confirmed during a congressional hearing in the early 1930s. As Table 1–1 shows, until the late 1950s the budget of the Food and Drug Administration has been

[32] James Turner, *The Chemical Feast* (New York: Grossman, 1970), pp. 121–122.

[33] Young, *Medical Messiahs,* p. 100.

extremely parsimonious, leaving the agency in a constant state of in-
ability to do an effective job of consumer protection.

Table 1–1   Total Enacted Appropriations of the Food and Drug Admin-
             istration for Selected Years, 1925 to 1959

1925	$ 1,409,731*
1930	1,521,000
1935	1,642,741
1940	2,389,182
1945	2,947,580
1950	5,824,354
1955	6,303,617
1956	7,285,585
1957	7,798,909
1958	10,932,000
1959	12,198,000

* Bureau of Chemistry

SOURCE: *The Budget of the United States Government for the Fiscal Year Ending
June 30* . . . 1927, 1932, 1942, 1947, 1952, 1957, 1958, 1959, 1960, 1961. (Washington,
D.C.: U.S. Government Printing Office).

The history of the Federal Trade Commission is not unlike that
of the FDA. Formed by the Federal Trade Commission Act of 1914,
its basic objective has been "to prevent the free enterprise system from
being stifled or fettered by monopoly or corrupted by unfair or deceptive
trade practices."[34] Like the other regulatory agencies, the FTC was
full of regulatory fervor during its "youth," and the original members
of the commission shared the Progressive skepticism toward big business. However, as in the case of the ICC and the FDA, a different
orientation took hold in the 1920s during the period of Republican
domination of the national government and a general public sentiment
favorably disposed toward business. Although the composition of the
five-man commission had already begun to swing toward the right, the
most notable change in the commission occurred in 1925 when President Coolidge appointed William E. Humphrey to the FTC and re-

[34] *United States Government Organization Manual—1970–71* (Washington,
D.C.: 1970), p. 440.

versed the voting balance. Humphrey had, prior to his appointment, been sharply critical of the FTC as "an instrument of oppression and disturbance" to business and thus sought to correct the commission's orientation.[35] As in the FDA, the change came in the form of reliance on voluntary and informal methods of obtaining compliance. Enforcement activities relying on sanctions were applied only to the worst offenders.

Although the FTC had originally been concerned only with antitrust work, the agency had almost since its inception also been concerned with false advertising—a concern which was initiated and backed by advertising associations which considered false advertising as a species of unfair competition. With the backing of the advertising associations, the commission became increasingly involved in false advertising cases and by 1925 this type of case was dominant. In its approach to this area, the FTC was in no way antibusiness. Rather, the aim of its policies was to protect competitors rather than consumers. This is evidenced by the increase in false advertising actions during the Republican era on the commission. The commission was therefore more of a participant in a system of self-regulation than an exclusive regulator itself.

The commission's regulation of advertising and its rationale for doing so were struck down in a federal circuit court decision upheld by the Supreme Court. The circuit court held that the FTC had to demonstrate positive damage to competitors resulting from deceptive ads. Otherwise it had no jurisdiction over advertising.[36] Given the great favor with which most of the business community viewed the FTC, it is no surprise that its authority over advertising was shortly restored by the 1938 Wheeler-Lea act partly as a result of that favor and also to head off advertising regulation by the less-trusted Food and Drug Administration. Thus, deceptive practices along with antitrust law came under the scope of FTC responsibilities. Although other amendments afixed new responsibilities particularly with regard to fabric labeling, these two are still the major areas of concern.

Since the problems of the FTC have not changed greatly since it assumed its present responsibilities and since it got into the pattern of

[35] Quoted in Young, *Medical Messiahs,* p. 114.

[36] *Raladam Co.* v. *Federal Trade Commission,* 42 Fed. (2nd) 430 (1930).

voluntary enforcement, these matters will be dealt with in Chapter 2. Suffice it to say that the FTC early on discarded a strict sanction approach and opted for voluntarism (or, critically, lax enforcement). The agency has been the subject of a long series of congressional and other studies which are unanimous in their assessment that the FTC has for years been an inadequate agency of consumer protection. Its weak enforcement policy has been a major component of that inadequacy.

Summary

To facilitate drawing historical comparisons in later chapters, this chapter concludes by setting forth explicitly the major themes which underlie consumer protection in the past.

The alignment of sides on legislative matters has been strikingly consistent in the major battles. The affected industry with its steadfast congressional supporters were on one side, while the legislation was being pressed by congressmen generally regarded as progressive or liberal with support from large or mass-based organizations that have only a subsidiary or temporary interest in consumer protection. This seems natural—like all social phenomena sanctioned by the usage of time. But why is it thus? The one notable group of exceptions were the meat grading and inspection laws of the nineteenth century. These were enacted at the behest of the large domestic manufacturers to protect their own competitive position. Is it not equally plausible to expect other industrialists to accept regulation in the interest of higher standards—as long as everyone was so regulated? There are of course psychological and economic reasons why industry usually fought consumer protection measures strongly. The point here is only that such an alignment is by no means obvious or inevitable, but is an historical development of some importance.

In the legislative process itself, there was usually a trend toward weakening the legislation. Industry rarely suffered a complete defeat. This was particularly true in the two major food and drug bills.

Finally, a crisis or scandal was frequently, but not always a factor in moving long-stalled legislation to eventual passage. A Supreme Court decision made the Interstate Commerce Act essential; revelations of danger and actual death from food and drugs immediately preceded the food and drug acts. However, less extensive and less hotly contested measures such as the Federal Trade Commission Act proceeded in a less dramatic fashion.

In terms of implementation, the administrative process has proved to be the key element in consumer protection policy and the implementation of that policy invariably has taken a different path than that envisioned by the original proponents of the legislation. The agencies charged with administering consumer protection policy have conformed to Marver Bernstein's model of the life cycle of agencies as they go from vigorous youth to the debility and decline of old age.[37] It turned out that it did not matter whether the agency was an independent commission or a part of the normal Executive structure like the Food and Drug Administration. This decline has generally been manifested by two phenomena. The first is an abiding belief in the good faith of the regulated industry and the agency's eventual identification with the members of that industry. Secondly, after an initial period of vigorous enforcement, the agencies have come to rely on various forms of voluntary compliance with compromise rather than sanction being the key element in the administration of the law.

An additional problem in consumer protection administration has been the constantly low financial resources which have placed definite limits on how much could be done no matter how internally vigorous the agencies had been.

Not only has the administration of legislation been inadequate, but attempts to provide direct bureaucratic representation of the consumer interest during the New Deal also proved unsuccessful.

Apart from these specific themes, there is a more general historical pattern seen in the chronology of consumer protection issues. The earlier episodes of consumer protection controversies were not simply the products of the actions of concerned groups nor were they independent of the times. Rather, the important controversies of the past were all part of larger social movements. The ICC was an outgrowth of populism and the Granger movement. The Pure Food and Drug Act was a major accomplishment of Progressivism on the national scale, and the Food, Drug, and Cosmetic Act of 1938 was in the con-

[37] Bernstein, *Regulating Business by Independent Commission,* pp. 74–102.

text of the New Deal. Thus, in the past, consumer protection activity did not emerge alone nor was it perceived as an independent issue. Rather, it was part of a cluster of issues of major social movements and it drew most of its supporters from the active participants in the larger movement.

chapter 2

The Development of Consumer Protection as an Issue

The Beginnings of the Present

Like much of the rest of the New Deal, interest and activity in consumer issues was a casualty of World War II. The consumer issues of the war years were unique to the times as Americans had to cope with rationing and other dislocations of the consumer goods economy.

In the remaining years of the 1940s, consumer issues still tended to be related to the economic problems caused by the war and reconversion. In those years, there was a tone to consumer issues which was entirely different from the previous and later eras of "consumerism." Public attention was focused on such consumer problems as inflation and price stabilization, housing shortages, rent control, and proposed social security legislation. This conception of consumer protection can be seen in the "Program for Action" recommended to Congress by *Consumer Reports* in 1949. The recommendations included a cut of military spending, price and rent controls, an excess profits tax, an improved farm price program, new antitrust laws, and others.[1]

During the late 1940s, and through the 1950s, the only consistent voice of consumer interests was Consumers Union which published

---

[1] "Consumers and the 81st Congress: A Program for Action," *Consumer Reports* 14 (January, 1949): 38–40.

Consumer Reports. While *Consumer Reports* began to run articles on chemicals in foods, meat inspection, and finance rackets, it was largely a voice in the wilderness and the period was one of general quiescence for consumer protection (as well as many other later reform issues) until the early 1960s.

One intervening issue during those years is the exception that proves the rule—automobile safety. Auto safety emerged in 1965 as a major consumer issue which, in the opinion of many consumer activists, was the "breakthrough" issue. Yet it was also an issue on the congressional agenda, although with much lower public visibility, in the 1950s. From 1956 until his defeat in 1964, Congressman Kenneth Roberts, Democrat of Alabama, held hearings on automobile safety. During those years, however, Roberts was the only consistent advocate of federal safety standards for automobile design. From 1956 until 1966, congressional response consisted of passing three piecemeal auto safety bills, all of them in the years from 1962 to 1964. The most important bill of those years required the General Services Administration to set safety standards for all cars purchased by the government. (Twice previously the House had passed this bill sponsored by Roberts, but the Senate did not act until 1964). Nonetheless, this legislation and the years of hearings went forth with no fanfare; there was practically no publicity given to Roberts' hearings.[2]

After these years of quiescence since the New Deal, consumer protection again emerged as an issue on the public agenda in the 1960s. Since the personalities and issues involved constitute the bulk of the analysis in the remainder of this study, only a brief sketch of the unfolding of consumer protection as a present-day political issue is presented here. The development of specific issues and the roles of the major participants are treated in greater detail in later pages.

The real origins of consumer protection as an important congressional political issue at the present time are to be found in the hearings on the prescription drug industry held by Senator Estes Kefauver's Antitrust and Monopoly Subcommittee. The hearings were held intermittently from 1959 through 1962. Although the original

---

[2] The causes of this lack of publicity were peculiar to Roberts' own orientation toward Congress and, together with the importance of publicity, they are discussed more fully in Chapter 4.

focus of the hearings was drug prices, the revelation that Americans had narrowly missed the mass marketing of thalidomide, a drug which produced birth defects when taken by pregnant women, turned the hearings around, brought widespread public attention, and caused a previously emasculated bill to emerge in reasonably effective form. As in the previous two eras of consumer protection activism, drug safety was a central issue touching on public emotion and creating a public demand for action. The drug amendments of 1962 became law on December 10, 1962. However, these events did not lead directly to an increased consumer activism or the expansion of a generalized consumer protection issue. There was no presidential package of consumer proposals until 1965 and no outpouring of legislation until 1966.

The one issue which both preceded the late 1960s period of consumer activism and was also a link with it was truth-in-lending, originally championed by Senator Paul Douglas. Senator Douglas began hearings on a bill to require full disclosure of interest costs in 1960, but it did not become law until 1968—two years after Douglas was defeated for reelection. The chronology of truth-in-lending is illustrative of the development of consumer protection as an issue although there are unique reasons as well for the length of time it took for the bill to pass.[3] Nonetheless, while it had not even been able to get out of committee for eight years, by the time it passed in 1968, the bill was actually more comprehensive and stronger than the one which had originally been introduced.

In general, the years 1966 through 1968 were the major years of congressional action. Table 2–1 shows the development of the congressional issue.

In the two major consumer eras of the past, the President was prominently associated with the consumer issue at hand. While the relative degree of support varied, there was no question that Presidents Theodore Roosevelt and Franklin Roosevelt publicly supported the food and drug measures under consideration. In the development of the present era, varying degrees of presidential support are also seen. However, Lyndon Johnson was the first President to adopt a set of legislative consumer protection proposals as his own and make them a major part of his overall legislative program.

3 See pp. 130–137 below.

Table 2–1   Number of New Consumer Protection Laws Enacted by
            Congress

1962	1
1963	0
1964	1
1965	0
1966	5
1967	4
1968	6
1969	1
1970	2

The examination of the role of the President as proponent of consumer protection starts with John Kennedy. It is an understatement to
say that consumer issues were not among the major concerns of his
predecessor's administration. President Eisenhower fully shared the
congressional apathy and negative attitude toward consumer protection. The administration took no position on the Roberts auto safety
proposals and, in 1960, opposed the Douglas truth-in-lending bill.
Thus the Democratic administration inherited a tradition of the President sharing the general indifference to the issue and potential of consumer protection.

The first major presidential articulation of the consumer interest
since the New Deal was President Kennedy's 1962 consumer message
to Congress, the first such message delivered by any President. Although, in that message, President Kennedy proclaimed four "rights of
consumers" and announced his commitment to consumer protection,
his only major intervention in consumer politics was to aid in opposing
some sections of Senator Kefauver's original drug amendments—an
effort which was quickly reversed in the wake of the thalidomide
episode.

Regardless of the specific instances of support and opposition to
legislation, from 1965 onward, consumer protection had become an
issue on the public agenda which was legitimated by annual presidential
messages to Congress and legislative proposals. Indeed, President
Johnson made consumer protection a major part of his legislative program and, in 1968, included consumer proposals in his state-of-the-

union address. By 1969, the legitimacy of a governmental role and the need for further action was so widely accepted that a conservative Republican President, Richard Nixon, delivered his own consumer message. While there is no available survey data to permit a precise analysis of the growth of the consumer protection issue in the public mind, we can at least establish a rough measure of public exposure to consumer protection issues simply to illustrate the growth of consumer protection as a *public* political issue. Table 2–2 lists the number of general consumer protection stories in popular magazines from 1963 through 1970. While it is hazardous to infer from these figures the state of public awareness, at the very least media exposure makes public awareness possible, and it is possible to see the chronology of that potential awareness.

Table 2–2   Number of Consumer Protection Articles in Popular Magazines

1963	4
1964	9
1965	6
1966	14
1967	24
1968	24
1969	32
1970	48

SOURCE: *Readers Guide to Periodical Literature,* for the years indicated. (Includes only stories listed under general heading of "consumer protection.")

In general, the present era of consumer protection began slowly with two specific issues in the early 1960s. Presidential support, congressional action, and public attention converged in 1966, by which time one could speak in terms of consumer protection itself as a general issue. Perhaps the event which most dramatically symbolized this maturing of the issue was a *Newsweek* cover story which proclaimed Ralph Nader as "Consumer Crusader." Just as with Ralph Nader, the issue was no longer automobiles or other separate issues, but was consumer protection as a generalized category of issues.

Why Now?

In discussing the background of the present focus on consumer protection, one major unanswered question is why this should become an issue at the present time after it was a "non-issue" for so long. While it may be impossible to resolve this problem definitively and to assign the precise weight to each causal factor, still something can be said about the causes which will satisfy our present purposes. Beyond being interesting in their own right, the causes behind the present concern with consumer protection are significant because they are important ingredients in determining the shape of policy outcomes. Policy emerging from a cluster of causes labeled "A" will be different from policy emerging from cluster of causes "B" if A and B differ from each other.

We can view the making of an issue from two perspectives: the perspective of the participants in the policy, or a more detached perspective based on the investigator's own assessment. Taking the former first, several of the interview respondents were asked to make their own assessment of why the consumer issue developed. Although this group consisted of only eleven persons, it was a carefully selected group of consumer activists who themselves participated in making consumer protection a political issue. Their responses are summarized in Table 2–3. The response "good politics" usually meant that the political

Table 2–3   Activists' Perception of the Rise of Consumer Protection as an Issue

Cause	Number of Responses
Good Politics	8
Necessity	5
Need for low-cost program	3
Consumer demand	3

N = 11

climate was now able to sustain the issue and to profit those who were active in it. The category of "necessity" generally referred to the increased complexity of the marketplace and the relative powerlessness of individual consumers. "Consumer demand" was a judgment that the issue arose in response to a spontaneous public demand for government action. "Need for a low-cost program" is closely related to "good politics" but more specifically indicates a belief that some sort of liberal or reform program was desired by the administration, and consumer protection was pushed because it had the advantage of low cost to the government. The responses total to more than the number of respondents because most individuals cited more than one major factor.

As can be seen, most participants felt that the fact that the issue was profitable politically was a major factor in its rise to prominence. This does not imply a cynical attitude—few people are so cynical about their work. Rather, it simply is a recognition by political realists that a good cause is helped if it is also good politics. Indeed, many a worthy cause will get nowhere if it is not good politics. On the other side of the spectrum, it is interesting that so few participants attributed the issue to public demand. Apparently, the champions of this cause view themselves as being in the business of generating that public demand.

But the story does not end there. While the participants directly involved are in the best position to assess the causes, it may be that they cannot see the forest for the trees. In any case, a more detached perspective is useful not only to assess the validity of the participants' judgments but to elaborate upon them.

Perhaps the most basic cause of consumer protection becoming an issue was that this was an area where government intervention was necessary and, more importantly, was perceived as necessary by the public and policy makers alike. In a variety of important ways, the marketplace had become more complex and more removed from control by the consumer. In the 1960s there was a greater number of new or modified products of greater complexity than ever before. This increased complexity meant that there was more that could go wrong and that the consumer was less knowledgeable about each product. Poorly made electric can openers were not an irritation in the early 1950s. Service problems with color television sets were of a complexity and cost unknown in the 1950s. A myriad of examples point to consumer confusion arising from increased complexity. Nor are they limited to relatively trivial consumer goods. Prescription drugs also became more complex, more potent, and, hence, more dangerous. The need for rigorous FDA regulation was greater than ever before. In the

purely financial sphere, the 1960s brought to fruition a host of new
consumer problems. The use of consumer credit increased greatly with
the introduction of bank credit cards and the widespread distribution
of unsolicited credit cards. Outstanding consumer installment credit
rose from $21.5 billion in 1950 to $56.0 billion in 1960 and to $87.9
billion in 1965.[4] In the face of increased traffic and soaring court judgments, automobile insurance rates continued to rise and coverage was
restricted. One of the most frustrating developments of the decade was
the rise of computerized billing. No longer could the consumer obtain
direct redress from human error by a human billing clerk. The impersonality and intractability of computers became the subject of many
a magazine article replete with horror stories of people whose credit
ratings were ruined by a random hole in an IBM card and who could
not obtain redress for years.

Both the complexity and the increased impersonality of a computerized market certainly created a need for a regulatory system more
in tune with the times. However, while there was widespread consumer
frustration with various aspects of the modern market, it is interesting
that so few of the participants viewed public demand as a causative
factor in creating the issue. Indeed, necessity was only the second-
ranked factor. This leads to the second type of cause—the politics of
the situation. There is a difference between societal needs and public
issues, and there are many needs which are not issues or which do not
become issues for a long time. The question then becomes: Granted
that there was a need for consumer protection legislation, why did it,
out of all the other needs, become an issue on the public agenda?

The modern Presidency has been the single most important factor
in defining the national political agenda; thus the political factors behind the issue can best be seen in light of presidential action. Basically,
presidential activity in behalf of consumer protection from 1966 on
can be seen as a presidential response to a need for a new issue. The
condition of the President's program and relations with Congress are
relevant in this regard.

The impressive legislative outpouring of the 88th and especially
the 89th Congresses in 1964 and 1965 is well known. President Lyndon

---

[4] U.S., Bureau of the Census, *Pocket Data Book, U.S.A. 1969* (Washington, D.C.:
U.S. Government Printing Office, 1969), p. 318.

Johnson was lavish in his praise of the progress and programs of the first session of the 89th Congress. In those two years Congress completed favorable action on much of the original program of the late President Kennedy—most notably in the form of the Civil Rights Act of 1964. Furthermore, with the help of substantial congressional majorities, in 1965, President Johnson largely realized his goal of completing enactment of programs long on the agenda of goals of the (Northern) Democratic party—some since the New Deal. Thus the "Fabulous 89th" enacted Medicare, aid to elementary and secondary education, voting rights, immigration reform, establishment of the Department of Housing and Urban Development, and the poverty amendments. This was a dramatic and impressive record but it presented the proverbial problem of being a hard act to follow.

Nor was President Johnson content to rest on his laurels even if he was presented with that opportunity. The same 89th Congress, however, became recalcitrant in 1966, and the President fared poorly in comparison with the preceding session. He was defeated in his attempt to secure passage of the District of Columbia home rule bill and to repeal the right-to-work section of the Taft-Hartley Act. Several other of his measures were passed in very diluted form.

In 1967, the President had a still harder time with the 90th Congress and its reduced Democratic majorities. Although his requests were generally more modest, he met with less success than previously. His *Congressional Quarterly* legislative success "score" (the percentage · of presidential requests enacted by Congress) declined from 68.9 percent in 1965 to 47.6 percent in 1967.[5]

In addition to the decreasing success with Congress, although related to it, was the war in Vietnam and the resulting economic problems. Throughout 1965 and 1966, the conflict in Vietnam escalated into a full-scale American war. This was clearly reflected in the January, 1966, budget presentation in which President Johnson called for an appropriation of $15.2 billion to finance the expansion of the war in fiscal year 1966–67. At that time there was almost no slack left in the economy and the inflationary pressure of new war-related spending was reflected in an increase in the consumer price index of 2.9 percent

[5] 1967 *Congressional Quarterly Almanac* (Washington, D.C.: Congressional Quarterly Service, 1968).

during 1966 (compared to 1.7 percent during 1965). By the end of 1967, the index had hit 117.5. Although most economists advised that a tax increase was essential to stem the inflationary tide, the President resisted such a measure and continued to conduct the war without wartime economic controls. In spite of the pledge of the President in the state-of-the-union message in early 1966 to provide both guns and butter, it was apparent by year's end that the war and related inflationary pressures, had made costly domestic programs a luxury whose implementation was highly improbable.

In short, during 1966, two factors converged which created a need for a new domestic issue. First, while the President had already enacted a substantial program of major domestic reform legislation, he was facing an increasingly recalcitrant Congress as he desired to push forth with new programs. Second, it was clear that the war and inflation dictated that no *costly* new programs be enacted. Consumer protection fit these two needs precisely. While it was not a brand new issue at that time, it had never been seriously pushed by the administration beyond a recitation of legislative endorsements in the consumer messages of 1962 and 1964. This is borne out by the fact that there was no consumer message in 1965—the year of the "Fabulous 89th." During that time, the President still had bigger fish to fry. Thus, while consumer protection was already on the presidential agenda, its elevation as a public issue and increased administration activity on its behalf came at the same time that the need for a new such program was developed.

Furthermore, the type of legislation being pushed was extremely cheap compared to such programs as the War on Poverty or pollution control. No major new government bureaucracies were to be created nor was substantial revenue sharing with the states contemplated. The new agencies which were created had budgets so modest they created no noticeable dent in the federal budget. For example, in fiscal year 1968, the National Transportation Safety Board received an enacted appropriation of $4,050,000, and the President's Committee on Consumer Interests received a mere $345,000. New programs such as expanded federal inspection of meat processors could be accomplished by relatively modest increments to the already small budgets of the relevant inspection agencies. In the main, the costs of these programs would eventually be absorbed by consumers or industry and would not be reflected in a noticeable increase in the federal budget.

As an issue, consumer protection had one important advantage in addition to novelty and low cost: it is a "concensus" issue. At a time when divisions were beginning to appear on the Vietnam War and the poverty and civil rights issues were becoming subject to increasing tension, consumer protection presented itself as a reform issue not subject to those same divisions. Merely to state the fact that poultry should be safe and wholesome is to gain overwhelming public support for that position. To champion an issue as inherently popular as consumer protection was an irresistible opportunity for a President concerned both with getting new programs and with achieving concensus.

The political appeal and political dividends of the issue went beyond the White House, of course. As will be shown later in the study, the Congress was a major center of activity and there the issue also filled political needs.[6] For now, suffice it to say that several members of Congress who were to become key activists seized upon the issue to broaden their base of support by being identified with an issue with wide public appeal and reap a good deal of personal publicity by bringing forth dramatic problems or incidents the resolution of which also had wide public appeal.

Looked at from another perspective, in saying that congressmen were attracted to consumer protection because it was good politics, we are really saying that the issue coincided with their career maintenance needs. From that same perspective it becomes more clear why the issue achieved a fair amount of publicity. Publicizing it was not only good for politicians, it was also good for the journalists who brought the news directly to public attention. The issue was the source of many important exclusive stories which furthered the careers of reporters. In short, just as with the members of Congress, the consumer issue filled the career maintenance needs of several reporters all of which increased the coverage of the issue.

Given the appeal of the consumer issues, initial success in pressing one issue led to more activity and further success on other issues. While it may be impossible to pinpoint one "breakthrough" issue which led to increased activism on other issues, most activists are probably correct in assigning this role to the auto safety bill. In passing legislation

---

[6] The manner in which the issue was harmonious with the political needs of various members of Congress is explored in greater detail in Chapter 4.

to specifically regulate an industry which had never before known government regulation specifically aimed at it, Congress dramatically proved that it could be done—which had previously been in doubt. The auto safety legislation demonstrated that a powerful industry could be defeated in Congress, that the public supported such legislation, and that political careers could be enhanced by championing such causes. One important element in the auto safety case which made it a breakthrough was the involvement and rise to fame of Ralph Nader. Having come to prominence by playing a major part in enacting auto safety legislation, Nader was able to work for legislation in other consumer areas more effectively. This brings us to yet another factor behind the development of the issue—the rise of Nader himself.

Ralph Nader quickly became a personal symbol of the drive for consumer protection policy. He has been extremely effective in getting his message across to the public as well as to governmental decision makers. His role in the auto safety bill was largely one of spearheading a successful drive toward enactment of legislation, and he was clearly the most important individual participant. However, the question of whether there would have been a consumer movement without Ralph Nader is analogous to the classic historical question of whether great men make events or whether events make great men—and perhaps as unanswerable. Clearly Nader had a major role in developing the issue and bringing it to public attention. However, he came along at a time when other conditions also pushed the issue forth. Whether Nader could have done it without the coincidence of other factors is an unanswerable question. Suffice it to say that the other factors discussed above made the success of individual activists like Nader possible—or at least much more probable.

All the above factors are specific to the current interest in consumer protection. But there are deeper contextual reasons which lay behind the emergence of consumer protection as an issue. While consumer protection became an issue essentially because it was good politics, there are underlying reasons why it was good politics. These factors are found in the fact that beyond all the groups and individuals involved, consumer protection was one part of a much larger reform movement. Some scholars have argued that such periods are cyclical and culminate in new policy after a long period of agitation and gradual public acceptance.[7] While the years of the Kennedy administration may be seen as the final stages of building support, the first part of the Johnson administration was the culmination of that cycle. Public support existed for Johnson's version of completing the New Deal, and he had the political resources equal to the task. Consumer protection must be seen in the context of this larger scene. It was not on the agenda of the Eisenhower administration because major reform legislation in general was absent. The reasons underlying the growth of reform movements themselves is beyond the scope of this study, but the relation between the issue of consumer protection and those movements is relevant.

This situation is of course parallel to the earlier major episodes of consumer protection policy making which occurred during the Progressive era and the New Deal. Those previous eras like the short-lived era of the "Great Society" were periods of popular support for an expanded or different government role in economic, political, and social life. It was this underlying base of support which made consumer protection good politics and politically feasible then and now. In short, the most fundamental reason for the emergence of consumer protection was most likely the "temper of the times." The specific factors outlined above can only account for the development of the issue when the temper of the times is such as to make those factors important components in the rise of any public policy issue.

[7] For example, see James L. Sundquist, *Politics and Policy: The Eisenhower, Kennedy, and Johnson Years* (Washington: The Brookings Institution, 1969).

chapter 3

The Federal
Bureaucracy
and Consumer Protection

While public and congressional concern with consumer protection has fluctuated through the years, it is the bureaucracy which has had the constant responsibility for administering consumer protection policy. It has long been recognized that the bureaucracy is not simply the neutral servant of congressional will, but exercises an independent influence on public policy. It is therefore the performance of the bureaucracy which most directly affects consumers in their everyday lives. This chapter will examine three selected consumer protection bureaucracies and assess them in terms of the representation of the consumer interest. The basic line of inquiry of this chapter concerns the effectiveness of these bureaucracies in protecting and promoting the interests of consumers. To what degree have they been effective and what accounts for that effectiveness? In pursuing these questions, we will consider the relevant activities of the bureaucracies, their response to consumer protection as a political issue, their priorities, and their coordination with each other.[1]

[1] The information presented here is based primarily on open-ended interviews in these bureaucracies, supplemented by public and private documents which are cited where applicable. In choosing interview respondents, my purpose was to

There are three major "points of leverage"[2] for consumer protection in the Executive Branch—the President's Committee on Consumer Interests (PCCI), the Federal Trade Commission (FTC), and the Food and Drug Administration (FDA). This leaves out a variety of agencies and bureaus which could legitimately be considered to have major consumer protection responsibilities. Indeed, nearly all the independent regulatory agencies are nominally oriented in this direction. Nevertheless, this is a book about consumer protection and not only about regulatory agencies. Obviously a narrowing of focus is necessary. Since no agency can be said to be "typical," and not all agencies can be covered, it is logical to focus on agencies with the widest scope of consumer protection responsibilities. While other regulatory agencies such as the Interstate Commerce Commission concentrate on specific fields or on problems which are one step removed from the ultimate consumer, the agencies discussed here are more directly concerned with problems of comprehensive consumer protection—problems which directly affect consumers through a wide variety of goods and services. The PCCI is theoretically the overall coordinating agency for consumer protection activities in the national government. The FDA has primary jurisdiction over products which are used daily by all citizens. The FTC has jurisdiction over trade practices in all industries which directly affect consumers.

Response to a
Resurrected Issue

Widespread public interest in consumer protection is a recent phenomenon. The automobile safety bill, considered by many to be the "breakthrough" legislation, was passed in 1966. Not since the prewar

---

interview all personnel with policy-making responsibilities in the selected consumer protection bureaucracies. This was both possible and desirable since I was dealing with a small universe of respondents—approximately thirty officials. Of these, I interviewed twenty-five, plus several lower-ranking bureaucrats.

[2] This apt term describing decision-making centers is from Kenneth Gergen, "Assessing the Leverage Points in the Process of Policy Formation," in *The Study of Policy Formation,* ed. Raymond Bauer and Kenneth Gergen (New York: Free Press, 1968).

Roosevelt administration and Rexford Tugwell's campaign to amend the Pure Food and Drug Act has consumer protection been given much attention by the Executive Branch. For purposes of this study consumer protection is a new issue whose present form is not a continuation of the earlier controversies because more than thirty years had elapsed before the issue again surfaced. Also the great changes in the economy and in technology substantially changed the form of consumer protection issues from what they were in prewar depression days.

Given the novelty of the issue, the first set of questions in this chapter revolves around the response of the Executive Branch to the new consumer protection issues—many of which originated in Congress. An analysis of this response is essential to a thorough consideration of the representation of the consumer interest. The center of public attention for regulatory policy (of which consumer protection is a type) had traditionally been the Congress. It is now a commonplace that such enacted legislation is generally changed in the implementation by administrators and is steadily weakened as time goes by.[3] The attentive public follows the controversy in Congress and may exert pressure on behalf of the regulatory measure, but once the policy is out of the legislative mill, it generally is also out of the public eye. The reform coalition which fought for the policy dissolves, and the administrator is left to confront only the groups immediately affected by the legislation.

Murray Edelman has argued that this political quiescence by citizens results from their being manipulated by political symbols. That is, having witnessed the successful course of legislation through Congress, citizens assume that the administrative agency will in fact implement that legislation in accord with their perception of legislative intent. This conception of symbolic politics extends beyond regulatory legislation. By extension, the administrative system as a whole is a symbol to citizens of government faithfully protecting their interests.[4] The citizenry may believe a policy is being implemented in a certain way when in fact it is being implemented in an entirely different fashion. From the standpoint of the citizens, when this state of affairs prevails

[3] See Marver Bernstein, *Regulating Business by Independent Commission* (Princeton: Princeton University Press, 1955).

[4] Murray Edelman, *The Symbolic Uses of Politics* (Urbana: University of Illinois Press, 1967), pp. 22–43.

the policy may be said to be symbolic rather than operational. Thus, the citizens are represented only symbolically. This symbolism may proceed without any conscious attempt by the administrators to manipulate the public. Inaction by an agency due to lethargy or inertia may proceed alongside feverish activity within Congress on issues directly related to the agency's responsibilities. The more general case occurs in the absence of any publicity when the public assumes that the government is taking care of some particular problem when no one is actually responsible.

The first section of this chapter therefore considers the extent to which activity and changes in Congress were paralleled by administrative changes. The extent and manner in which participants in the Executive Branch reacted to the newly popular issue of consumer protection is an important component of their performance in representing the consumer interest.

The President

Consumers are a natural constituency for any President. No constituency could be wider, and it is a commonplace that the Presidency is the most representative single actor in the governmental process. Harry Truman is quoted as saying, "There are a great many organizations with lots of money who maintain lobbyists in Washington. I'd say 15 million people in the United States are represented by lobbyists. The other 150 million have only one man who is elected at large to represent them—that is, the President of the United States."[5] The large body of literature on the Presidency is unanimous in assigning this overall representational role to the American President. For example, Edward Corwin argues that inherent in the ascendency of the executive is the notion that the people are embodied in the Executive. Clinton Rossiter posits the "Voice of the People" as one of the unofficial roles of the President.[6]

Theoretically, then, the President would be expected to spearhead

[5] James Deakin, *The Lobbyists* (Washington, D.C.: Public Affairs Press, 1966), p. 42.
[6] Edward S. Corwin, *The President: Office and Powers* (New York: New York University Press, 1948) chap. 1; and Clinton Rossiter, *The American Presidency* (New York: Harcourt, Brace, & World, 1956), chap. 1.

a consumer movement. However, the President, if he is so disposed, must get beyond the platitudes, and operationalize his representational role. His potential leadership can be expressed primarily in four courses of action which are closely related. These are: attempting to set the public agenda;[7] sending legislative recommendations to Congress; exerting public or covert pressure on executive agencies; and creating new administrative machinery by executive order. Presidents Kennedy and Johnson utilized each of these avenues in order to advance consumer interests.

As noted in Chapter 2, the first major presidential articulation of the consumer interest since the New Deal was President Kennedy's 1962 consumer message to Congress, the first such message delivered by any President. It was both an attempt at agenda setting and a request for legislation. The "bully pulpit" aspect of the message is seen in Kennedy's pronouncement of the four essential consumer rights: The right to safety, the right to be informed, the right to choose, and the right to be heard. The implication, of course, was that the government was the ultimate guarantor of those rights. Thus, the speech lent executive authority and a further aura of legitimacy to attempts to intensify the role of the government in a variety of consumer protection programs.

Actually, the 1962 message seems more important in retrospect than it was at the time it was delivered. While the four rights of consumers which it defined are now frequently referred to by consumer activists,[8] and prominent mention is often made of the fact that it was Kennedy who first articulated those rights, consumer protection was not a high priority item of the Kennedy administration.

The consumer message of 1962 requested new food and drug regulation, truth-in-lending legislation (requiring accurate and complete disclosure of credit costs), the manufacture of all-channel (UHF) tele-

---

[7] By "setting the agenda" is meant the President's impressive power to shape and mobilize public opinion not only in terms of opinion toward the issues, but in shaping perceptions of what the issues are. Theodore Roosevelt's adage that the presidency is a "bully pulpit" has been consistently echoed by scholars of the Presidency. See, for example, Louis Koenig, *The Chief Executive* (New York: Harcourt, Brace & World, 1968).

[8] For example, eight years later, the *Washington Post* editorially referred to this declaration of consumer rights in support of a package of consumer bills. *Washington Post,* July 6, 1970, p. A18.

vision sets, and the strengthening of the antitrust laws. None of these was an original proposal and all had been advocated some time earlier by members of the Congress. There was no consumer message in 1963, although several proposals to strengthen the Food, Drug and Cosmetic Act were included in President Kennedy's health message. In 1964, President Johnson sent a comprehensive consumer message to Congress in which six of the thirteen proposals were original. Taking the origin of proposals as a guide, it is safe to say that in 1964 consumer protection had become part of the administration's own legislative program. There was no message in 1965, but the messages resumed on an annual basis from 1966 through 1968. Indeed, by 1968, the issue had become so important that the President presented most of his consumer proposals in the state-of-the-union address. The tradition was continued after the change in party control of the White House, and President Nixon issued a consumer message in October, 1969. However, by this time the consumer movement had outrun the President and consumer activists including Ralph Nader and the Consumer Federation of America criticized the proposals in the message as inadequate. This criticism was partly a result of a change in function of the consumer message. Previously, the President simply endorsed legislative proposals either initiated or managed by Democratic consumer activists in Congress. With a Republican as President and the Democrats still in control of Congress, there was competing legislation on this as on many other issues. Thus, instead of endorsing an agreed upon consumer agenda, the President used the consumer message to advance his own consumer program as against that of the competing Democratic congressional consumer activists—a competing program preferred by all independent consumer activists.

Presidential administrative directives are also generally embodied in the consumer messages, but they do not comprise any sort of comprehensive program. Rather, they consist primarily of announcements of previous executive regulatory agency programs and investigations, directives to certain agencies for studies, and a general exhortation to heed the consumer interest.

The President's Committee on Consumer Interests

The most distinct presidential response to the newly popular consumer protection issue was the creation of new administrative forms, particularly the President's Committee on Consumer Interests (PCCI) which was formed by President Johnson by executive order on January 3, 1964. The PCCI was an outgrowth of the Consumer Advisory Council that had been appointed by President Kennedy in 1962 as an adjunct to the Council of Economic Advisors. Kennedy's action was the delayed redemption of a pledge he made in a campaign speech shortly before the presidential election in which he promised to appoint a consumer counsel in the Office of the President. The counsel was to "scrutinize" the activities of regulatory agencies, represent consumers before congressional committees, keep the President informed about deficiencies in consumer protection administration and participate in the formation of new legislative proposals.[9]

The Consumer Advisory Council consisted of persons from outside the federal government and was "blue ribbon" in nature. It included a sprinkling of academicians, state officials, and representatives of consumer organizations—eleven individuals altogether.

The council's term of office lapsed in 1964 and, after some delay, President Johnson reconstituted it as part of the PCCI. Technically, the PCCI consists of "high level" officials of ten major federal agencies. A later amendment included the secretaries of the involved departments, a change which was billed as an upgrading of the PCCI. The President's special assistant for consumer affairs was chairman of the PCCI and, after 1966, the Consumer Advisory Council. It was explained that she thus wore three hats. In reality, the PCCI has rarely met as a body since there are few problems which cut across the wide range of interests represented on the PCCI. Also, as Richard Fenno found, cabinet members rarely meet together to coordinate the activities of their departments in any policy areas.[10] Both the Consumer Advisory Council and the PCCI are serviced by the same staff and although the Consumer Advisory Council is technically part of the PCCI, the council's existence is only a formality.

In the words of a PCCI publication, "The PCCI was to represent no organized sector of American society, but the millions of individuals —wealthy or poor, young or old, educated or uneducated—who as

[9] U.S., Congress, Senate, Committee on Commerce, *The Speeches of John F. Kennedy, Presidential Campaign,* 87th Cong., 1st sess., 1960, pp. 900–901.
[10] Richard Fenno, *The President's Cabinet* (Cambridge: Harvard University Press, 1959).

consumers purchase more than two-thirds of all the goods and services produced by the Nation."[11]

The first special assistant to the President to head PCCI was Esther Peterson, an assistant secretary of labor who kept her Labor post and worked half-time in the PCCI. Mrs. Peterson undertook duties with vigor—somewhat greater vigor than the political climate could sustain. A *New York Times* editorial noted that "she fought valiantly, but it became increasingly plain that hers was a lonely voice, unsupported by any resolute backing from the administration."[12]

It was uniformly reported in the press that Mrs. Peterson's activities in behalf of consumers caused sufficient business hostility to make her a political liability to the administration. A typically hostile statement came from the Advertising Federation of America which advised member firms that Mrs. Peterson was creating "unwarranted suspicion" of business. This hostility reached a peak when Mrs. Peterson publicly supported a national supermarket boycott in 1966.

Mrs. Peterson was replaced by Miss Betty Furness, a former television personality, whom the President appointed to the post in March, 1967. The appointment aroused considerable consternation among consumer groups and consumer-oriented politicians. Most observers felt that the appointment was a sham and that nothing more was to be expected from the administration in support of consumer protection legislation.[13] For approximately five months these activists kept their distance and continued being suspicious. However, many of them began to take a more positive attitude later in the year. She favorably impressed and surprised other consumer activists by taking a strong stand in support of truth-in-lending legislation in late October, 1967, when it was tied up in the House Banking and Currency Committee. But most activists agree that the breakthrough to general acceptance and respect of Miss Furness was her public support of a strong meat inspection bill in the Senate Agriculture Committee hearings. Her testimony in those hearings can be considered the breakthrough for two reasons. First, the

[11] PCCI, *A Summary of Activities, 1964–1967,* p. 1.

[12] *New York Times,* March 17, 1967.

[13] For example, the *New Republic* stated that the President had "signaled loud and clear . . . that representation within the government of the consumer as an economic force comparable to business and labor is out." March 18, 1967, p. 8.

bill she supported was stronger than the one originally backed by the Agriculture Department. When Senator Joseph Montoya, Democrat of New Mexico, asked Miss Furness who was speaking for the administration, she or the Agriculture Department, she maintained that her position enjoyed the support of the President and was *the* administration position. It turned out that she was right. It was Secretary of Agriculture Orville Freeman who backed down, and not the supposedly powerless Miss Furness. Secondly, it was widely believed by the participants in this controversy that her support was an important factor in the passage of a stronger bill than could otherwise have emerged. This was not a tribute to her personal power, but to her ability to publicize the issue effectively. Her appearance before the committee received wide publicity and the public was made aware of the existence of the two competing meat inspection bills (the original administration bill sponsored by Senator Montoya and the final administration bill sponsored by Senator Walter Mondale). From that point on, both her professional and her public stature, to use Neustadt's dichotomy, were considerably enhanced.[14]

Prior to his inauguration, President Nixon gave no indication as to whether, or in what form, he would continue the Office of Special Assistant to the President for Consumer Affairs. The success of Miss Furness had made the office visible and had given it a built-in constituency of consumer groups who were demanding that the President fill the post. In February, 1969, the President had his first lesson in the politics of consumer protection when he announced the appointment of Willie Mae Rogers, director of the Good Housekeeping Institute, as his part-time consultant on consumer affairs. She was to remain with the Institute, the department of *Good Housekeeping Magazine* which dispenses the Good Housekeeping Seal of Approval. The President's press secretary, Ronald Ziegler, said that there was no official concern about possible conflict of interest between her functions at Good Housekeeping and her official duties. However, many consumer activists were not so sanguine.[15] In addition, regardless of who was appointed, the downgrading of the position from special assistant to

---

[14] See Richard Neustadt, *Presidential Power* (New York: John Wiley & Sons, 1960), pp. 58–107.

[15] *Washington Post,* February 12, 1969, p. A6.

part-time consultant was bound to engender considerable opposition. The opposition was led by Congressman Benjamin Rosenthal, Democrat of New York. He called a press conference at which he urged the President to "reconsider" his selection of Miss Rogers charging that she could not serve two masters—Good Housekeeping and the President. Apparently unknown to the administration, the staff of Rosenthal's consumer subcommittee of the House Government Operations Committee had been investigating government and private product testing organizations, especially Good Housekeeping. Rosenthal cited several specific abuses of the Good Housekeeping Institute, all of which tended to show that the Good Housekeeping Seal was a sham and merely an advertising gimmick unrelated to the worth of the product.[16] Congressional criticism also came from senators William Proxmire and Harrison Williams, but the media focused most attention upon Rosenthal's continuing and extensive attacks.[17] Within a week, Miss Rogers withdrew herself from consideration and "a palpable air of relief settled over Richard Nixon's White House."[18]

After a respectable time had passed, the President appointed Mrs. Virginia Knauer to be special assistant for consumer affairs in April, 1969. Mrs. Knauer, a Republican, had been head of the Philadelphia office of consumer protection. While two instances may not constitute a firm pattern, nonetheless Mrs. Knauer followed the tradition of finding and publicizing a single issue to establish her credentials as a sincere and aggressive advocate of consumer interests. Much to the chagrin of some consumer activists, she choose the fat content of hot dogs. Without first securing an agreement within the administration, Mrs. Knauer publicly urged that the fat content of hot dogs be held down to 30 percent. The Agriculture Department had been willing to grant a higher allowance. While the issue was not crucial, it was important for low-income consumers and for those on low-fat diets. Since little good could be said for high-fat hot dogs, the President was really forced to back Mrs. Knauer. Although the issue wasn't nearly as dramatic,

[16] Morton Mintz, *Washington Post,* February 15, 1969, p. A5.

[17] E.g., The CBS Evening News with Walter Cronkite on February 12, 13, and 14, gave extensive coverage to the controversy and prominently featured interviews with Rosenthal.

[18] *Newsweek,* February 24, 1969, p. 25.

the parallels between it and Betty Furness's initiation are obvious. The parallel, however, ends there. While Betty Furness was part of an administration seeking to produce a record in consumer protection as part of its overall legislative record, Mrs. Knauer met considerable opposition within her administration. Her position was bound to be difficult if for no other reason than she was joining an administration whose first act in consumer affairs was to attempt to downgrade the office she eventually held.

The pressures and problems facing Mrs. Knauer can be seen in relief in the context of the class action issue. Briefly, the concept of class action is one which would allow a group of consumers of a single product to bring suit as a class against the sellers of goods or services which were defective, unsafe, overpriced, or generally not delivered as advertised. Thus, consumers with relatively small claims could aggregate those claims thereby making it economically rational to incur the costs of legal action. Senator Joseph Tydings, Democrat of Maryland, introduced a class action bill in the Senate and hearings were held on it in July, 1969. Mrs. Knauer testified at that hearing on July 28 and warmly supported the concept of class action and the principle behind the legislation. Her support was not qualified by specifics regarding implementation or limitations. She reiterated her stand on August 23 in a speech she delivered before the Consumer Federation of America.

Business interests were opposed to the concept of class action, fearing a wave of harassment suits and, more importantly, a basic realignment in the traditional relationship between individual buyers and sellers. As the opposition of the business community was mobilized by the American Retail Federation and the Chamber of Commerce, their position was effectively represented by the Commerce Department. However, Mrs. Knauer's public position had committed the administration to some sort of class action bill. According to one close observer of the issue, administration staff members felt painted into a corner by Mrs. Knauer and would not have put forth a class action bill otherwise.[19]

According to the *Washington Post,* Mrs. Knauer's legislative

[19] Ronald Kessler, "Class Action Bill: Its Rise and Fall," *Washington Post,* April 27, 1970, p. A1.

director drafted a strong class action bill incorporating her original unqualified endorsement of the class action principle.[20] The Justice Department's legislative section originally endorsed the bill in a letter which was to be sent to the Senate Committee on the Judiciary. However, that Justice Department position was quickly changed. The chief of the Justice Department's antitrust division, Richard McLaren, recommended that the bill allow class action only for a limited number of enumerated violations of existing law. A new draft to this effect was prepared. However, the Commerce Department still would have none of it and represented its constituency in opposing the very concept of class action. There was a need for a decision since the previously announced date of the President's consumer message was approaching. Although Secretary of Commerce Maurice Stans was still opposed, it was clear that some bill would have to be presented. The bill which finally emerged from the White House tried to mollify the Commerce Department with a "triggering device" requiring action by the Justice Department or the FTC. That is, a class action suit could be brought only after the Justice Department or the Federal Trade Commission had successfully prosecuted a company for one of an enumerated list of violations. Given the almost legendary delay in these kinds of proceedings, the bill provided small comfort to consumer activists.

Mrs. Knauer supported the compromise measure and the President presented it in his October consumer message. Mrs. Knauer has maintained that she never really changed her position. Rather, she stated that she originally supported the basic concept in the Tydings bill, but always thought that it needed improvement. Publicly, she states that the administration bill is an improvement since it protects honest businessmen and prevents clogging the courts with trivial suits. However, interviews with some of those involved indicate that she was indeed overruled in a compromise struck between her original position and the adament opposition of the Commerce Department.

This incident indicates the general pattern of relationships confronted by Mrs. Knauer during her tenure of office. She originally was separated by two levels from the President—reporting to an assistant to presidential aide Peter Flannigan who in turn was responsible to the President. As one disgruntled former PCCI staff member put it, "It

---

[20] Ibid. Also independently confirmed in personal interviews.

seems to me incredible that the Special Assistant to the President on Consumer Affairs should have to report to a kid 28 years old, two years out of law school, who in turn reports to Peter Flannigan, who in turn reports to the President—neither one of whom has had as much as a day's work in consumer problems." After being in office for about a year, Mrs. Knauer was invited to attend regularly the daily morning briefings held by Counsel to the President John Ehrlichman to whom she then reported directly. Nonetheless, the nemesis of the PCCI continued to be the Commerce Department. While there were no further about-faces in recommendations, this was most probably due to a law of anticipated reaction. At any rate, no one in consumer affairs outside the administration shared Mrs. Knauer's opinion that the administration was committed to consumer protection and that she was not restrained by representatives of business within the administration.

Mrs. Knauer is very sensitive to the almost universal reports that she is restrained and is quite defensive about the Nixon administration's consumer protection posture. In sorting out the various perspectives on events, it seems that she is caught in what some critics of bureaucracy have called "the effectiveness trap." She is sincerely committed to consumer protection and her original unqualified support of the class action concept reflected that commitment. Confronted by an administration less aggressive in pursuit of the consumer interest than she would prefer, she has opted to keep battles internal and to be a "team player" in order to maximize her effectiveness. This orientation is reflected in her strong opinion that any federal consumer office should be connected with the White House so that it could attempt to exert its influence directly at the highest level. There is, of course, a fine line between compromise in pursuit of effectiveness and cooptation by the ineffective, and the side of that line occupied by any presidential consumer advisor will continue to be subject to question. In February, 1971, the President's Committee on Consumer Interests was given the more realistic title of Office of Consumer Affairs although its functions remain largely the same.

The Departments

Following the example set by the President, several of the major Executive departments responded to the newly popular issue by appointing consumer advisors. They were given titles such as consumer program advisor (Labor), or special assistant to the secretary for consumer affairs (Health, Education, and Welfare). Their main responsibility is to advise the secretaries of their respective departments on present or proposed programs with a consumer interest. However, they have only marginal influence within their departments, and in no case has a close working relationship been established with the secretary.

While their limited influence prevents them from effectively shaping legislative proposals and major new programs, consumer advisor offices are still able to undertake that time-honored bureaucratic mission of coordination. They attempt to perform a clearing house function for all the consumer protection activities of their departments by increasing liaison between bureaus, linking up with related activities in other parts of the government, and presenting each department's programs as a coherent package. The epitome of this coordination function is the President's Committee on Consumer Interests which serves as the chief coordination agency of federal consumer activities. As in other aspects of bureaucratic behavior as well as other areas of consumer politics, this coordination is more in the nature of labeling old activities rather than any sort of systematic adjustment of resources and priorities to achieve common goals.

The main thrust of all these newly created posts was to increase and improve "consumer representation" in each of the major Executive departments. At the same time, however, the duties of such offices were highly amorphous in character. Betty Furness in defining the responsibilities of her office stated, "It was explained loosely to me by the President. He told me to do two things: Go out and tell the consumers that their government cares about them. We're also supposed to find out what's on the consumer's mind."[21] She went on to state a variety of possible programs for the future, but it was evident that there was little if any guidance from the top. The central feature of these advisory offices is their lack of guidance and, consequently, their self-definition of function.

A "bandwagon" effect is clearly visible in the recent proliferation of consumer protection activities within the national bureaucracy. In 1967, the PCCI published a *Guide to Federal Consumer Services* as a response to the President's 1964 directive to the PCCI "to develop

---

[21] Personal interview.

means of keeping the public continuously informed of developments of importance in the consumer field." The booklet lists the consumer activities of various governmental agencies. Included are the Department of Defense, the Coast Guard, the Veterans Administration and various other agencies with only the most peripheral and broadly defined consumer responsibilities.

Actually, in their official statement of responsibilities, virtually all government agencies claim to be performing services for the public, as can be ascertained from a review of the *United States Government Organization Manual*. Now, instead of service to citizens or the general public, it has become fashionable for the agencies to stress service to the consumer. It is not surprising that government agencies adopt the popular term, but it is significant that a wide variety of agencies can claim to represent the same interest. This shows that when an interest is shared by nearly all citizens, everyone can claim to be furthering that interest if it becomes more salient and more popular. To the extent that it is diffuse and lacking in clear definition, the consumer interest, like the public interest, can be all things to all people.

Response by Existing
Consumer Protection Agencies

At this point it should be pointed out that although the consumer protection issue has become politically popular only recently, several government agencies have long had direct and clear responsibilities in this area. Indeed, the "granddaddy" of regulatory agencies, the Interstate Commerce Commission, was created in response to demands by consumers of railroad services. In the previous section the discussion centered on the creation of new administrative offices in response to the popularity of consumer protection. We now turn to two agencies which existed prior to the 1960s and which have always had direct and unambiguous consumer protection responsibilities—the Federal Trade Commission and the Food and Drug Administration.[22]

---

[22] In discussing "response" I am not assuming that the activities so discussed conform to any strict model of causality. For my purposes it is sufficient that the interview respondents consider these activities as the agencies' response. Being perceived as a response, it is a moot question whether or not certain programs would have emerged anyway.

The Federal Trade Commission: Preliminary Response

The Federal Trade Commission has a wide variety of statutory responsibilities revolving around its basic objective of maintaining "free competitive enterprise as the keystone of the American economic system." However, traditionally the two major responsibilities of the commission are the enforcement of antitrust laws and the prevention of unfair and deceptive practices. These dual responsibilities were lodged in the original Federal Trade Commission Act, and the FTC also shares responsibility with the Justice Department for enforcing the Clayton Antitrust Act. While the prevention of deceptive practices was once restricted to deceptive trade practices (false advertising, deceptive promotions, etc.) in which damage to competitors could be demonstrated, the FTC can now act against those practices which are deceptive and unfair to consumers regardless of their effect on competition. In addition the commission has been given the responsibility for enforcing truthful labeling of textile and fur products. More recently, the FTC has been given enforcement responsibilities for several consumer protection measures of the 1960s. These include the Flammable Fabrics Act which provides for the establishment of flammability standards in most textile products; the Fair Packaging and Labeling Act ("truth-in-packaging") which sets information requirements for grocery packaging; and the truth-in-lending sections of the Consumer Credit Protection Act which require detailed written disclosure of actual finance charges by all consumer creditors. In carrying out its enforcement responsibilities the commission may, after appropriate administrative hearings, issue a cease and desist order against an offending business. While the cease and desist order itself carries no sanctions, the FTC can recommend civil actions (which carry penalties) to the Justice Department. Furthermore, the FTC can recommend criminal action in deception cases involving food, drugs, flammable fabrics, or furs. The other major technique of law enforcement is to secure voluntary compliance, through advisory opinions, trade regulation rules, and industry guides. While this is not an exhaustive description of the agency's functions, anything more might be exhausting. The lay reader can find a more detailed listing of the FTC's responsibilities in the most recent volume of its Annual Report.

Change was slow in coming to the Federal Trade Commission, and the response to the burgeoning interest in consumer protection came in two stages. The first was the independent actions and record of the commission during the late 1960s when the FTC was making its own way and its own record as one of the participants in the newly salient issue. In light of what follows, this might be called the "preliminary response." As will shortly be demonstrated, the preliminary response was totally inadequate. In a time of increasing concern with consumer protection, it was inevitable that outside attention should be directed toward the agency. Although subject to criticism before, beginning in late 1968 the FTC was subject to an almost continuous flood of publicized criticism which was remarkably consistent in its findings. The first salvo in this series was contained in the "Nader Report"—a study of the FTC carried out by a small group of law students brought together by Ralph Nader (and dubbed Nader's Raiders by the press.)[23] This criticism continued up to and including an American Bar Association study undertaken at the request of President Nixon.[24] While all this criticism arose as part of the general political trend in consumer protection, the later actions of the FTC were influenced at least as much by the surrounding bombshells as by the more generalized trend of consumerism. Therefore, we can consider the later actions of the FTC as a sort of "crisis response," consisting in part of the series of reactions of a tension-filled bureaucracy under external attack.

The earliest visible response by the commission was the establishment of a deceptive practices program in the District of Columbia. While the FTC has always had plenary jurisdiction in the District, it was only in 1966 that it inaugurated a program to handle complaints against merchants in that area.

An even more visible response of the FTC consisted of hearings on consumer protection which were held in November and December, 1968. There were nearly ninety witnesses including forty representatives of various governmental agencies, twenty-one trade association representatives, and eighteen representatives of consumer groups.

[23] Originally released in mimeographed form, it has been revised and published as Edward Cox, Robert Fellmeth, and John Schulz, *The "Nader Report" On The Federal Trade Commission* (New York: Baron, 1969).

[24] *Report of the ABA Commission To Study The Federal Trade Commission* (New York: American Bar Association, 1969).

With regard to agency action, the hearing itself constituted the generalized response by the FTC to the consumer protection problem. Other than the usual report, it soon became clear that no action would result from the hearing. That being the case, the hearing can be viewed as an exercise in symbolic politics.[25] Just as the very existence of a consumer protection agency nurtures the belief that something is being accomplished for consumers, so too can hearings create the belief that something will be done once the agency knows of the problems. Various episodes that occurred during the hearings lend weight to this hypothesis. Thus, witness after witness brought forth matters not within the legal jurisdiction of the commission. They spoke as though they believed that by airing the problem before a government agency some progress has been made toward alleviating it. This is not to attribute any Machiavellian motives to the commissioners. The chairman several times reiterated that the commission did not have the legal power to deal with some of the matters being discussed. Furthermore, attempting to prevent anyone from speaking would not have been worth the grief which surely would have resulted.

The two responses discussed above were the primary visible and objective preliminary responses by the FTC. However, interviews with the commissioners revealed that they had no unified conception of the agency response. While the former chairman mentioned the hearing, the D.C. program, and the establishment of a federal-state liaison bureau he was alone in mentioning all these programs. The other commissioners gave answers ranging from their impression that the agency had become "more consumer minded" to the mention of particular programs being initiated, evaluated, or expanded. Although there was no agreement on the specific measures by which the FTC was responding to the new interest in consumer protection, all the commissioners believed that the FTC was responsive in good measure. This assessment was shared even by the three commissioners who were most critical of the commission. However, it is the lack of agreement on just what policy or program constitutes the commission response that is significant in terms of the representation of the consumer interest. If the individual commissioners themselves were not clear on the specific

[25] Edelman, *Symbolic Uses of Politics,* pp. 44–72.

nature of the commission response, how could consumer organizations, let alone the individual consumers, know what is being done on their behalf?

Federal Trade Commission: Post-Crisis Response

It is not merely a matter of convenience to divide the actions of the FTC into preliminary and crisis response periods. While there were some objections to the Nader report and charges of bias against it, the ABA report plus critiques written by some of the commissioners provided ample evidence of the inadequate performance of the agency. By all accounts, agency morale was low, and a majority of the commissioners were keenly aware of the agency's deficiencies and were anxious to remedy those deficiencies. The feeling of crisis came at a time when change could be expected anyway—a change of administrations. Thus, reform-minded personnel in the agency looked to the President's appointment of a new chairman as the first step in any change.

In terms of visibility and effect on future events, the appointment by President Nixon of Casper Weinberger as chairman of the commission can be viewed the major response to the crisis. Weinberger was appointed by the President on January 13, 1970. His background in Republican politics, caused his appointment to be greeted with some suspicion and disappointment by consumer advocates. However, it was not long before Weinberger was cloaked in the image of a hard-driving, committed, and imaginative chairman. Thus, in testimony before the House Committee on Foreign and Interstate Commerce, Weinberger not only endorsed the administration proposals to increase FTC enforcement authority, but urged that it be still further broadened to include authority to assess civil penalties and to award damages to consumers who have been injured by acts found by the commission to be violations of the law. Furthermore, Weinberger led the commission in a unanimous recommendation that Congress pass an automobile quality control act in which the government would prescribe minimum standards of durability and performance for new automobiles. In the area of consumer protection, the first "crisis era" chairman seems to have merited a *New York Times* headline, "F.T.C. Shows Spirit of Toughness Under New Chief."[26] Weinberger's tenure, however, was brief. He left the FTC in August, 1970, for a top post in the Office of Management and Budget. He was succeeded in September by Miles Kirkpatrick who had been chairman of the American Bar Association Commission which produced the 1969 report on the FTC. Having been a critic of the agency, Kirkpatrick was even more committed to the revitalization and reform of the FTC than his predecessor.

An immediate consequence of the appointment of a new chairman was a healing of the rifts within the agency. Toward the end of the regime of Chairman Dixon, personal relations within the commission were extremely strained and nearly all actions were split decisions. In contrast, Weinberger was able to achieve unanimity in almost all decisions during his tenure. This change was of greater consequence than merely insuring a more pleasant time in the executive cafeteria since unanimous action increases agency influence and legitimacy.[27]

A second major response of the agency to crisis was a major reorganization. The existing functional bureaus were abolished or shifted into two new bureaus, Deceptive Practices and Consumer Protection, representing the two major responsibilities of the agency (the antitrust activities come under Consumer Protection). While this reorganization was greeted with enthusiasm by critics of the agency, one commissioner noted that its major purpose was simply to circumvent Civil Service rules to get rid of considerable dead wood at the top of the abolished bureaus. Furthermore, within a month of the reorganization, many critics began a sober second look and felt that the reorganization may well have been a change devoid of substance. Apart from easing out a few bureau heads, the reorganization brought about little change in operating procedures or personnel. Thus, Weinberger never did appoint a man to head the Bureau of Consumer Protection. Chairman Kirkpatrick, however, filled the post in October, 1970. (The new man, Robert Pitofsky, was also associated with the ABA report).

26 John D. Morris, February 7, 1970, p. 19.

27 For an analogous situation demonstrating the importance of unanimity and the means of achieving it, see David J. Danelski, "The Influence of the Chief Justice in The Decisional Process," in *Readings In American Political Behavior,* ed. Raymond E. Wolfinger (New York: Prentice-Hall, 1970), pp. 185–195.

A third response occurred in June, 1970, when the FTC established a council of legal experts to propose changes in the FTC's administrative procedures which have been notorious for their delays. The establishment of the council was, of course, a direct response to this criticism of the agency—a criticism which was the one most frequently made and which was included in every study of the commission.

In addition to these organizational changes, there were a number of individual substantive actions by which the commission indicated a new "toughness." A good example was a major FTC action announced on June 10, 1971, in response to a petition filed the previous December by Ralph Nader and other consumer advocates. The commission announced that it would henceforth require that all major industries provide substantive data in support of their advertising claims. Thus a claim that a tire "stops twenty percent quicker" would have to be documented with solid evidence—evidence which would be made available to the public. The orders are being drafted on an industry by industry basis with the automobile manufacturers being the first target. This assertion of authority, which has been vociferously denounced by businessmen, will probably have to be resolved by the courts. It should be noted that in taking action affecting the giant automobile industry the FTC has departed from its pattern of timidity toward large industry.

In short, there has been a very visible series of organizational and substantive actions in specific response to the widespread criticism of the commission. However, there are serious questions as to whether these actions represent a fundamental change in the agency. At least one other commission member, Philip Elman, concluded after Weinberger left the commission that the FTC and other independent regulatory agencies were still not responsive to the public interest and needed a "radical structural reform."[28]

Part of the problem is that FTC actions can readily be viewed as a specific response to criticism of their performance in consumer protection. The most visible area of this criticism (to the press and to the public) has been in regard to deceptive practices. Therefore, the most dramatic recent actions of the agency relate to deceptive practices. However, there has been no correspondingly urgent action in the antitrust area even though chairman Weinberger publicly labeled this as

---

[28] David Vienna, *Washington Post,* August 12, 1970, p. A2.

the area of paramount importance. This can be seen in the case of the automobile industry. Weinberger received a flurry of publicity for his unprecedented suggestion that the physical quality of automobiles, even beyond safety, be subject to regulation. This was indeed a striking proposal in the area of consumer protection. However, the FTC did not issue equally striking proposals in the antitrust field. Thus, Ralph Nader and others have argued that one of the major reasons for the problems of automotive quality is the oligopolistic nature of the industry. Yet there have been no FTC suggestions on how to deal with the quality and cost problems resulting from the automobile oligopoly. Therefore, to a large extent the FTC response to consumer protection has been limited to problems in such visible areas as deceptive practices rather than weighty but low-visibility problems in the antitrust area.

A second problem is in the area of priorities to be discussed shortly. Although, the vacancy at the head of the program planning office of the commission was filled, there was little sense of urgency in the area of systematic program planning, and the small staff of the office was increased only slightly. In terms of a permanent institutional change, one would expect a key role to be played by a revitalized program planning office. This has not come about, however.

It is possible that what might be described as a new aggressive tenor at the FTC may represent a fundamental reorientation. Especially in 1971, the commission has been vigorous in making important and extensive proposals to curb deceptive practices. The institutional base which is needed to carry through that orientation, however, is still very fragile. In view of the nearly fifty years of FTC stagnation, it is too early to make any final judgments on the permanence of the FTC's "new look."

The Food and Drug Administration

It is more difficult to identify the response of the Food and Drug Administration since it is an integral part of the Department of Health, Education and Welfare. The agency's response is thus influenced by the political executives in the department and ultimately by the President.

The FDA is a natural place to analyze a bureaucratic response to consumer protection. Its areas of responsibility have traditionally been at the heart of public concern about consumer protection, and the two previous eras of consumer consciousness resulted in the Pure Food and Drug Act of 1906 and the Food, Drug, and Cosmetic Act of 1938. More recently, the first stirrings of consumer protection as a current public issue can be traced to the hearings on drug prices and safety conducted by the late Senator Estes Kefauver—hearings which led to the revelation of the thalidomide birth-defect episode and to the 1962 Kefauver-Harris amendments to the Food, Drug, and Cosmetic Act. The involvement of the FDA was more than a matter of its subject area. The competency and zeal with which the agency carried out its responsibilities has been a subject of contention since the agency's establishment—a subject that always emerges to the fore during periods of concern with food and drugs.

The FDA was established as the Food, Drug, and Insecticide Administration in the Agriculture Department in 1927, and took over administration of the 1906 act from the Bureau of Chemistry. In 1931, it was given its present name and, in 1940, transferred out of Agriculture into the Federal Security Administration where it remained when that agency was succeeded by the Department of Health, Education, and Welfare.

In its own statement of its mandate, the agency declares: "The Food and Drug Administration is responsible for ensuring that foods are safe, pure, and wholesome; that cosmetics are safe; and that all of these are honestly and informatively labeled and packaged. In addition, it has broad responsibilities in other areas of consumer protection: hazardous substances, poisons and pesticides, as well as other products which may present hazards to the user."[29]

In practice, this gives the FDA an enormous range of responsibilities. It routinely inspects food processing plants whose products are in interstate commerce and has extensive programs of voluntary compliance and agreements with state inspection units to aid in the inspection task. The FDA can seize contaminated foods, order recalls of food which has left the plant, and can ask for criminal prosecution of flagrant violators. In addition to regulation after the fact, the FDA certifies for safety all coloring agents used in foods, drugs, and cosmetics; estab-

[29] U.S., Department of Health, Education, and Welfare, *Annual Report 1968* (Washington, D.C.: U.S. Govt. Printing Office, 1969), pp. 315–316.

lishes standards of quality and identity for commonly used foods such as grape juice, pork and beans, etc.; and establishes pesticide residue tolerances for produce. The greatest part of the FDA's activities is in the field of drugs. No new prescription drug can be marketed unless approved by the FDA for safety and, since 1962, for efficacy. The FDA also has authority over the advertising and labeling of drugs and may send out "corrective letters" to physicians informing them of misleading claims made for drugs. In addition to approving new drugs, the FDA continually supervises the manufacture of all antibiotics and insulin.

Although the trend has been toward a decreasing emphasis on cosmetics, several cosmetic products a year are seized for being harmful or for failing to have labeling which warns consumers of potential hazards. With the exception of the coloring agents in the products, cosmetics are not required to be approved prior to marketing and cosmetic manufacturing plants are not inspected.

The FDA has considerable responsibilities under the Hazardous Substances Act originally passed in 1960. It is responsible for the requirement that all household products be labeled with proper warning about any hazards involved in using the product. In addition, the FDA may ban any product it deems too hazardous for household use—as it did with carbon tetrachloride. It may also seize products where unreasonable hazards have been found.

Finally, the FDA provides services even beyond its regulatory authority such as providing a variety of consumer information on such topics as drugs and food additives.

In assessing the FDA response, the scope of this study excludes the possibility of giving a comprehensive overview of all facets of agency activity. Rather, several components of the agency's response will be identified as indicative of the agency's posture. In the present context, "response" means the reactions to various political pressures. Thus the essential question is whether the renewed public and congressional interest in consumer protection constituted effective political pressure to which the FDA reacted.

Like the FTC, the response of the Food and Drug Administration can be viewed during two successive periods. The first period covers the first burst of attention focused primarily on drug safety and is roughly the years 1960–1965. The second, 1966 to the present, begins with the firing of a much criticized FDA commissioner and is coincident with the current period of generalized interest in consumer protection. The earlier period was the era in which George Larrick was commissioner of FDA. The general tenor and lack of vigor of Larrick's tenure in office can best be described by the fact that in 1958 he received an award from the Pharmaceutical Manufacturers Association for "devoted service to the public welfare" and for his "understanding of mutual problems."[30] Since its creation, the FDA's dominant assumption has been trust of industry and a reliance on voluntary methods. Until very recently, the agency did not have the funds to do anything else. However, it is unusual that after the rapid increase in appropriations beginning in the late fifties, Commissioner Larrick maintained the same faith in industry and in a 1963 interview stated that "by and large people in industry are just about as honest as people in Government." Since this statement came a year after it was revealed that the chief of the FDA's antibiotic division had received over one quarter million dollars from the drug industry during the preceding eight years, Larrick was hardly reassuring on either count. As a further indication of the rather comfortable relationship between FDA and industry, an FDA Citizens Advisory Committee (whose members were chosen by Larrick) issued an October, 1962, report urging that mandated self-inspection and self-regulation should eventually supercede formal regulation and enforcement by the agency. Although the report was prepared during the time that the shape of the thalidomide tragedy was emerging into the public press, no mention was made about new drug testing problems. Perhaps this was due to the fact that the chairman of the drugs subcommittee of the advisory committee was James B. Mintener, a former HEW assistant secretary who was then engaged in private Washington food and drug law practice and whose clients included Richardson-Merrell, Inc., the American manufacturer of thalidomide. Not surprisingly, the report was hailed by the Pharmaceutical Manufacturers Association.[31]

At the very least, one would expect a temporary top-level reaction to the results of the thalidomide story. But even that was lacking as indicated by a hearing held by the House Intergovernmental Relations

[30] Morton Mintz, *By Prescription Only* (Boston: Beacon Press, 1967), pp. 95–96.
[31] Ibid., pp. 129–130.

Subcommittee chaired by L. H. Fountain. In April, 1963, C. T. G. King of the National Institute of Dental Research sent a memo to Commissioner Larrick advising him that the antihistimines meclizine, cyclizine, and chlorcyclizine had been found to cause congenital abnormalities in rats. These drugs had been sold as nonprescription drugs under the brand names Bonamine, Bonadettes, and Bonadoxin by Charles Pfizer & Co. and Marezine and Perazile by Burroughs Wellcome & Co. Two of the drugs were for nausea—and were promoted for the relief of nausea in pregnant women.

After consulting outside experts, on May 7, 1963, the Bureau of Medicine recommended that nonprescription sales of the drugs be halted, that consideration be given to sending a warning letter to all physicians, and that a specific warning regarding use by pregnant women be added to the label. Larrick, however, did not act. In reply to the subcommitee's natural curiosity as to why he took no action, Larrick claimed that the experts who had been consulted would not be available as witnesses in any eventual court action. In fact, internal FDA memos showed this statement to be false. Instead of acting, Larrick and Assistant Commissioner Rankin convened an ad hoc committee for recommendations. On April 20, 1964, a year after the initial warning, the group recommended unanimously that nonprescription sales should be discontinued and that a warning be added to the prescription labeling. But the commissioner's office still took no action. The reason offered for the delay was that in some fashion the committee's action was not yet "official." On January 18, 1965, the official report was transmitted to the commissioner by the ad hoc medical director, Dr. Joseph Sadusk, who endorsed the recommendations of the committee. However, within three days, Dr. Sadusk withdrew his recommendation for the stated reason that more review and data were necessary. Thus, even in the wake of the thalidomide episode the attitude was, as Morton Mintz put it, "When there is, or is claimed to be, a doubt, give the benefit of it not to the pregnant woman and her embryo, but to the manufacturer."[32] The ad hoc committee was reconvened on April 22, 1965. However, the reconvened committee (with several members absent) voted 8–1 to reverse its previous recommendation in light of certain controlled studies presented which indi-

[32] Ibid., p. 264.

cated no risk in the antihistimines. Unfortunately, the congressional subcommittee later found out that the studies relied on most heavily by Dr. Sadusk were still in progress and, indeed, the researcher in one of them had written that progress so far permitted no conclusions about safety. Furthermore, Dr. Sadusk's views that the antihistimines should be marketed as before were contrary to the opinion of several of his subordinates in the Bureau of Medicine—subordinates whose views were not transmitted to the commissioner. Finally, after all of the preceding had been revealed in the Fountain subcommittee hearing, in October, 1965, Sadusk announced that the FDA would require an over-the-counter label warning against use by women who are or may become pregnant.[33]

The purpose of the foregoing vignette is not to dramatize an isolated incident. Rather, the purpose has been to examine the record for an indication of FDA response to sharply focused congressional and public attention. It might be expected that the crisis of confidence in the agency would produce large-scale changes in procedures and personnel. At the very least the normal bureaucratic reaction to be expected would be to remedy the particular conditions which had been most visible and which had been the precipitating cause of most criticism of the agency. Thalidomide was clearly such an event. Yet, when faced with another drug suspected of producing fetal deformities, there was almost no change in the attitudes and perspective of the top-level personnel of the agency.

Furthermore, the incident is not isolated. At least eight volumes of congressional hearings by two committees (subsequent to the Kefauver hearings) demonstrate little in the way of an identifiable programmatic response during the initial period of consumer protection concern. An advisory committee study of the FDA commissioned by Health, Education, and Welfare Secretary John Gardner and released in January, 1966, condemned the agency for failing to keep pace with its expanded responsibilities.

What might be termed a "new era" (at least in terms of public image) began at the Food and Drug Administration in 1966, with the appointment of Dr. James Goddard as commissioner. Indeed, after years of criticizing his predecessor, *Science* magazine praised Goddard

---

[33] Ibid.

for achieving a "bureaucratic miracle" at FDA and announced that FDA was where the action is.[34] In point of fact, Goddard started out in a most unorthodox way and set a new public tenor for the agency which was a far cry from the mutually admiring relation between Larrick and the regulated industries. Early in his tenure of office, Goddard signaled an about face from the attitudes of Larrick by denouncing the drug industry as irresponsible and not worthy of trust. Furthermore, in a much publicized speech given before the convention of the Pharmaceutical Manufacturers Associations he asserted that already he had "seen evidence that too many drug manufacturers may well have obscured the prime mission of their industry: to help people get well." Specifically he denounced the quality of investigational new drugs and new drug applications and charged that manufacturers had been guilty of faulty testing and deliberately trying to withhold unfavorable information.[35] The important point is that there was a general aura surrounding Goddard's appointment which indicated a top-level response to increased consumer awareness. Goddard was able to capitalize publicly on that awareness and reaped a harvest of publicity with picture spreads in *Time, Life,* and the *New York Times Magazine.* The image projected was one of a dynamic, public-spirited commissioner shaking up the agency.[36] Even though the image exceeded the reality, Goddard did respond to the new political climate more than any other agency head. His increasingly strained relations with the drug industry were both symptomatic and a by-product of that response. Under Goddard, the agency shifted to a greater emphasis on enforcement and stricter inspection of drug houses.

Unfortunately, one commissioner does not an agency make. It is necessary to analyze the elements beyond merely the image of the "tenor" of the agency. It is this kind of inquiry which yields a less encouraging picture of agency response.

Structurally, the initial response was a reorganization which placed FDA in a new division called the Consumer Protection and Environmental Health Services (CPEHS) and brought together con-

---

[34] "Goddard at FDA: New Rules for the Game," *Science,* June 10, 1966, p. 1487.

[35] Mintz, *By Prescription Only,* pp. xxxi–xxxii.

[36] See, for example, George Boehm, "He is Shaking FDA Well," *New York Times Magazine,* May 15, 1966, p. 234.

sumer protection, pollution control, and medical research functions under the Public Health Service. This reorganization took place in July, 1968. The change brought FDA down one notch in the organization chart, but the Department of Health, Education, and Welfare argued that the realignment created a greater potential for a coordinated program to deal with a greater range of environmental hazards. It should be noted that the reorganization was not entirely prompted by increased awareness of consumer problems. Rather, it was part of an attempt to introduce program budgeting (PPB) in HEW. Since PPB is based on the combination of related programs and functions, the reorganization was a natural result.

HEW officials also thought that by making FDA part of a larger entity in the regular chain of command, it would be more insulated from pressures directed from the food and drug industries. However, the former FDA commissioner, Dr. Herbert Ley, Jr., complained that he had been under "constant, tremendous, and sometimes unmerciful pressure" from the drug industry after the reorganization occurred.[37] In other respects also, reorganization turned out to be a failure. The drug industry has repeatedly charged the agency with not acting fast enough in licensing new drugs while consumer advocates such as Ralph Nader complain about laxness in new product licensing.

A shake-up in FDA occurred in December, 1969. Dr. Ley and two other top officials (who had been criticized by Nader and others for laxness) were removed and the reorganization was virtually rescinded. FDA was taken out of the Consumer Protection Environmental Health Service and placed directly under the authority of the assistant secretary for health and scientific affairs. Dr. Ley was offered a new post as deputy assistant secretary for health and scientific affairs, but declined it.

Procedural and personnel changes can be superficial and transitory things. Although the appointment of Goddard and the successive reorganizations of the Food and Drug Administration might indicate a new responsive posture, an examination of specific cases indicate that in fact the basic problems continue. In short, the more things change, the more they stay the same.

The first of these episodes involves the story of the artificial

37 *New York Times,* December 31, 1969, p. 1.

sweetner, cyclamate, and is symptomatic of the response at FDA during both the "old" and "new" eras.[38] Cyclamates first came to the attention of the FDA in 1950 when Abbot Laboratories filed a new drug application for Sucaryl Sodium which it originally intended to market as a drug for use by those who had to restrict their intake of sugar. The FDA promptly disallowed the test data submitted by Abbot, but conducted tests of its own. Cyclamate was approved on the basis of those FDA tests even though a normally rare malignant tumor was noted in six out of the 100 rat tests. Although this might have been taken as a warning, it was not interpreted as such. In the following nineteen years, there were a number of other such warnings which were ignored.

A series of warnings began in 1954 when the National Academy of Sciences-National Research Council warned the FDA against the uncontrolled distribution of cyclamates. This warning was repeated with no effect in 1955, 1962, and 1968.

In spite of these warnings, in 1959, the FDA included cyclamates in the Generally Recognized As Safe (GRAS) list under the authority of the Food Additives Amendment of 1958. This meant that cyclamates, like all GRAS substances could be added to food without prior proof of safety. This listing is what unleashed the flood of cyclamates into food. Prior to that time the FDA had restricted cyclamate use to special dietary food where it was listed on the label as being intended for people who must restrict their intake of normal sweets.

As noted before, in 1962, the National Academy of Sciences repeated its warning about cyclamates and again no action followed. From the preceding discussion, this might have been expected of the FDA in the "old era." However, as the rest of the story shows, the response to the hazards of cyclamates was no better during the years of supposed change and pro-consumer posture in FDA.

Indeed, one could argue that the FDA behaved even more badly in the later years since it was then that the most damaging evidence on cyclamates came in. In 1966, two Japanese scientists discovered that cyclamates in a person's body could cause a chemical reaction resulting in the production of cyclohexylamine, a chemical already regarded as

[38] For a more detailed account of the cyclamate story see James Turner, *The Chemical Feast* (New York: Grossman, 1970) on which I base this summary.

dangerous by the FDA. Indeed, it later turned out that this reaction occurred in about one-third of the people ingesting cyclamates.

In 1968, an FDA biochemist, Dr. Helen Verrett, reported that she had discovered a significant relationship between cyclamates injected into eggs and embryo deformities. Although this was specifically brought to the attention of Commissioner Ley in April, 1969, he made no effort to remove the additive from the GRAS list. An even more indicative episode also occurred in 1968. An FDA cell biologist, Dr. Marvin Legator, discovered that cyclohexylamine, the chemical produced by cyclamate in the bodies of many people, could cause chromosome damage. He sent an urgent message to Commissioner Ley urging that cyclamate use be curtailed. However, without Legator's knowledge, this message was changed by his superior, Dr. Edwin Howe, in such a manner as to greatly reduce its urgency.

In sum, by 1968, at least ten other warning signals about cyclamates in addition to the ones mentioned had been received by the FDA including possible damaging effects on the liver, the intestinal tract, and on blood anticoagulants.

However, in 1968, there also appeared a report by a committee of the National Academy of Sciences which played down the dangers of cyclamates after reviewing all the studies. This report was criticized severely by the Food and Drug Administration's own scientists. Nonetheless, based on this report, Commissioner Ley decided to keep cyclamates on the GRAS list.

Finally, one year later, in October, 1969, Robert Finch, Secretary of Health, Education, and Welfare, announced a ban on the use of cyclamates. Might this be an indication of a reawakening of responsibilities? Not quite. Cyclamates were banned on the basis of the flimsiest evidence of their harm—that they might be carcinogenic and thus subject to prohibition under the Delaney clause of the 1958 additives amendment. In his press conference, Finch conveyed the impression that he was somewhat reluctantly banning cyclamates and that this rather weak evidence of their carcinogenic character was the only possible harm arising from them. The other studies were not mentioned. In fact there were better studies done which showed that, even in low doses, cyclamates could be carcinogenic.

The first ban did not remain for long. One month later, Secretary Finch rescinded the total ban and allowed distribution of cyclamates when labeled as such in dietary foods and in tablet and liquid form as a sweetner. Cyclamate-sweetened food products were then officially considered as "drugs" by the Department of Health, Education, and Welfare. The FDA approved interim applications for cyclamate marketing which contained no evidence of safety. It later turned out in congressional hearings in June, 1969, that this action was bitterly protested by FDA scientists and was instigated by HEW officials including Secretary Finch; Roger O. Egeberg, the assistant secretary for health and scientific affairs; and the surgeon general, Jesse L. Steinfeld.[39] The whole sorry story came to an end in August, 1970, when the FDA finally returned to a complete ban on cyclamates after releasing a report showing cyclamates to be of little or no value in controlling diabetes or obesity—conclusions for which evidence had been abundant for years. Thus, the critics of agency performance on cyclamates were vindicated by the FDA itself.

There are two points to be made about the cyclamate episode. First, the ban announced by Secretary Finch was preceded by material in the popular media on cyclamates which appeared the month before. In one instance, popular magazines such as *Newsweek* featured Dr. Legator's evidence of the relationship between cyclamates and chromosome damage.[40] Also, in early October, 1969, Dr. Helen Verett, an FDA scientist, discussed her embryo studies and cautioned against cyclamate use by pregnant women. Thus, warnings about cyclamates were appearing in the media for a short period of time prior to official FDA action. In can thus be speculated that the agency was reacting to a specific situation where an increase in public pressure was perceived.

The second point stems from the above reaction. That is, the reaction was a specific one. The agency had ignored warnings on cyclamates for almost twenty years, including the recent years of great public interest in consumer protection. But the chronology of the situation points to the conclusion that the agency reacted only to the potential of a public outcry specifically relating to cyclamates. The generalized external concern with consumer protection apparently had no bearing on agency action on cyclamates—and by implication none on other aspects of food additive control.

[39] *Washington Post,* June 11, 1970, p. A3.
[40] *Newsweek,* September 29, 1969, p. 83.

The above episode is not presented to show that the FDA is stifled by one or two venal men. Rather it is one of a series of episodes which demonstrate a variety of problems affecting the Food and Drug Administration. The extent of those problems can be seen in another episode—this one involving Panalba, a fixed-ratio combination of two antibiotics, tetracycline and novobiocine, manufactured by Upjohn Company. The opinion of independent medical researchers had long been that such fixed-ratio antibiotics were not more effective than their component antibiotics used separately and the combination only increased the risk without increasing the benefit. The FDA, in July, 1969, received a study it had commissioned by the National Academy of Sciences-National Research Council which judged at least fifty such combinations to be dangerous. But even prior to final release of that report, the FDA had begun a campaign to remove such drugs from the market. On March 26, 1969, the FDA's Bureau of Medicine recommended that the FDA stop certifying Panalba because its novobiocine component created serious risks without offsetting benefits. On April 30, Commissioner Ley sent Secretary Finch a memo to inform him that at a scheduled meeting the next day he would inform Upjohn that Panalba was being immediately decertified. This he did at the May 1 meeting. Needless to say, Upjohn was completely opposed to this action and wanted an administrative hearing which would have delayed matters while permitting the continued marketing of Panalba. Ley was not willing to grant a hearing with sales continuing since the issue was safety as well as efficacy.

Intercession by Congressman Garry E. Brown from Kalamazoo, Michigan (where Upjohn's headquarters are located), resulted in a meeting between Upjohn representatives, Finch, and HEW Undersecretary John Veneman. That same day, Veneman phoned the HEW deputy undersecretary, Winton Rankin, urging him to consider granting Upjohn a hearing, resuming certification of Panalba, and to have no publicity about the Panalba controversy.

On May 6, Ley responded that the evidence was overwhelming and he could not in good conscience certify Panalba. Nor could he suppress publicity since Congressman Fountain and Senator Nelson had already scheduled public hearings on the matter.

From there, the affair moved quickly and in a confusing manner. On the morning of May 9, Ley was informed by his immediate superior,

C. C. Johnson, the administrator of the Consumer Protection and Environmental Health Service, that the surgeon general had approved Ley's recommendation for immediate removal of Panalba. However, fifteen minutes later Ley was informed by FDA General Counsel William Goodrich that Secretary Finch had ordered a hearing. At 10:30 that morning an investigator for Fountain's subcommittee notified FDA that he wanted to examine their files regarding Panalba. After first being told the files would be ready shortly, he was advised that there would be a delay until the secretary could review the situation. Finch authorized that the files be opened. According to Fountain, the files made it clear that the decision was being made by the secretary rather than the FDA commissioner. At 3:10 on the same day, after the files documenting his involvement were opened, Finch rescinded his earlier decision and went along with the course of action recommended by Ley.

Thus, in 1969, a time of great concern with consumer protection, the FDA was subject to top-level political interference with action based on unanimous medical opinion. The only intervening event between that interference and the withdrawal of interference was the knowledge that it would be found out and publicized by a congressional committee.

It is worth noting two other aspects of the Panalba case which illustrate the problems of bureaucratic response to popular pressure. First, on May 27, Upjohn filed suit in federal district court in Kalamazoo seeking a temporary restraining order and an injunction to stop FDA from decertifying Panalba without a hearing. The judge, W. Wallace Kent, granted the injunction in spite of the fact that FDA final action had not been officially completed and that even if it had, the law requires that the company may carry its complaint to a court of *appeals* and not a lower court. Indeed, on February 27, 1970, the court of appeals ruled against Upjohn and held that when the FDA had officially declared a drug to be dangerous or ineffective, it could remove it from the market without being required to hold a public hearing. Manufacturers would now have to show reasonable grounds for requesting a hearing. Shortly after this ruling, Upjohn halted its sales of Panalba.

Apart from this later judicial interpretation, it is interesting to discover that Kent, the original district court judge, is the unpaid chairman of the Kalamazoo Science Foundation, half of whose trustees are connected with Upjohn Company. A second interesting aspect is that the law firm representing Upjohn before the federal court was Congressman Garry Brown's old firm from which he received at least $1,000 during 1968, which he claimed to be in settlement of his severance. While these facts may only hint at certain improprieties, they do illustrate some of the tangled obstacles which must be hurdled by a consumer protection bureaucracy even when its officials are seeking to respond to the public interest.[41]

While the episodes discussed above are not conclusive in themselves, they are indicative of a trend, especially when they are considered in the context of other evaluations of the Food and Drug Administration.

There is no doubt that the performance of the FDA was totally inadequate prior to the 1960s due to lack of resources and mismanagement of existing resources. The Kefauver hearings and a citizens advisory committee report make that abundantly clear. In this respect, the FDA fully participated in the general disregard of consumer protection. The relevant question now is whether the agency adequately partook in the resurgence of the consumer interest.

Fortunately, there is adequate documentation which confirms the trends indicated by the individual episodes. First, there have been several extremely well-researched investigative congressional hearings, which show that many of the inadequacies of the FDA continued into the period of reawakened public concern with consumer protection.[42] Second, in 1969, two internal reports were issued by FDA and the Department of Health, Education, and Welfare which, although contradictory in placing the blame, point to the same conclusion—that the consumer protection performance of FDA has been inadequate. The first of these reports was prepared under the leadership of Maurice Kinslow who was then director of FDA's Baltimore office. It was critical of the performance of the agency and confessed that FDA was not able

---

[41] See Morton Mintz, "Panalba: A Conflict of Commercial and Therapeutic Goals?" *Science,* August 29, 1969, pp. 875–881.

[42] The most comprehensive are: U.S., Congress, House, Committee on Government Operations, *Drug Safety, Hearings before a subcommittee of the Committee on Government Operations,* 88th Cong., 2nd sess., 1964; and U.S., Congress, Senate, Committee on Small Business, *Competitive Problems in the Drug Industry, Hearings before a subcommittee of the Committee on Small Business,* 90th Cong., 1st sess., 1967.

to assure consumers of the purity of the FDA-regulated products that they bought. This report was not in the nature of a mea culpa however. Rather, it blamed the agency's shortcomings on insufficient appropriations, personnel, and legal authority. Thus, the report implied that the agency was doing the best it could with what it had. The problem was that it didn't have enough.

Dissatisfied with the Kinslow report, Secretary Finch commissioned one of his own by a review committee under the direction of HEW Deputy Undersecretary Frederick V. Malec. While the Malec report also found substantial inadequacies in the agency's performance, it found a major cause of these inadequacies to be internal organizational problems and incompetency.

In one sense the Kinslow and Malec reports can be viewed as political documents serving the ends of those who commissioned them. In the case of the Kinslow report, the agency could not really brush off the mounting criticism directed at it. It would be to the advantage of the agency's management to frankly admit to the obvious problems as part of an appeal for greater authority and appropriations. Similarly, Secretary Finch's Malec report came at the same time that Finch fired Commissioner Ley and reorganized the agency once again. However, the true import of both documents should not be obscured by the political jockeying which may have prompted them. The point to be remembered is that the FDA has not been able to do an adequate job of protecting the consumer of the products under its jurisdiction. The political appeal of consumer protection as an issue only highlighted this problem. It did not remedy it.

Summary

In summarizing the nature of agency response, it should be remembered that the central concern here is the response of bureaucracies to what was generally perceived as a new and widespread public concern with consumer protection. Thus, the question is not whether or not the agencies have been doing an adequate job in protecting the consumer—all observers agree that they have not—but whether and in what manner they improved their performance. In short, did these bureaucracies respond to the demands of a newly articulate constituency?

There are striking parallels in the response of the Food and Drug Administration and the Federal Trade Commission—parallels which lead to speculation about the generality of the response of agencies undergoing a crisis of public confidence. First, there have been changes of personnel at the top levels. In both agencies, the President chose a new chairman; in both a number of old-time executives were eased out. A second response has been reorganization. This was both a change of personnel and a manifestation of the old Progressive belief in the ability of structures to shape behavior. Both agencies were the subjects of critical studies by Congress and independent bodies and both responded by commissioning studies of their own. Indeed, the study commission is a time-honored bureaucratic response to outside pressure. Finally, there has been a programmatic response of high visibility. The agencies have held hearings, partially reallocated resources, and instituted new programs. Viewed in the larger context of the potential for action, the action changes were rather modest.

In a recent work, Francis Rourke emphasizes that the "first and fundamental source of power for administrative agencies in American society is their ability to attract outside support."[43] Given the new public concern with consumer protection the agencies were surprisingly reticent in mobilizing that concern to their benefit. They failed to seize constituency-building opportunities—a failure which can be seen in two potential activities that never really materialized.

First, the agencies made only slight increases in their efforts to make the public aware of their activities and of their efforts in the public's behalf. This is less true of the FDA which partly had the services of the Department of Health, Education, and Welfare consumer advisor who would go out on the hustings to arouse local public support. But a second failure resulted in a lack of follow-through for whatever public support was being mobilized. Rourke points out that general public support may be extremely volatile and that it is thus essential for an agency to have the continuing support of attentive groups. This is particularly essential for organizations like the State Department which have no natural constituency. The FDA and, to some extent, the FTC have no natural attentive constituencies in *sup-*

---

[43] Rourke, *Bureaucracy, Politics, and Public Policy* (Boston: Little, Brown & Co., 1969), p. 11.

port of their activities. Other organizations including the departments of Defense and Agriculture have purposely built support groups.[44] The consumer protection agencies, however, have not fulfilled the potential ability to build a coalition. Liaison between the agencies, consumer groups, and congressmen was spotty and not directed toward the establishment of an effective consumer coalition.

To summarize, the bureaucracy was aware of and did respond to the increased consumer protection concern in other political arenas. However, that response consisted of increments to ongoing activities. Their behavior fits into Herbert Simon's conception of "satisficing."[45] Simon asserts that administrators decide among alternatives on the basis of what is good enough rather than what is best, and that this is the only realistic decision-making model for an administrator. However, Simon's model has its best fit in a situation where there is a constant level of political interest in an agency's activities. This is not the case with consumer protection. Where there is a rapid increase in the political popularity of an agency's functions, administrators have the opportunity to do more than "satisfice." The consumer protection agencies, however, have done little more than that, and have not grasped the opportunities which are available. In "satisficing," they have failed to enlarge and intensify their capacity to represent the consumer interest.

Resources and Response

FDA officials point to the dramatic rise in their budget as the most tangible indication of the agency response. Of course, they do not determine the budget, but the budget is the essential indicator of the *ability* of an agency to function. Previously the analysis dealt with the way the agencies utilized their resources. The budget indicates whether

[44] See, for example, Samuel Huntington, *The Common Defense: Strategic Programs in National Politics* (New York: Columbia University Press, 1961), pp. 384–404. Huntington discusses the ability of the military services to utilize civilian "backstop" organizations to bolster their political power. Also, Rourke points out the experiences of the departments of Labor and Agriculture in building clientele organizations. *Bureaucracy,* p. 17.

[45] Herbert Simon, *Administrative Behavior,* 2nd ed. (New York: Macmillan Co., 1957).

the agencies were given resources commensurate with the new political interest in consumer protection. Viewing the matter in terms of the representation of the consumer interest, the budget figures demonstrate the extent to which governmental consumer protection policy and surrounding publicity is substantive or merely symbolic at the implementation level. Table 3–1 presents the annual budgets of the FTC, and FDA, and the total of all non-defense spending with the annual percentage rise from the previous year for each. As can be seen, the trend

Table 3–1   Annual Increase in Enacted Appropriations, 1960–1969

Fiscal Year	Food and Drug Administration		Federal Trade Commission		Total Non-Defense Appropriation	
	Amount (million)	Increase	Amount (million)	Increase	Amount (billion)	Increase
1960	$15.5	27.2%	$ 6.8	5.4%	$ 46.3	1.9%
1961	20.5	31.9	8.0	17.1	50.4	8.8
1962	26.4	29.2	10.3	28.8	55.7	10.5
1963	30.9	17.2	11.5	14.6	59.1	5.9
1964	40.1	29.5	12.2	6.5	65.0	10.1
1965	51.2	27.8	13.5	10.2	68.9	5.9
1966	58.7	14.5	13.8	3.0	77.9	13.1
1967	64.4	9.7	14.4	3.7	88.3	13.4
1968	62.8	−2.4*	15.3	6.3	98.3	11.4
1969	58.9	−6.1*	16.9	10.9	102.7	4.4

* Decrease reflects transfer of functions in reorganization of HEW.
SOURCE: U.S. Bureau of the Budget, *The Budget of the United States Government, Fiscal Year* [1960–1970], (Washington, D.C.: U.S. Government Printing Office [1960–1970]).

is irregular. However, it is clear that the FDA budget is reflective of the concern with the safety of foods and drugs. The period of rapid growth of FDA actually began in 1956 and continued following the dramatic revelations of the Kefauver investigation. While the period of rising appropriations through the 1960s can be attributed to the interest sparked by the Kefauver hearings, the earlier rise, of course, cannot be so explained. Actually, that change came about when control of Congress reverted to the Democrats in 1955, with a consequent shift in the Appropriations committees. The importance of the shift in party control for FDA appropriations is evidenced by the behavior of the last Republican chairman of the House Appropriations Committee. Angered by an FDA decision to prohibit a canner from cutting large beets into little balls and calling them baby beets, he cut half a million dollars from the FDA budget. At the time, this represented almost a 10 percent cut. Therefore, the increase in funding for the FDA was probably due at least as much to shifts in partisan control over Congress as to response to consumer protection interests.

The FTC budget also shows a curious pattern in that the years of greatest increase, 1961, 1962, and 1963, preceded the period of greatest public interest in consumer protection. Indeed, during this later period the rise was considerably more modest. The budget increase in the early 1960s resulted in a sizable staff increase, but was itself not a result of new statutory authority. Nor does the FTC annual report explain the increase.

Looking at Table 3–1 as a whole, it is apparent that the budget increases of the two consumer protection agencies are chronologically unrelated to the increased interest in consumer protection in other spheres of activity. As can be seen from Table 3–2, the agencies were granted resources far in excess of those they had previously and the increases were considerably greater than the increase in all non-defense spending. However, these increases were independent of the *current* concern over consumer protection. Viewed in terms of this relationship, this current concern is more symbolic than operational since Congress did not grant financial resources commensurate with the publicity surrounding consumer protection.

Total resources are of course only the most indiscriminate indica-

Table 3–2   Total Budget Increase, 1959–1969

Fiscal Year	FDA (million)	FTC (million)	Non-defense Budget (billion)
1959	$12.2	$ 6.0	$ 45.5
1969	58.9	16.9	102.7
Percent Increase:	383%	161%	126%

SOURCE: U.S. Bureau of the Budget, *The Budget of the United States Government, Fiscal Year* [1960, 1970], (Washington, D.C.: U.S. Government Printing Office).

Table 3–3   Division of Food and Drug Administration Budget

Fiscal Year	Foods	Drugs	Cosmetics	Hazardous Substances
1966	38.0%	48.0%	1.7%	1.3%
1967	34.9	48.1	1.6	1.2
1968	33.4	51.9	1.3	1.8
1969	32.5	41.3	1.3	17.6

SOURCE: U.S. Department of Health, Education, and Welfare, *Annual Report* [1966–1969], (Washington, D.C.: U.S. Government Printing Office [1967–1970]).

tion of an agency's response to a new political situation. Of even greater importance arc the uses to which those resources are put. Thus, the budget is also a useful indicator of the utilization of resources. Instead of looking at the total amount of money available, we can look at the internal breakdown of the budget as the first step in assessing the programs and priorities of the agencies.

For example, in Table 3–3, the allocation of funds in the Food and Drug Administration for a four-year period is shown. This is the most tangible evidence that greater weight is given to drugs than to foods and of the new importance of the agency's hazardous substances responsibilities (over which it has had legal authority since 1960).

The budgetary breakdown is but one element of an agency's priorities and to some extent it reflects the expense of some activities as much as their relative importance to the agency. Other explicit criteria must also be considered. But why worry about priorities at all? The answer is that the priorities of an agency as demonstrated by the budget and other criteria constitute the operational determination of which aspects of the consumer interest are represented by the agency and the efficacy with which they are represented.

The Food and Drug Administration has a rather explicit operational priority system. As one might expect, highest priority is given to urgent public health problems. The breakdown of this priority system is most concisely stated in a memorandum by former Commissioner Goddard:

> The fundamental strategy reflected in the choices between objectives
> and in the adjustment of objectives required by the low funding ceil-

ing is to give priority to those programs where the consumer risk is most acute and most obvious to the consumer. Thus greater emphasis is being given to drugs than to food and within the food area to the problem of acute disease states resulting from pathogenic bacteria rather than to those associated with long-term ingestion of toxic or potentially toxic chemicals in small amounts. The low ceiling, therefore, forecasts no increase in areas of food sanitation, food economics, cosmetics, or hazardous substances.[46]

Beyond this, there is a more general three-level priority system for the allocation of FDA resources. The FDA gives greatest attention to immediate health and safety hazards, secondly to sanitary considerations such as insect parts in food, and thirdly to economic adulteration.

In the case of the Federal Trade Commission, the internal breakdown of the budget provides additional evidence of the insensitivity of the agency to the new political popularity of consumer protection. Commissioner James Nicholson complained that year after year the approach to the budget has been in terms of the total budget with no new consideration of priorities within that budget. Each division's share is based on reasons that are historical rather than reasons based on current needs or potential for new programs.[47] Table 3–4 demonstrates

Table 3–4   Divisional Shares of Proposed FTC Budgets

	1966	1967	1968	1969	1970
Restraint of Trade	16.6%	16.7%	15.6%	15.8%	14.2%
Deceptive Practices	11.1	11.1	10.8	12.9	13.6
Textiles and Furs	7.8	6.9	7.5	7.5	11.0
Field Operations	19.6	20.2	20.1	19.2	16.9
Industry Guidance	4.3	4.3	4.8	4.6	4.0
Economics	7.7	7.7	8.8	7.7	6.8

SOURCE: James M. Nicholson, commissioner, to Federal Trade Commission, Memorandum, August 11, 1969, p. 30.

[46] James L. Goddard, commissioner of Food and Drugs, to William Gorham, assistant secretary for program coordination, memorandum regarding program objectives for 1973, May 29, 1967.

[47] James M. Nicholson, commissioner, to the Federal Trade Commission, Memorandum, August 11, 1969, pp. 25–36. Government budgeting generally is incremental and historically based, but the situations confronting the FDA and FTC were not normal. See Aaron Wildavsky, The Politics of the Budgetary Process (Boston: Little, Brown, & Co., 1964).

the remarkable continuation of the existing budget percentages during the period of greatest consumer protection activity elsewhere.

An unchanged internal budget allocation would not present any problem if it reflected activities and priorities which were adequate to the agency's responsibilities. However, the lack of a clear policy and a rational priority system have been among the oldest and most frequent criticisms of the Federal Trade Commission. Twenty years ago the Hoover commission charged:

> As the years progressed, the [Federal Trade] Commission has become immersed in a multitude of petty problems. . . . The Commission has largely become a passive judicial agency, waiting for cases to come up on the docket. . . . In the selection of cases for its formal dockets, the Commission has long been guilty of prosecuting trivial and technical offenses and of failing to confine these dockets to cases of public importance.[48]

This criticism was substantially echoed in every succeeding study of the FTC. Lack of systematic priorities was a major criticism of the Nader report, and the American Bar Association report found that four of the commissioners and many of the senior staff members generally agreed that, "the agency's review of its own mission, goals and priorities continues on an ad hoc basis only, and two Commissioners indicated that efforts to improve planning in recent years had failed."[49]

The specific difficulties were succinctly discussed in a detailed memorandum written by Commissioner James Nicholson prior to his leaving the commission. While not written directly in response to the Nader report, it does cite and corroborate most of its themes. Most of the FTC difficulties examined by Nicholson revolve around the problems of priorities and rational planning, and he concludes that the "first need of the FTC is the institution of strengthened coherent policy planning." Specifically, he identified and analyzed the following problems:[50]

---

[48] The Commission on Reorganization of the Executive Branch of the Government, *Task Force Report on Regulatory Commissions* (Appendix N), (Washington, D.C.: 1949), p. 128.

[49] *Report of the ABA Commission*, p. 12.

[50] Nicholson, Memorandum to the FTC.

1. The FTC burdens itself with trivial matters and is "bogged down in a quagmire of trivia."
2. Although not required to do so by law, the FTC lets its priorities be determined for it according to the complaints it receives— "mailbag" complaints.
3. There is excessive delay in all aspects of FTC action.
4. There is no evaluation of past FTC experience.
5. Once an investigation begins, it continues regardless of whether or not it is a losing cause.
6. Economists are not given an adequate role in agency planning.
7. The agency lacks a rational overall view in budgeting.

In defense of the FTC, it could be argued that the FTC, unlike the FDA, does not have the type of responsibilities that are amenable to a "natural" priority system. Obviously, the FDA's primary responsibility must be to prevent the poisoning of the public by food or drugs. The FTC has a variety of statutory responsibilities, none of which have the urgency of FDA tasks. However, this argument neglects some potential priorities which are nearly as obvious as those of the FDA. For example, as the Nader report asserted, the FTC could concentrate on the largest corporations since their deceptions affect the greatest number of people by advertisements in the mass media. In fact, the FTC did not even consider this as an element of a rational priority system until 1971. Thus, in response to a request for the size in terms of annual sales of firms in certain nonlitigated cases, the chairman replied:

> Annual sales are not maintained as general information in deceptive practice matters. This is simply because sales volume is frequently only one of the many considerations in assessing the impact of a particular practice.[51]

Furthermore, the commission does have public health responsibilities relating to flammable fabrics and food and drug advertising. Thus, the FTC does have a basis for a rational priority system which is as natural and obvious as that of the FDA.

While there is no formal priority system, a look at the record shows the priorities which are implicit in the operations of the commission. In assessing the internal priorities, the Nader report relied on

[51] Paul Rand Dixon to John Schultz, October 25, 1968, quoted in Cox, Fellmeth, and Schultz, *Nader Report*, p. 57.

the commission's own data and thus it cannot be accused of lacking objectivity in this respect. The two primary measures which are applied are size of firm and type of case. The data show that 33 out of 37 deceptive practices cases litigated during the first four months of 1968 involved small firms (net worth below $500,000). Half of the 26 restraint of trade cases during this period involved small to medium-sized firms (sales below $100 million).[52] The report argues that these figures reveal that the implicit priority system is the reverse of what it should be in that the FTC concentrates its attention on the small firms even though, as in the case of television advertisements, the largest corporations are the transgressors. In 1971, however, the FTC finally focused its attack on deceptive advertising in the automobile industry because of its size and importance to consumers.

The Nader report also charged that the FTC has a wool and textile "fixation." This assertion was borne out by comprehensive data later presented in the ABA study. Table 3–5 shows that while the

Table 3–5 FTC Formal Investigations Opened

	Restraint of Trade	Deceptive Practices	Textiles and Furs	Totals
1961	884	899	241	2,024
1962	741	897	157	1,795
1963	301	854	156	1,311
1964	351	686	346	1,383
1965	236	615	216	1,067
1966	249	748	160	1,157
1967	352	666	174	1,192
1968	218	388	146	752
1969	181	192	238	611

SOURCE: *Report of the ABA Commission to Study the Federal Trade Commission* (Chicago: American Bar Association, 1969), p. 17.

number of new restraint of trade and deceptive practices investigations has been declining, textile and fur cases wavered up and down around

[52] Cox, Fellmeth, and Schultz, *Nader Report*, p. 22.

the two hundred mark. Thus, the number of textile and fur cases grew from around 11 percent in 1961 to nearly 40 percent of the total in 1969. Table 3–6 shows that the number of complaints issued by the FTC has declined for both restraint of trade and deceptive practices, but has fluctuated with an eventual increase for textile and fur cases. The net result has clearly been an increase in textile and fur complaints as a percentage of all complaints issued by the commission.[53]

Table 3–6   Complaints Issued by the FTC

	Restraint of Trade	Deceptive Practices	Textiles and Furs	Totals*
1961	121	177	115	410
1962	49	93	91	232
1963	230	127	74	431
1964	95	129	85	309
1965	26	66	69	161
1966	94	48	52	194
1967	24	108	89	221
1968	16	45	62	123
1969	28	65	127	220

* Discrepencies reflect discrepencies in original FTC data.

SOURCE: *Report of the ABA Commission to Study the Federal Trade Commission* (Chicago: American Bar Association, 1969), p. 20.

Of course, a social scientist might look aghast at this interpretation of the data. Indeed, there are two major flaws. First, the concentration on smaller firms might be justified on the grounds that small fly-by-night outfits are the most vicious and do the most harm, as with home improvement rackets. Indeed, this is the viewpoint of Chairman Dixon. Secondly, there is a statistical problem. The data could be merely a reflection of the fact that there are more small firms than large ones regardless of who is more likely to run afoul of the law. Similarly, there might be more textile and fur violations than any other kind in the population as a whole although this is doubtful. It would be helpful

53 For a comprehensive statistical measure of FTC performance, see *Report of the ABA Commission*, p. 12.

to have this data stated in terms of percentages of all business of a given size and in terms of percentages of applications for complaint. The Nader report and the ABA report cannot really be faulted for not presenting the data in this fashion since the FTC does not prepare it in that way. Thus there is no definitive analysis of FTC priorities. However, it is the commission's lack of a priority system and lack of data essential to such a system that makes even the more extreme accusations of the Nader report possible and plausible.

There are two further aspects of agenda setting by the agencies which are applicable to both agencies. The first such aspect is the role of Congress in setting priorities. The Nader report charged the FTC with being overly obsequious toward Congress. Any letter which comes to the commission from a member of Congress is marked with a sticker saying "expedite." This assures the congressman of an answer within five days. The FTC gets about 110 of these a month, most of them from constituents of the congressman which are routinely bucked over to the FTC. This tends to interrupt other work. The Nader report contends that this situation is especially foolish since anything a congressman deems important will be handled by phone or in person, but it is rather naive on this point. While a congressman may only want a letter from the FTC saying a particular matter is being looked into, he certainly wants to be able to reply quickly to his constituents. Given the possessive feeling of congressmen toward the independent regulatory agencies, the agency has no choice but to cooperate. Furthermore, the Food and Drug Administration has the same imposition on its priority system. The FDA has a congressional services unit which tries to expedite matters, such as drug clearance, on the request of congressmen. These requests have priority over other current work.

A second aspect of agenda setting is that the influence of consumer groups is nil. At the very least, private interests are a normal factor in agency agenda setting due to their legitimate demands for agency reaction to their business activity. For example, the agenda of the Interstate Commerce Commission is largely determined by who asks for how much of a fare increase, by who wants to merge and so on. This is a minimum. Depending on the agency and on the interest, the influence on the agenda can be much greater and usually is. But consumer groups exercise almost no perceptible influence on the agencies. There is no reaction to consumer groups comparable to the priority attached to congressional intervention in behalf of more particular interests. This will be discussed in greater detail later in this chapter under the subject of representation.

Cooperation and Coordination

The next aspect of the Executive Branch to be considered is liaison within the Executive. The center for communications was the PCCI. It was frequently the only source of intra-Executive liaison for agencies. This was to be expected since the PCCI is composed of the heads of the executive departments. But beyond that formality, there was advantage to be gained from enlisting the PCCI. Even before the days of greater publicity attendant upon Miss Furness's tenure, agencies sought PCCI support. According to a former high-ranking official, many agencies tried to use the PCCI and wanted statements in support of their side of an issue. "They twisted a lot of issues to make them look like consumer issues when that had become the magic word." Given the increase in popular publicity gained by Betty Furness, agencies were even more eager to get PCCI support.

The PCCI staff believe that their relations with agencies were good due to several factors. The key factor seems to be that the PCCI was not in competition with any agency. They did not have an industry constituency and thus did have considerable freedom of movement. A second factor was their professional reputation. They were "in favor," first with President Johnson and then with the public, and this was known by other participants who then knew they would not be tainted by cooperating but, on the contrary, could even share the halo. Finally, the PCCI performed a service for other agencies by leading the charge for programs and policy that the agencies usually favor. The PCCI reached a constituency that the agencies cannot reach. The PCCI had far greater exposure to the public than the agencies which usually have communications only with people in the regulated industries. Being an official celebrity, Betty Furness could give exposure and publicity to agency programs. She regularly appeared on both daytime and evening "talk shows" and thus opened a further avenue of publicity for little-known government programs. Following Miss Furness's tenure, the post itself conferred celebrity status.

While the PCCI could sometimes take industry heat off an agency, a former PCCI executive director indicated that they sometimes put the heat on. For example, on the meat bill the PCCI successfully pressed for a stronger bill than that favored by the Agriculture Department. According to the director, ". . . the public wanted a stronger meat bill than the Agriculture Department proposed. It wasn't a question of the administration talking with two voices. Once people realized that not all meat was federally inspected, they demanded more."

A second type of liaison is intradepartmental. Theoretically, that is the chief function of the consumer advisor within the department. This is generally an information function. The advisor will present the overall consumer stance of the department in congressional hearings or special administrative hearings. This also facilitates informational liaison with the PCCI.

Both types of liaison have an informational and support function. Participants are made aware of the activities of other participants, and a variety of consumer protection functions are given support by the PCCI or the consumer advisors within the departments. What is lacking is goal-directed liaison beyond occasionally putting the heat on for a stronger bill at a single point in time. This is not unique of course; the federal bureaucracy rarely works with such singleness of purpose. However, the lack of goal-directed liaison has policy implications different than in other areas. It keeps the diffuse consumer interest served at a depressed level. A unified program has the potential of increasing consumer awareness in the public's range of personal priorities. The lack of such a program does not decrease consumer awareness; it simply keeps it at the same level.

A third type of liaison can only be loosely labeled as such. This consists of "working agreements" between agencies which share statutory authority for enforcing certain laws. For example, the FTC and the FDA both have concurrent jurisdiction over the labeling of food and drugs. By the working agreement, however, and outside the authority of the statute, they divide the responsibility. The FDA handles all labeling abuses while the FTC handles advertising abuses. Theoretically, this should eliminate wasteful overlap. The problem is that the FDA has little interest in economic mislabeling of foods. When the FTC gets a complaint of that nature, they send it over to the FDA which then does nothing. Consequently, in effect no one is responsible. Ap-

parently even the commissioners cannot overcome the working agreements, and no one is quite sure how they started nor does anyone have
ultimate responsibility for jurisdictional decisions.

Representational Problems
and Effectiveness

The problem of representation demonstrates the unique characteristics
of a diffuse interest. In that representation is one of the key issues in
this study, a more detailed analysis of the problem appears in Chapter
7. But some of the considerations affecting bureaucratic representation
may be presented here.

The first issue is the determination of consumer desires by the
agencies. The Interstate Commerce Commission has no problem in
ascertaining what the railroads want and the same is true in the relations
between most other regulatory agencies and the industries they super-
vise. The most typical answer, indeed the universal answer, to the
question "How do you determine consumer opinion?" is, to paraphrase
all the answers: "We get mail, and I give talks to consumer groups and
usually talk to individual consumers and groups and find out what is on
their minds." Determination of consumer input is thus based on an
impressionistic analysis. There is no survey and no codification of in-
coming mail.[54] Notice is taken when mail is extremely heavy on a single
topic. Betty Furness was able to report to Congress that she was flooded
with mail in support of a strong meat bill. Only at a time when a legislative controversy is highly visible is consumer opinion mobilized and
perceived in a single direction.

The reader may object, "It does not matter what consumers think;
it is what they need that is central." This is precisely the rationale behind agency activities in behalf of consumer interests. The needs are
felt to be obvious. The abuses are known. Representation is thus perceived not to lie in ascertaining opinion, but in acting on behalf of consumers in seeking to correct well-known abuses.

However, consumer expectations are not neglected, and there

---

[54] The PCCI eventually began dividing mail by states, but this reveals greater
sensitivity to political considerations than consumer problems.

can be conflict between needs as interpreted by consumers and by agencies. The priority system of the Food and Drug Administration has already been noted. Objectively it might be argued that the long-term ingestion of toxic materials in food should have higher priority than hazards of drug side effects since everyone eats food and the long-range effects might be irreversible and more hazardous precisely because they are less visible. These are scientific and moral questions. But a politically sensitive agency knows that it simply cannot downgrade programs where "the consumer risk is most obvious to the consumer."

Part of the problem is that while most people want sanitary food, only the professionals are competent to make judgments regarding requirements of sanitation, bacteria count, etc. Taking the case of the FTC, the average man might be upset if a widely advertised product does not live up to its billing. He thus takes notice when he hears of an occasionally publicized FTC action against such false advertising. But the "man on the street" has little idea of what level of economic concentration is unacceptable. This tendency leads to agency emphasis on visible areas at the expense of more important long-range problems. Dramatic issues come to the fore.

Finally, the agency itself often has conflicting goals. The Agriculture Department serves both the consumer and the producer of agricultural products. Economic conflict between these interests is inevitable. There is also no clear policy for resolving that conflict. The Federal Trade Commission has even more direct conflict. Enforcement of certain sections of the antitrust laws is one of its primary responsibilities. However, under the Robinson-Patman Act, the FTC takes action against discriminatory pricing agreements which work to the advantage of large volume businesses and permit them to charge lower prices on certain items. The FTC is thus caught between furthering competition as an aid to the consumer and preventing competition which is too vigorous. The conflict is rationalized by the majority of the commissioners as being merely two aspects of the same policy. That is, in the long run, it is necessary that competition not be so severe as to drive smaller firms out of the market. Hence a short-range restriction on price competition is justified because its long-range objective is a preservation of competition. Nonetheless, the Antitrust Division of the Justice Department and a minority of the FTC see this as a very real conflict.

The conflict is not in a vacuum. It stems, as do most other administrative conflicts, from serving more than one constituency. Thus, the FDA has the drug industry as well as consumers as its clientele. As former FDA Commissioner Goddard wrote, "A consumer protection agency can, only at its peril, afford unconcern with legitimate and fundamental problems of the industry it is charged with regulating."[55] Indeed, within the food and drug industries, there is conflict based on a division between large and small firms.

The FTC receives a large number of complaints from competitors. Theoretically, all deceptive practices harm both the consumer constituency and the business constituency of FTC. However, pricing discrimination is another matter. The complaints are typically brought by the firm not given the special pricing arrangement. In acting on that complaint, the commission benefits the complainant, but the consumer interest may actually be better represented by the defendant who passes on to the consumer the saving he has received. Thus the consumer interest may coincide with either the plaintiff or the defendant in many FTC actions. Although it has been alleged that most governmental assistance to the consumer has resulted from a coincidence of goals between consumer interests and those of better-organized groups,[56] this is often impossible in the course of present regulatory procedures due to the delay involved. The years of delay involved in FTC cases is legendary.[57] Deceptive advertising campaigns are often long since ended before final commission action. The Nader report points out that FTC procedures make it nearly impossible for businessmen to remain honest. One of the major ways of detecting violations is complaint from competitors. But if a competitor's action is limited only to a complaint, he will be severely disadvantaged since the dishonest businessman can continue the deceptive practice for years before final action. "Under the present regime at the FTC, a businessman who suffers because of a competitor's unethical practices must either adopt the same practices or commit economic suicide."[58]

[55] Goddard, Memorandum.

[56] Merle Fainsod, Lincoln Gordon, Joseph Palamountain, Jr., *Government and the American Economy*, 3rd ed. (New York: W. W. Norton, 1959), p. 214.

[57] For example, by 1969, slightly over half of the pending formal FTC investigations were over two years old. *ABA Report*, p. 29.

[58] Cox, Fellmeth, and Schultz, *Nader Report*, p. 38.

In view of the fact that an agency has conflicting constituencies, the question then becomes: How are these conflicts resolved? Who has the greater weight in this balancing act? It is widely held that regulatory agencies tend to be the captives of the regulated groups and are responsive only to them rather than to the public interest. Indeed, Marver Bernstein asserts that capture of the agencies by the nominally regulated groups is the final phase in the "life cycle" of regulatory agencies.[59] The life cycle of agencies within cabinet-level departments is, however, different and varies as a result of other political factors. The Food and Drug Administration has varied considerably under different Presidents and under different commissioners. One low point was reached in the late 1950s. A former FDA drug examiner testifying before the Kefauver committee claimed that the drug industry had more influence with the agency than its own medical officers. She testified that on one occasion, after she had urged the FDA to require a manufacturer to issue strong warnings about a tranquilizer to physicians, one of her superiors told her, "I will not have my policy of friendliness with the industry interfered with."[60] However, in the late 1960s the FDA was a different agency under the stewardship of Commissioner Goddard who was less solicitous of the industry and whose stance was uniformly described as "tough." Although there were lapses such as the failure to act on cyclamates, there was no longer the complete identity of interests between the agency and industry as there had been earlier. However, Executive Branch agencies such as the FDA are more susceptible to pressure to help pay the political debts of the administration in power. Thus, former Commissioner Herbert Ley, himself accused of lax enforcement by Ralph Nader and others, charged that there had been a "total lack of top-side support from the current [Nixon] Administration" for the enforcement efforts of FDA.[61]

Unlike the FDA, the Federal Trade Commission acts primarily on complaints which originate outside the agency. Although the greatest

[59] See Samuel Huntington, "The Marasmus of the ICC: The Commission, The Railroads, and The Public Interest," *Yale Law Journal* 61 (April, 1952): 467–509; and Bernstein, *Regulating Business by Independent Commission.*

[60] Testimony of Dr. Barbara Moulton, quoted in Richard Harris, *The Real Voice* (New York: Macmillan Co., 1964), pp. 106–107.

[61] Quoted in the *New York Times,* December 31, 1969, p. 1.

number of complaints comes from the general public, the most important and actionable complaints come from competitors. *Who* is complaining is not as important as what happens to complaints and the commission's record has been poor in that regard. Only a fraction of applications for complaint are acted on—a fraction which has been steadily declining. The percentage of avowed applications for complaint which were investigated dropped from 30 percent in 1961 to 11 percent in 1967. Applications which resulted in the FTC's issuance or approval of a formal complaint went from 8 percent in 1961 to 3 percent in 1967.[62] Viewed in that light, the agency has been decreasingly responsive to the complainant constituency.

Of course, the question of representation includes not only whom the agency responds to, but what the nature of the response is, and who benefits from the response. A major criticism of the Nader report revolves around FTC collusion with business interests. The report, however, does not allege the existence of a conspiracy or other dramatic collusion. Rather, it is a matter of the commission's being too solicitous of business at the expense of a broader public interest. While the charge may be too harsh, the evidence certainly points in that direction. At the very least, there is no firm adversary system with the representation of the interests of those that business might be abusing. For example, the reports of assurances of voluntary compliance do not tell the public what practice the offending business has agreed to cease—only that it has agreed to stop doing something objectionable.

There are industry guides to tell business what is prohibited, but there is no campaign to give the public the same information. While in theory the recent FTC emphasis on voluntary compliance and industry guides is preferable to enforcement after the fact, it is preferable only if it does prevent abuses. However, there are no sanctions to enforce the guidelines, and a firm which violates the guidelines is treated as though it erred in innocence. Moreover, even formal cease and desist orders, the basic FTC sanction, are not followed through. The ABA report cited the notorious Geritol case as an example of what it termed the "failure to put some bite into enforcement." In 1962, the FTC issued a complaint against Geritol's manufacturer, the J. B. Williams Company for false advertising, but did not seek a preliminary injunc-

---

[62] Cox, Fellmeth, and Schultz, *Nader Report,* p. 223.

tion. After Geritol failed to mend its ways, the FTC issued a cease and desist order in 1965, which was affirmed by the U.S. Court of Appeals in 1967. After receiving a compliance report in 1968, the commission found that Geritol was still violating the cease and desist order. However, the commission did not seek civil penalties, but instead merely directed the Williams Company to submit yet another compliance report. In 1969, the FTC found that some Geritol commercials *still* were in violation, but not until the end of the year did it ask the Justice Department to take action. Since this type of enforcement permits known abuses to continue, it is fair to say that the business constituency of the commission is represented with greater efficacy than the consumer constituency.

So far, I have concentrated on the agencies' attentive constituency. However, as Rourke points out, many agencies have a "potential public" that far exceeds the size of their normal constituency. The activities of these agencies, such as the FDA and FTC, affect the public at large in vital parts of daily life. The public may be unaware of these agencies until there is a crisis situation.[63] Given this definition of a potential public, it would seem that agencies would be less attentive to it than to the attentive publics if a choice had to be made, as it usually does. This, in fact, is the case. Agencies respond not only to attentive publics in preference to inattentive publics, but they must prevent a crisis which would rouse the potential public. Thus the FDA gives greater priority to "those programs where the consumer risk is most acute and *most obvious to the consumer*" (italics added) than to long-term and cumulative problems.[64] Similarly, I have argued that the FTC reciprocates in kind the attentiveness of business and the inattentiveness of consumers.

There are serious problems involved in this mode of representation. Health and environmental problems are not less serious because they are not obvious to consumers; indeed they are often more serious. The FTC is available to its potential public through "mailbag notice" —relying on consumers' complaints by mail. But this provides inadequate representation for several reasons. As with food and drugs, many problems go unnoticed since the consumer does not know he is being

63 Rourke, *Bureaucracy,* p. 14.
64 Goddard, Memorandum.

deceived or defrauded in situations where technical complexity is involved. There is little impetus to complain since the FTC does not have the power to obtain a refund for consumers nor can a civil suit be based on an FTC order. Finally, in ghetto areas, the consumers who are injured most seriously have probably never heard of the FTC.

While a bureaucracy may want to prevent the arousal of a potential public by a crisis created by its own failure, certain bureaucracies seek to mobilize this potential public. The failure of FTC and FDA to do that effectively has already been discussed. However, it should not be thought that this was a general failure of the bureaucracy. Whatever its original purpose, the main effect of the PCCI was to increase the salience of the consumer interest among the public. Betty Furness must be given primary credit for this, not because of any particular program but because of who she was. She was a celebrity before her appointment, and her celebrity status was often evoked by the press, especially in the early part of her tenure, to give greater visibility to consumer problems. Congressional hearings which might otherwise have gone unnoticed were extensively reported because she testified. Furthermore, she made the complete circuit of the television "talk shows" and handled herself with the aplomb of a professional performer. Advertisers have long tried to sell dull products, like toothpaste, by associating them with interesting things, like sex. President Johnson, probably inadvertently, utilized this same technique in appointing Betty Furness as his consumer advisor. Thus her role was an informational and supportive one in an attempt to increase issue awareness in a potential public.

But in the final analysis, the representation of the consumer interest in the bureaucratic policy process must be assessed as a sometime thing. While an increasing number of people are aware of their interests as consumers, the bureaucracy has not fully capitalized or followed through on this awareness. There has been insufficient assessment of priorities in this bureaucratic world of scarce resources. Most importantly, there is no regularity in the bureaucratic representational process with the result that certain classes of consumers are insufficiently represented and important aspects of the consumer interest are neglected. Things are far better than they were in 1960. But there has not been sufficient substantive and procedural change to assure that conditions will not revert to the "bad old days."

chapter 4

Congress
and Consumers

The most publicized and dramatic arena of consumer protection policy making is the Congress. In analyzing the formation of consumer policy in Congress this chapter will focus on the identity and characteristics of those who have been most active in pursuing this type of policy, the patterns of support and opposition, and the strategies used in support of consumer protection policy. Three case studies will be presented to illustrate the patterns of policy formation.

You Can't Tell the Players Without a Scorecard

In this first section of the chapter, the discussion revolves around the factors associated with support for consumer protection policy. In identifying these factors, the basic form of data used is the eleven non-unanimous Senate roll call votes on consumer protection between 1962 and 1968. These votes are spread over six separate bills and all but one occurred in the 89th and 90th Congresses (1965–1968). Therefore only the 107 members of the Senate during these two Congresses are considered.[1]

[1] There were a total of thirty-one roll call votes on consumer protection between 1962 and 1968, out of which sixteen were unanimous. In this section on individual

In analyzing support for a general policy area, the first thing to establish is whether there is indeed something to analyze. That is, can the selected votes be objectively classified together under the general category of consumer protection? Is a consumer protection orientation reflected in the votes or are the votes like apples and oranges—nonadditive and independent of each other?

One way of determining the presence of underlying traits is cumulative scaling, with the Guttman Scale being the best-known technique of this type. A Guttman Scale is a measure of whether a series of scores held by different individuals are cumulative. That is, it determines whether an individual with, for example, higher scores on a series of test items has more of some underlying traits than an individual with lower scores. It thus measures whether there is an underlying trait and ranks individuals by their score on that trait. In our case the scores are roll call votes in the Senate and the trait is consumer protection as an issue. The results of the scale are presented in Table 4–1 while Table 4–2 lists the votes on which the scale is based.[2] The scale scores run from one to twelve with higher scores being more "pro-consumer." The measure used to determine whether these scores are scalable is the coefficient of reproducibility which is the proportion of responses on scale items that could be predicted from knowing a legislator's scale position. The obtained coefficient of .918 indicates that consumer issues are indeed scalable, although not perfectly so. Nonetheless, we can be reasonably sure that there is an underlying issue which is reflected in these eleven roll calls.

In analyzing the results of the roll call votes, the first question concerns the identity of the consumer-oriented senators. Are they

---

congressmen, only the Senate is considered because only four of those roll calls were in the House and one of those four is barely in the nonunanimous category, having 93.2 percent voting in support of consumer protection. With only three roll call votes, the kind of analysis of individual members that I use would not be meaningful when applied to the House since cumulative scaling is impossible with so few votes and there is not enough differentiation for any sort of revealing correlation.

[2] The computer program used was BMDO5 in W. J. Dixon, ed. *BMD, Biomedical Computer Programs* (Berkeley and Los Angeles: University of California Press, 1967), pp. 379–389.

Table 4–1   Guttman Scale Scores of Senators

Guttman Scale Scores	Rank	Senator	State	Party
12	1	Metcalf, Lee	Montana	D
12	2	Magnuson, Warren	Washington	D
12	3	Burdick, Quentin	North Dakota	D
12	4	Brewster, Daniel	Maryland	D
12	5	Nelson, Gaylord	Wisconsin	D
12	6	Morse, Wayne	Oregon	D
12	7	Ribicoff, Abraham	Connecticut	D
12	8	Dodd, Thomas	Connecticut	D
12	9	Mansfield, Mike	Montana	D
12	10	Church, Frank	Idaho	D
12	11	Yarborough, Ralph	Texas	D
12	12	Neuberger, Maurine	Oregon	D
12	13	McCarthy, Eugene	Minnesota	D
12	14	Gore, Albert	Tennessee	D
11	15	Hart, Philip	Michigan	D
11	16	Randolph, Jennings	West Virginia	D
11	17	McGee, Gale	Wyoming	D
11	18	Jackson, Henry	Washington	D
11	19	Proxmire, William	Wisconsin	D
11	20	Inouye, Daniel	Hawaii	D
11	21	Clark, Joseph	Pennsylvania	D
11	22	Muskie, Edmund	Maine	D
11	23	Bible, Alan	Nevada	D
11	24	Symington, Stuart	Missouri	D
11	25	Byrd, Robert	West Virginia	D
11	26	Pastore, John	Rhode Island	D
11	27	Case, Clifford	New Jersey	R
11	28	Mondale, Walter	Minnesota	D
11	29	Williams, Harrison	New Jersey	D
11	30	Long, Edward	Missouri	D
11	31	Javits, Jacob	New York	R
11	32	Lausche, Frank	Ohio	D
11	33	Kennedy, Robert	New York	D
11	34	Hayden, Carl	Arizona	D
11	35	Kennedy, Edward	Massachusetts	D
10	36	Moss, Frank	Utah	D
10	37	McIntyre, Thomas	New Hampshire	D

Table 4–1—*cont.*

Guttman Scale Scores	*Rank*	*Senator*	*State*	*Party*
10	38	Smathers, George	Florida	D
10	39	Young, Stephen	Ohio	D
10	40	Long, Russell	Louisiana	D
10	41	Bartlett, E. L.	Alaska	D
10	42	Hartke, Vance	Indiana	D
10	43	Smith, Margaret	Maine	R
10	44	Douglas, Paul	Illinois	D
9	45	Monroney, A. S. Mike	Oklahoma	D
9	46	Byrd, Harry	Virginia	D
9	47	Aiken, George	Vermont	R
9	48	Spong, William	Virginia	D
8	49	Harris, Fred	Oklahoma	D
8	50	Anderson, Clinton	New Mexico	D
8	51	Cannon, Howard	Nevada	D
8	52	Pell, Claiborne	Rhode Island	D
8	53	Robertson, A. Willis	Virginia	D
8	54	Russell, Richard	Georgia	D
8	55	Tydings, Joseph	Maryland	D
7	56	Stennis, John	Mississippi	D
7	57	Bayh, Birch	Indiana	D
7	58	Montoya, Joseph	New Mexico	D
6	59	Ervin, Sam	North Carolina	D
6	60	Talmadge, Herman	Georgia	D
6	61	Griffin, Robert	Michigan	R
5	62	Holland, Spessard	Florida	D
5	63	Fong, Hiram	Hawaii	R
5	64	Jordan, B. Everett	North Carolina	D
5	65	Boggs, J. Caleb	Delaware	R
5	66	Hill, Lister	Alabama	D
5	67	Fulbright, J. William	Arkansas	D
5	68	Sparkman, John	Alabama	D
5	69	Cooper, John Sherman	Kentucky	R
5	70	Williams, John	Delaware	R
5	71	Thurmond, Strom	South Carolina	R
5	72	McClellan, John	Arkansas	D
5	73	Ellender, Allen	Louisiana	D

Table 4–1—*cont.*

Guttman Scale Scores	*Rank*	*Senator*	*State*	*Party*
5	74	Bass, Ross	Tennessee	D
4	75	Scott, Hugh	Pennsylvania	R
4	76	McGovern, George	South Dakota	D
4	77	Dominick, Peter	Colorado	R
3	78	Mundt, Karl	South Dakota	R
3	79	Pearson, James	Kansas	R
3	80	Cotton, Norris	New Hampshire	R
3	81	Young, Milton	North Dakota	R
3	82	Eastland, James	Mississippi	D
3	83	Saltonstall, Leverett	Massachusetts	R
3	84	Kuchel, Thomas	California	R
3	85	Hickenlooper, Bourke	Iowa	R
3	86	Brooke, Edward	Massachusetts	R
3	87	Percy, Charles	Illinois	R
3	88	Hollings, Ernest	South Carolina	D
3	89	Hatfield, Mark	Oregon	R
3	90	Baker, Howard	Tennessee	R
2	91	Jordan, Len	Idaho	R
2	92	Miller, Jack	Iowa	R
2	93	Morton, Thruston	Kentucky	R
2	94	Murphy, George	California	R
2	95	Allott, Gordon	Colorado	R
1	96	Fannin, Paul	Arizona	R
1	97	Bennett, Wallace	Utah	R
1	98	Tower, John	Texas	R
1	99	Dirksen, Everett	Illinois	R
1	100	Hruska, Roman	Nebraska	R
1	101	Curtis, Carl	Nebraska	R
1	102	Carlson, Frank	Kansas	R
1	103	Prouty, Winston	Vermont	R
1	104	Simpson, Milward	Wyoming	R
1	105	Gruening, Ernest	Alaska	D
1	106	Hansen, Clifford	Wyoming	R
1	107	Russell, Donald	South Carolina	D

Coefficient of Reproducibility = .918

Table 4–2   Senate Consumer Roll Call Votes. Listed in descending order
             from "hardest" to "easiest"

Issue	"Pro-Consumer" Position
AUTOMOBILE SAFETY (1966). Amendment providing for criminal penalties for violations of the act.	Yes
DRUG AMENDMENTS (1962). Motion to table Kefauver amendment imposing strict licensing requirement for drug patent holders.	No
NATURAL GAS PIPELINE SAFETY (1967). Amendment providing for criminal penalties.	Yes
DECEPTIVE SALES (1968). Amendment to delete the provision of the Deceptive Sales Act which would allow the FTC to seek temporary restraining orders to prevent fraudulent or deceptive practices.	No
GAS PIPELINE (1967). Amendment to include natural gas gathering lines in the group to be regulated by the Secretary of Transportation.	Yes
AUTO SAFETY (1966). Amendment to eliminate the bill's requirement that patents, information, uses, and processes developed with federal aid be fully and freely available to the general public.	No
TRUTH-IN-PACKAGING (1966). Amendment to delete weight and quantity standardization sections.	No
TRUTH-IN-PACKAGING (1966). Motion to table "fair trade" amendment to the bill.	Yes
WHOLESOME POULTRY ACT (1968). Amendment to eliminate committee-inserted provision allowing poultry and meat processed under state inspection standards which are at least equal to federal standards to be shipped between states even though it had not been federally inspected.	Yes
TRUTH-IN-PACKAGING (1966). Motion to refer packaging bill to Judiciary Committee for further consideration.	No
TRUTH-IN-PACKAGING (1966). Passage of the Fair Labeling Act.	Yes

grouped together only on this issue or do they share other traits and the same position on other issues? The obvious place to start is with the political parties. A brief glance back at Table 4–1 indicates that the top scorers are Democrats, Northern Democrats with the exception of senators Yarborough and Gore. Table 4–3 confirms this more precisely and shows the scale positions of the parties (and regions in case of the Democrats). Table 4–3 shows that votes on consumer protection vary

Table 4–3 Percentages of Senators Within Each Scale Group by Party

	Scale Score		
	1–4 (Most favorable to consumer protection)	5–8	9–12 (Least favorable)
Northern Democrats	79.2% (38)	26.9% (7)	6.1% (2)
Southern Democrats	12.5% (6)	53.9% (14)	9.1% (3)
Total Democrats	91.7% (44)	80.8% (21)	15.5% (5)
Republicans	8.3% (4)	19.2% (5)	84.9% (28)
Totals	100% (48)	100% (26)	100% (33)

The percentages in the cells are the percentages of each scale category occupied by each political party.

both by party and by region within party. The Northern Democrats are the most favorable to consumer protection, the Republicans are least favorable, and the Southern Democrats occupy a middle ground.[3] As

[3] Partisanship and regionalism also vary with the particular consumer issue under consideration. See pp. 146–151 below.

might be suspected from this clear partisan and regional division, the strongest supporters of consumer protection legislation are senators currently defined as liberal. The Guttman Scale scores of senators correlate highly ($r = .69$) with their scores on the liberalism index of the Americans for Democratic Action and also with the *Congressional Quarterly* scores on support for an enlarged federal role ($r = .71$). Thus, analysis of the data confirms the impression that the consumer-oriented congressmen are likely to be part of the "liberal coalition" and, by implication, that consumer protection is an issue favored by liberals.

The Activists

Who Are They

The previous sections have shown the consumer "coalition" in broad outline. Of course, there are differences among members of even the highest scoring groups, and some are more actively involved in this type of legislation than others. Since the roll call vote is only the final aspect of the legislative process, the key participants are those who are active in the early stages in ways that go beyond voting. Both by their activities and their reputations, certain members are closely identified with consumer protection or with particular issues under this general category. For purposes of analysis, these members may be called the congressional consumer activists. In addition to having high scale scores these members fulfill two of the following criteria: (or one of the following twice): Chaired favorable hearings, was primary sponsor of a bill, introduced a strengthening amendment, was floor manager of a bill, wrote a book or article on consumer protection. These criteria are the same for the House and Senate except that in the House, as noted earlier, no scale could be constructed. In following previous procedures, the activists are listed only for the 89th and 90th Congresses. These leave out the earliest recent activist, Estes Kefauver, but his role in the prescription drug controversy is covered later.

Within these criteria the consumer activists in the Senate are:

Philip Hart (D–Mich.)	Joseph Montoya (D–N.M.)
Warren Magnuson (D–Wash.)	Gaylord Nelson (D–Wisc.)

Walter Mondale (D–Minn.)
Paul Douglas (D–Ill.) *

William Proxmire (D–Wisc.)
Abraham Ribicoff (D–Conn.)

* 89th Congress only.

In the House, the activists are:

Thomas Foley (D–Wash.)
Benjamin Rosenthal (D–N.Y.)
Richard Ottinger (D–N.Y.)

Harley Staggers (D–W.Va.)
Leonor Sullivan (D–Mo.)
Neil Smith (D–Iowa)

The most obvious characteristic of this group is that they all are Democrats. This might be due to the increased opportunities for Democrats to assume any type of activist role in Congresses with Democratic majorities. However, these activists are also Northern Democrats at a time when disproportionate power and committee chairmanships are held by Southern Democrats. Furthermore, as Table 4–3 shows, Democrats are far more predisposed to vote for consumer protection legislation. So, although half of the activists are subcommittee or committee chairmen, their activism is not merely a reflection of this fact. Thus Allen Ellender, chairman of the Senate Committee on Agriculture and Forestry, is not an activist even though his committee reported out the meat inspection bill while committee members Walter Mondale and Joseph Montoya are included in the activist category.

As would be expected from the earlier data presented regarding liberalism, the activists have a far higher liberalism rating than other members. When compared only to other Northern Democrats, however, the differences in liberalism dissolve as seen in Table 4–4.

Table 4–4 Mean ADA Liberalism Scores for Activists and Other Northern Democrats

	Senate	House
Activists	70	84
Other Northern Democrats	80	85
All Other Members	45	37

1968 scores were used for all members except Senator Douglas in whose case the 1966 score was used.

SOURCE: Individual scores reported in *Congressional Quarterly Almanac,* 1966 and 1968 (Washington, D.C.: Congressional Quarterly Service, 1967 and 1969). Computation and table are by the author.

Consumer Protection and the Congressional Career

Almost by definition, the consumer activists are specialists in consumer protection issues. This does not, however, mean that consumer protection is their only or even their most important area of interest. Only two activists, both in the House, rated consumer protection as their number one interest. This is natural since House members tend to specialize in fewer issues than senators. They have a smaller staff and fewer committee assignments. While, from time to time, a consumer protection issue will be at the center of attention and have the highest priority for a senator or congressman, in general it is simply one of several issues in which they invest time and effort. The real specialization takes place at the staff level and a busy senator's commitment to consumer protection is usually represented by a staff member working almost full time on that one area. In terms of the total activity of a congressional office, the amount of time spent on consumer protection depends on which bills are up for consideration and what the competing issues are.

One of the factors which influences the importance a congressman attaches to an issue is his perception of the importance or popularity of the issue with his constituency. First and foremost, the consumer activists believe that the legislation they sponsor is necessary and in the public interest. They additionally believe, however, that consumer protection is good politics and gives them a net benefit.

The issue is good politically because it has inherent features making it popular. It is nearly impossible to argue against an incumbent's stand in favor of consumer protection. This is particularly true in the case of health and safety issues. Staff members are fond of asking, "Who can be in favor of diseased meat?" or "Who can champion high utility rates?" In order for the issue to be good politically, constituents must know about the issue and must be made aware of their representative's position on it. It is, however, doubtful that any appreciable number of citizens are aware of their congressmen's role in this or other policy areas.[4] Nonetheless, it is significant that all the activists used

4 Warren E. Miller and Donald E. Stokes, "Constituency Influence in Congress," in *Elections and the Political Order,* ed. Angus Campbell, Philip Converse, Warren E. Miller, and Donald E. Stokes (New York: John Wiley & Sons, 1966), pp. 366–367.

their role in consumer protection as one of their campaign themes. One bemused observer recounted that after flying to Seattle, he was greeted by a string of billboards proclaiming, "Magnuson's Law—Auto Safety," "Magnuson's Law—No Flammable Fabrics," etc. Magnuson's slogan during the 1968 campaign was "Keep the Big Boys Honest."

The process of favorably impressing constituents is not limited to the formal campaign. Sponsorship of an important and popular bill carries with it publicity advantages. More importantly, committee and subcommittee chairmen can capitalize on their position to achieve a steady flow of favorable publicity. When the right issues and the right witnesses are present, the presiding congressman can reap a gold mine of publicity. Senator Ribicoff is one of the acknowledged masters of this technique. The hearings he holds in the Subcommittee on Executive Reorganization of the Senate Government Operations Committee only nominally consider substantive legislation. They are designed to focus the spotlight on particular issues and, incidentally, on the chairman himself. The vaguely defined and omniscient jurisdiction of the committee allows him to review any subject to see "what the government is doing about it." After he assumed the chairmanship in 1965, hearings were held on the consumer topics of automobile safety (with the then-unknown Ralph Nader as a star witness), automobile pricing, and the statutory establishment of a Department of Consumer Affairs.

Aside from hearings overflowing with reporters and covered on television, identification with the issue is perceived to be politically advantageous. Consumer protection is seen to be a popular issue and one which broadens a congressman's base of support. The case of Warren Magnuson is especially interesting. In the Senate since 1944, Magnuson was closely identified with Boeing Aircraft, the largest employer in Seattle. His previous campaigning emphasized how much new industry he had brought into the state. Then he had a close call in winning reelection in 1962. His winning proportion of the vote was only 52.1 percent. This close margin alerted him to the need to expand his base of support. As he approached the middle of his fourth term, two of his aides pressed him to embrace consumer protection as a good policy area that would reap political dividends. The first issue was the combined auto and tire safety bill. From there, the issues sailed forth. Magnuson apparently had so much faith in the power of consumer protection that he gave up his chairmanship of the Subcommittee on

Merchant Marine and Fisheries, an area vital to his home state, and assumed chairmanship of the new Subcommittee on the Consumer in in 1967. This indicates a shifting of representational focus from concern with a particular industry to identification with a popular interest of a wider constituency. In any case, Magnuson scored with a landslide victory in 1968, winning with 64.4 percent of the vote. Further testimony to the perceived drawing power of consumer protection is provided by the epilogue to Magnuson's success. In 1969, he gave up his chairmanship of the consumer subcommittee to Senator Frank Moss of Utah who hitherto had been a strong supporter of consumer protection policy but not an activist. Moss, a Democrat in normally Republican Utah, faced reelection in 1970, and had an uphill fight to retain his seat. After repeating Magnuson's strategy, Moss won with 54 percent of the vote. Whether such identification with consumer protection is actually related to increased victory margins will be considered shortly.

Several activists noted that activism was not without its dangers, and Senator Paul Douglas thought that it hurt more than it helped him. Although it cannot be proven, there is little doubt that the stands of senators Kefauver and Douglas on drugs and consumer credit respectively substantially enriched the campaign coffers of their opponents. The cost of consumer activism, however, cannot be measured in any way. Most activists believe that support is given to their electoral opposition by the industries affected by their particular consumer protection legislation. Regardless of how much or how effective such opposition is, the important point is that consumer activists perceive that their performance and reputations in this area do entail political costs even if the end result is a net gain.

Although the predominant feeling among activists is that their identification with consumer protection is politically helpful, no one is so naive as to think that that issue alone will result in electoral success, or even be the deciding factor. It is doubtful whether a congressional candidate's stand on this or any other issue makes any difference in the voting decisions of citizens. The voters simply are not very aware of particular issues let alone sufficiently concerned to base their votes on those issues.[5] Indeed, the degree of electoral success of

5 Miller and Stokes found that only three percent of the free answer comments they obtained from interview respondents had to do with *any* legislative issue. Ibid.

the consumer activists has not been different from that of other Northern Democrats and the electoral margins of the two groups were almost identical in 1968. This does not mean that the consumer activists are wrong in assuming that consumer protection is politically advantageous. Active identification with the issue does generate publicity which may increase recognition of the incumbent even after the issue is forgotten. Furthermore, quite apart from electoral considerations, the consumer activists add to their overall reputations as liberals among the attentive public and the Washington community. Politics, after all, does not end with getting elected.

Strategies and Techniques

While the consumer activists have a sense of shared purpose, there has been little overall coordination of strategy or activities. They do not work with each other any more frequently than they work with other liberals. Cooperation and coordination of strategy have occurred only on particular issues. However, as the consumer protection issue has developed, the trend has been toward more cooperation. Where contact among staff members had previously been only casual, by 1970, Democratic staff members had started holding regular meetings at which information and ideas are traded. In addition, the Democratic Study Group, consisting of liberal members of the House, formed a task force on consumer protection which introduced its own package of consumer proposals early in the 92nd Congress. The trend toward more cooperation stems partly from the fact that Democratic consumer activists now face a Republican administration with its own ideas on consumer protection. This naturally has increased the feeling of "we" against "they." Also, policy making has become more complex as issues such as class action law suits replace meat inspection, and thus it is less clear what measures would strengthen or weaken legislation. To avoid later trouble and embarrassment, it became necessary to have an exchange of views (and to maintain a real prospect of a change in positions) with those who have been passive allies in the past.

Nonetheless, there is still little overall purposeful coordination and no firm consumer coalition. There are three reasons for this. First, coordination is somewhat precluded by committee specialization. When a bill is in committee, active participation by outsiders is frowned upon. Second, the activist is associated with a small number of particular consumer protection issues. If he does not tend to these issues, no one else will. Time spent on someone else's bill reduces the time spent on his own. Third, few people perceive a need for any more coordination. In 1969, there were days when as many as three hearings were occurring simultaneously. None of the activists interviewed saw a danger of dilution of public interest through simultaneous hearings. Rather, most of them saw simultaneous hearings as advantageous and speculated that they would increase rather than dilute public concern. If there is no point of diminishing marginal returns in consumer activism or if that point is remote, an important motivating factor for coordination is missing. When and if bills and amendments reach the floor, there is still little coordination. The process of building support for a bill is not undertaken by any consumer coalition. Rather, it is handled by the supporting consumer activists in Congress aided by consumer interest groups and by the President's legislative liaison staff if the President has taken a position on the bill.

Greater coordination would create more opportunities for rivalry while at the same time muting the expression of that rivalry. In the past there was some rivalry between members active on the same issues, but this is not now prevalent and was never bitter. Indeed, the only real instances of rivalry came at the beginning of consumer protection activism in Congress during the events leading to the auto and tire safety bill. First, there was the rivalry between Senator Ribicoff, who held the first hearings on the general subject, and Senator Magnuson, whose Commerce Committee held hearings on the actual legislation. But, even here, there was a difference of function. Ribicoff's hearings were designed to generate publicity on the subject while the Commerce Committee hearings kept up the momentum and followed through with substantive legislation. Secondly, there was rivalry when Magnuson incorporated Senator Nelson's tire safety bill into a combined auto safety package. In effect, Magnuson pirated the bill. Nevertheless, if there was any bitterness in the past, it has faded and both sides claim there are no hard feelings.

If there is any teamwork on an issue it does not have to be limited to cooperation among members of Congress. Activists work with the Executive Branch, with whom relationships vary depending on time and issue. They vary with time in that the amount of attention given an issue by members of the Executive Branch is partly dependent on what other issues are competing for attention. Also, cooperation with Executive Branch participants depends on the stage of a bill's legislative history. Generally, technical expertise from specialized agencies is required during the early stages of staff research; political expertise and "clout" is required as the bill finally emerges from committee.

Naturally, contacts vary with subject area. There has been a great deal of staff contact between Senator Nelson's subcommittee investigating prescription drugs and the Food and Drug Administration. The Commerce Committee staff worked with the Federal Power Commission on gas pipeline safety. There has been a whole range of these ad hoc contacts and they generally fade when the issue passes from the congressional agenda.

The primary factor affecting the pattern of congressional-Executive relationships is the partisan composition of both branches. That is, the nature and extent of contacts was considerably different under the Johnson administration than under the Nixon administration.

During the Democratic administration, the President had his own consumer package which formed the basis of (and was formed from) congressional action by the Democratic consumer activists who, being the majority, controlled the committees. Particularly in the last two years of that administration there was relatively little disagreement on legislation between the White House and the consumer activists. The PCCI served to convey officially the support of the President. The actual bargaining and strategy sessions involved in marking up bills involved the regular White House legislative liaison staff—Joseph Califano and Larry Levinson in the latter months of the administration.

Two major changes in this pattern occurred with the change of administration. First, the administration and Democratic consumer activists had differing ideas about consumer protection which accentuated existing partisan differences. Thus, on several issues, there were competing bills—the administration bill sponsored by a string of Republicans and a Democratic bill. Where the tendency had previously been to compromise differences in an effort to get a bill both the administration and Congress could live with, the tendency in the situation of divided control was for both the White House and congressional consumer activists to put their own imprint on legislation and to accentuate differences. The greatest and most publicized differences were over the two major consumer measures considered in the 91st Congress, consumer class action law suits and the organization of consumer representation in the Executive Branch.

The second change was in the routing of contacts with the White House. Not surprisingly, the administration dealt almost entirely with Republican members. This was true both for the regular White House legislative staff and for the President's ·Committee on Consumer Interests. What is somewhat surprising is the almost total lack of contact the White House has with Democratic staff members—including the ones at the heart of the most important contested consumer legislation. This both results from and reinforces the competition with the White House.

In general, the consumer activists have had more freedom of action since 1969. The restraints of having a President of the same party necessarily took the edge off any criticism they might have directed toward Executive Branch bureaucracies. After 1969, this situation no longer prevailed. Instead there was a positive incentive to find areas to criticize and to push programs regarded as more aggressive and "pro-consumer" than those of the administration. Indeed, the Democrats have come to regard consumer protection as a better campaign issue since they have been able to capitalize on their new freedom of action.

Although the pattern of Executive-Legislative relations was dependent on who controlled which branch of government, this aspect of policy formation was not different in the area of consumer protection than in other areas. In both administrations the legislation was handled by the regular legislative liaison staff. Consumer legislation was one part of President Johnson's legislative program and was handled like other parts. Similarly, the White House during the Nixon administration was cut off from the Democratic liberals not only on consumer protection, but in most other issue areas as well. In short, in terms of Executive-Legislative liaison, consumer policy formation was handled like any other type of domestic policy.

The purpose of this discussion of the liaison arrangements of the consumer activists is to fill out the discussion of *who* represents the consumer interest. The lack of any purposeful consumer coalition with Congress or between Congress and the Executive highlights the fact that the representation of the consumer interest in Congress depends on the individual results of individual consumer activists, each surrounded by his own supporting staff rather than on any regular combined effort.

Committees

The real centers of power in Congress are the committees, and an examination of the committees indicates both the locus and extent of congressional action on consumer affairs. Since 1967, four consumer subcommittees were established within existing committees: The Subcommittee on Consumer Interests of the Elderly in the Senate Special Committee on Aging, the Subcommittee on Consumer Affairs of the House Banking and Currency Committee, and the Subcommittee on the Consumer of the Senate Commerce Committee. Within the House Government Operations Committee, a Subcommittee on Special Studies was primarily concerned with consumer affairs in the 90th Congress. These are not the only subcommittees which have handled consumer legislation, but the establishment of these subcommittees demonstrates the institutional recognition given to consumer representation.

An examination of the committees which have handled consumer legislation in the 89th and 90th Congresses shows the locus of the effective legislative process in this area. Table 4–5 lists all the consumer legislation passed by Congress since 1966 and the committees which held hearings on it. An asterisk denotes which chamber first held hearings. Where there is no asterisk, hearings began nearly simultaneously.

Two facts are obvious from this chart. First, the commerce committees are dominant in the area of consumer protection. They report out more consumer legislation than all the other committees combined. Although Table 4–5 does not show it, this is also true of bills which are

Table 4–5   Congressional Committees and Consumer Legislation in the 89th and 90th Congresses

---

Senate

Agriculture Committee
Wholesome Poultry Act
Wholesome Meat Act

Commerce Committee
Flammable Fabrics Act Amendments*
Radiation Control Act
Natural Gas Pipeline Safety Act*
Fair Packaging and Labeling Act*
National Commission on Product Safety*

Table 4–5—*Continued*

Fire Research and Safety Act
Automobile Insurance Study
Child Protection Act
Food Marketing Commission Extension

Committee on Judiciary
Truth-in-Packaging (original hearings)

Banking and Currency Committee
Interstate Land Sales Act*
Consumer Credit Protection Act
(Truth-in-Lending) *

Labor & Public Welfare Committee
Clinical Laboratories Licensing Amendment

House of Representatives
Agriculture Committee
Wholesome Poultry Act*
Wholesome Meat Act*
Food Marketing Commission Extension*

Interstate and Foreign Commerce Committee
Flammable Fabrics Act Amendments
Clinical Laboratories Licensing Amendment
Radiation Control Act
Natural Gas Pipeline Safety Act
Fair Packaging and Labeling Act
National Commission on Product Safety
National Traffic and Motor Vehicle Safety Act
Automobile Insurance Study
Child Protection Act

Science and Astronautics Committee
Fire Research and Safety Act

Banking and Currency Committee
Interstate Land Sales Act
Consumer Credit Protection Act

* Indicates committee which first held hearings on the legislation when Senate and House hearings did not begin simultaneously.

not reported out or not passed by Congress as a whole. Second, the Senate is the initiator of most of this legislation. Seven of the bills had original hearings in the Senate, four in the House and four had simultaneous hearings. Only the House Agriculture Committee was the initator more often than its Senate counterpart.

Among the committees which have reported out legislation, there are three notable absences. They are: the Subcommittee on Executive Reorganization of the Senate Government Operations Committee, the Special Studies Subcommittee of the House Government Operations Committee, and the Antitrust Subcommittee of the Senate Committee on Judiciary. Their absence is notable because these subcommittees have held extensive and well-publicized hearings on a variety of consumer protection issues. This situation illustrates the variety of roles played by congressional hearings. Hearings are held for reasons other than only considering a particular piece of legislation with the exception that it will pass. In the case of these three subcommittees, legislation has not been reported out, but to consider their efforts futile for this reason is to neglect the other roles played by hearings.

These committees, either by design or necessity, serve as an arena of activity for the particular consumer activists associated with them. It has been noted that one of the functions of subcommittees is to allow the less senior legislators an opportunity to gain prestige and to pursue matters of concern to them.[6] The Senate Executive Reorganization Subcommittee is chaired by Senator Ribicoff. The Special Project on Consumer Protection of the House Government Operations Committee is run by Congressman Benjamin Rosenthal. The Senate Antitrust Subcommittee is chaired by Senator Philip Hart. The subcommittees provide the arena for the activism of each man. They choose the topic, the timing of hearings, and the staff. Each of the three has utilized his position to accrue a great deal of publicity, both personal and topical.

Staff members of these three "nonlegislative" subcommittees agree that their most important function is the generation of publicity about the issues at hand. It is held as axiomatic that publicity could only reflect favorably on the cause they advocate. It is generally felt that such publicity is not an end in itself, but is preparatory to the eventual

---

[6] George Goodwin, Jr., "Subcommittees: The Miniature Legislatures of Congress," *American Political Science Review* 61 (1962): 597.

passage of legislation. "Pave the way" or "lay the groundwork" are typical of the descriptions of the function. The hearings have been designed to arouse public support or, at least in retrospect, they are seen as having had that effect.

It should be noted that these subcommittees are not necessarily nonlegislative by design. It is a typical congressional strategy to relegate controversial bills or bills with strong opposition to ineffectual subcommittees. One of the subcommittees is purposely publicity-oriented with the self-image of a ground-breaker for legislation. Hearings are held which are topically oriented. The political value of the issue is a greater concern than the possibility of getting substantive legislation enacted. A second subcommittee attempts to be legislatively oriented, but is confronted with an unfavorable situation in the full committee which makes the passage of consumer protection legislation nearly impossible. The subcommittee is thus nonlegislative by necessity. This subcommittee has usually held hearings on topics without considering any particular bill. Indeed, when it was perceived that a piece of legislation under consideration would be favorably received in the Senate as a whole, the chairman of this subcommittee led the effort to have the jurisdiction for this bill shifted away from his own committee. The third subcommittee falls somewhere between the other two. It conducts studies and holds hearings both on specific bills up before it and on general topics in the absence of concrete legislative proposals. It has not reported out any legislation, but it is by no means clear that, even if it had done so, such legislation would have cleared the floor.

The significant point about these nonlegislative committees is that, unlike other nonlegislative units in Congress, they are perceived to be an important and equal part in the total consumer protection legislative process. For example, the House Un-American Activities Committee was traditionally a self-contained sideshow with no reference to legislative ends. On the other hand, the Senate Subcommittee on Executive Reorganization held hearings on auto safety which led to consideration and reporting of the bill by the Senate Committee on Commerce.[7] Among other participants, no distinction is drawn between activists on legislative and nonlegislative committees. Rather, they are considered to be performing different functions toward the same end. Thus, once

[7] See pp. 137–143 below.

again it is important to note that the publicity function is considered to be an integral part of the legislative process in consumer protection.

Case Studies

So far, this discussion has considered the identity of those in Congress who represent the consumer interest, their similarities and differences to other congressmen and other identifying features. This still leaves open the manner in which these activists and their supporters operate. Although the general pattern of the consumer legislative process will be presented later in this chapter, a better grasp of the process may be had by examining some specific cases. Therefore, three brief case studies of bills have been selected. These are the Kafauver drug amendments of 1962, the automobile safety bill, and the truth-in-lending bill. These have not been selected because they are necessarily typical any more than any bill can be said to be typical of the legislative process. Rather, these are presented because they were among the early bills and each was surrounded by considerable controversy and opposition. For both these reasons, they demonstrate the full range of resources and techniques which were discovered and utilized by the activists.

Pure Food and Drug Amendments

The history of the 1962 drug amendments is instructive for a number of reasons. It was the first consumer bill of the 1960s and thus covered a good deal of virgin territory. It pitted against each other three classic figures in consumer politics. On one side was the late Estes Kefauver reveling in the role of the crusader for the public interest. On the other side were Everett Dirksen and Roman Hruska who would in the following years be the most frequent, vocal, and prominent champions of industry on a variety of consumer measures. Finally, it was a bill which had a widely publicized near-crisis as a catalyst.

The previous major consumer legislation in this century involved food and drugs and was aimed, almost entirely, at questions of safety.[8] The origins of the 1962 amendments to the Food and Drug Act were

[8] See pp. 7–19 above.

different, however, in that the cost rather than the safety of drugs was involved. A preliminary study of antitrust problems in the drug industry was begun in the Federal Trade Commission in the early 1950s, but was dropped without any further action.

In January, 1957, Senator Estes Kefauver of Tennessee became chairman of the Antitrust and Monopoly Subcommittee of the Senate Judiciary Committee. His two principal aides were Paul Rand Dixon, a former FTC lawyer, and John Blair, also formerly of the FTC, who became the subcommittee's chief economist. They decided to investigate the trend toward administered prices (pricing policies which are independent of market competition), and for two years the investigation concentrated on the steel and automobile industries.

In 1959, after some prodding by staff member Irene Till, another former FTC economist who had worked on the earlier FTC drug study, the committee decided to investigate administered prices in the drug industry. The hearings began in December, 1959. The first phase focused on drug costs and their relation to patents and licensing arrangements. The second phase focused on the high prices of tranquilizers. (This coincided with a Justice Department suit filed against Carter Products and American Home Products Corporation for conspiring to monopolize the mild tranquilizer market.) Until this point, the whole thrust of the investigation was economic. However, at the end of this second phase, two witnesses charged that advertising practices led to dangers of misprescribing drugs. In his concluding statement, Kefauver echoed this charge. Safety was now an issue, although a subsidiary one.

The hearings resumed in April, 1960, with the third phase concentrating on the general question of drug promotion. By the end of the month, the fourth phase was covering the pricing aspects of antidiabetic drugs. Then safety was once more discussed in relation to the antidiabetic drug Diabinese. The fifth phase, from May 10 through May 13, covered prescription practices, the naming of drugs and particularly the question of prescribing by generic name (as opposed to the manufacturer's trade name).

In the sixth phase of the hearings beginning in mid-May, 1960, the first major scandal surfaced. It was learned that Dr. Henry Welch, director of the FDA Antibiotics Division, had received $287,142 from outside publishing jobs connected with drug firms' promotion activities during his tenure. Evidence was presented at the hearings to show that he had solicited those fees. Although Welch was immediately fired, the FDA was criticized by Kefauver and the press in this phase of the hearings for general laxness in the performance of its duties.

The seventh phase focused on the prices of antibiotics. The hearings concluded in February, 1962, with assorted testimony given by organizational supporters of a bill to curb high drug costs.

The main emphasis of the hearings continued to be on economic factors, with drug safety a secondary matter discussed primarily in relation to advertising and promotion practices. This emphasis of the hearings was completely reflected in the subcommittee majority report, issued before the hearings were concluded.

The report contended, first, that drug prices are "generally unreasonable and excessive" and that profits have been "extra-ordinary." Secondly, in the case of *unpatented* drugs, prescribing by generic rather than trade name can effect large savings for the patient, in many cases over 100 percent. Most physicians do not prescribe generically because drug companies have: (1) persuaded physicians that this might result in their patients getting inferior drugs, and (2) established long and sometimes duplicate generic names. Thirdly, the report stated, "Advertising and promotion, as carried on by the drug industry has come to be an important source of monopoly power in that amounts spent by the major companies have reached such proportions as to be far beyond the resources of their smaller competitors." The safety issue was introduced here in the report's finding that advertising sent to physicians is frequently misleading and brushes over known side effects. Finally, the United States is the only major economic power that grants unlimited patents on drugs. This results in higher prices and a proliferation of drugs which are only slightly modified versions of existing drugs. The report concluded with a summary statement about the bill which is instructive in light of the eventual provisions in the enacted bill. The basic intent of the bill was to provide "relief from a monopolistic industry by infusing therein the force of price competition."[9]

This report was vigorously opposed by the Republican subcom-

[9] U.S., Congress, Senate, Committee on the Judiciary, *Drug Industry Antitrust Act. Hearings before a subcommittee of the Committee on the Judiciary on S. 1552,* 87th Cong., 1st sess., 1961, part 1, pp. 2–15.

mittee minority, primarily Hruska and Dirksen. They had an opposite conclusion on every major point and their dissenting report maintained that the public interest was best served by the existing research and marketing practices of the drug companies.[10] The controversy was reflected in the subcommittee by a 3–2 party line vote; the subcommittee reported S. 1552 in the form introduced by Kefauver to the full committee.

In March, 1962, Kefauver learned that President Kennedy was going to send a consumer message to the Hill shortly. Kefauver then met with one of the President's legislative aides and pressed for an endorsement of S. 1552, but the White House was noncommittal. When the message was delivered on March 15, it did not mention Kefauver or his bill. Several of Kefauver's proposals were presented as the President's own, but none which related to drug costs. Needless to say, Kefauver was disappointed.[11] However, as Kefauver requested, the administration did not send down its own drug bill.

The Judiciary Committee met the next day, and with only Kefauver and Hart objecting, the bill was referred to the Patents, Trademarks and Copyrights Subcommittee chaired by Senator John McClellan of Arkansas. Lack of overt administration support gave committee members complete latitude on this vote. Although it was generally believed that shuffling the bill off to another subcommittee effectively killed it, doing so on a jurisdictional question took everybody off the hook.

Although it had been thought that McClellan would kill the bill by inaction, the subcommittee voted on the patent provisions and rejected them 4–2 with Kefauver and Hart in the minority. The section most vehemently opposed by industry had been gutted.

Throughout this time, the administration had been under pressure in the press for not supporting Kefauver. The widely syndicated columnist Drew Pearson was particularly active and his columns claimed that the administration could, if it so desired, push the drug bill through. Then, the day after the patent provision vote, the Presi-

[10] Ibid., pp. 16–19.
[11] Richard Harris, *The Real Voice* (New York: Macmillan Co., 1964), 145–148. I rely heavily on Harris's account of individual actions during the legislative history. Several of the participants have validated the accuracy of his book.

dent sent a letter to Eastland supporting the bill with some changes. Richard Harris's analysis of the administration turnabout demonstrates the general pattern of consumer legislation:

> On Capitol Hill, the most widely held explanation for the administration's sudden interest in the Kefauver bill was that the President had become increasingly concerned about the sluggish progress of his legislative program. By this time, it was generally believed that the Medicare plan had almost no chance of getting through both houses that session. Moreover, the A.F.L.-C.I.O. and a number of other unions, which had strongly supported S. 1552 from the start were beginning to grumble about his apparent disinterest in the measure. Now, since the drug industry no longer opposed it so adamantly, the administration, it was commonly said, had everything to gain and nothing to lose.[12]

On April 23, to the surprise of Kefauver, the administration sent its own bill to the House sponsored by Oren Harris, then chairman of the Interstate and Foreign Commerce Committee. The Harris bill was weaker than Kefauver's original bill and did not concern drug prices.

The administration moved in the Senate also. The President's leg man on the bill, Myer Feldman, requested that the Department of Health, Education, and Welfare send a couple of aides to Eastland's office to participate in marking up the bill. The meeting consisted of staff members representing Eastland, the committee minority, and two men from the Pharmaceutical Manufacturers Association. Throughout the day they hammered out the bill that the committee would report. Kefauver was outraged when he found out about the meeting from which he had been excluded and he promised a floor fight to reinstate the provisions of his original bill. On July 12, the Judiciary Committee voted unanimously to approve the bill.

The provisions of the Kefauver bill which were weakened are good examples of the points of resistance to consumer legislation, and I shall describe the major provisions of the original bill and the changes made by the full committee with this in mind.

The first substantive section amends the patent sections of the Sherman Antitrust Act so that exclusive rights to drug patents would be granted only during the first three years of the patent. During the

12 Ibid., p. 153.

remaining fourteen years, the patent holder would be required to license other drug firms who would pay a percentage of sales fee to make the drug. Also, patents would be granted for modifications of existing drugs only if the Department of Health, Education, and Welfare decided that the change would significantly improve the drug's efficiency. This entire section, which Kefauver considered the heart of the bill, was dropped.

The rest of the bill consisted of amendments to the Federal Food, Drug and Cosmetic Act. The first provision required the licensing of all pharmaceutical drug manufacturers by the Department of Health, Education, and Welfare.[13] It required that applicants meet standards set by HEW for a license. The committee altered this into a form more in the nature of routine registration with biannual inspection, but without the required standards in the original language of the bill. The point of resistance can be seen in Senator Eastland's statement that by licensing of business firms the government would be "dealing in socialism."[14] However, the HEW secretary was empowered to determine proper manufacturing practices, and inspection was authorized.

The second provision required that a new drug be proven effective for the purposes which it is intended to serve. Any drug approved prior to the amendments could be withdrawn if shown to be ineffective. Previously, drugs had only to be proven safe. This was altered so that proof of efficacy was required only for newly developed drugs and not for claims of new uses for drugs previously cleared as safe. Also, the committee version would permit a claim of efficacy even when there was "preponderant" evidence against such a claim as long as some qualified studies support the claim. The main point of concentration seemed to be a desire of the committee majority not to burden drug firms with the necessity of proving claims for old drugs.

It should be noted that, throughout the legislative history, the opposition managed to keep the safety question within the bounds of the issue of side effects. Clearly, if a patient is given a useless drug for his disease, he suffers as much risk as is inherent in his disease if there

[13] The numbering of provisions is my own. Since the bill consists of amendments to two laws, its own numbering sequence is confusing.

[14] *1962 Congressional Quarterly Almanac* (Washington, D.C.: Congressional Quarterly, 1963), p. 204.

exists an alternate drug which would be effective. Although Kefauver touched upon this issue, the committee majority and the ultimate thrust of the final bill treated safety and efficacy as though they were separate problems.

The third section provided that an application for a new drug could not become effective unless specifically approved by FDA. (Under the law then in force, new drugs could become effective within 60 days unless the HEW secretary specifically postponed the final date in writing.) The committee eliminated the prohibition of clearance without approval but extended the minimum time from 60 days to 90 days which the Food and Drug Administration could extend to 180 days. Senators Kefauver, Carroll, Hart, Dodd, and Long specifically dissented from this provision.

The original bill's provision, permitting HEW to require manufacturers to keep records and make reports on drug tests, was kept.

The fifth provision required that the generic name of drugs be printed on the package as prominently as the trade name. In the committee version, the generic name had only to be conspicuous enough for the average person to read.

The original bill required that the manufacturers include in advertising materials sent to physicians a copy of the material required in the package insert. It also required that all advertisements contain the generic name as prominently as the trade name and contain a warning of side effects and a statement of the drug's efficacy. This section was completely revamped. The committee version required the manufacturer to send any physician the drug package insert for a particular drug, *when the physician requests it.*

Thus, S. 1552 had been thoroughly weakened. Although Kefauver promised a floor fight, at that point his chances of restoring the bill on the floor were extremely dim particularly since the administration could not be expected to take a new tack and back the original bill. Although Congressman Emanuel Celler had introduced a House bill similar to Kefauver's he had vitrually no chance of getting it out of committee.

Then, like the cavalry coming to the rescue in the nick of time, the thalidomide crisis broke and became front page news. On July 15, 1962, a front page story in the *Washington Post* by Morton Mintz revealed that the sedative thalidomide could cause deformities in fetuses and that only the protracted efforts of Dr. Frances Kelsey, an

FDA medical officer, had kept the drug off the American market. For our purposes, the importance of the thalidomide incident lies not in the facts relating directly to the case, but in the fact that the fortuitous timing was not accidental. An Antitrust subcommittee staff member had begun compiling information on thalidomide in April after John Blair came across a small article in the April 11 *New York Times.* The article concerned a speech given by Dr. Helen Taussig in which she pointed out the relation between thalidomide and birth defects. The article further reported her statement that the only reason thalidomide was not marketed in the United States was that William Merrell Company had submitted what the FDA considered insufficient data in its application to market the drug. This was three months before the episode received wide publicity.

What is most surprising about the thalidomide episode is that it was mentioned in hearings nearly two months before surfacing as a major issue. Chairman Emanuel Celler had earlier introduced a drug bill which everyone assumed was dead. At the urging of Kefauver, who did not want to settle for the bill the administration had sent to the House, Celler held four days of hearings in late May, 1962. Dr. Taussig testified at those hearings on the malforming effects of thalidomide. The testimony was dramatic, yet it received no press coverage since Celler's subcommittee staff had not alerted the press to cover the hearings. So here was a second opportunity for the thalidomide story to enter the public consciousness, and once again the media did not follow through. But Kefauver's staff was aware of the potential all along. John Blair wanted to wait for a more favorable time to disclose the story and he is quoted as saying, "I tried to talk Celler's people out of using Dr. Taussig. It's too early to spring this kind of story. All the various bills are still far from reaching the floor of either house, and it's clear that the thalidomide story, or something like it, is just what we need to ram through some legislation. In a situation like this, timing is vital."[15]

When the weakened bill was reported out of the Judiciary Committee, Blair alerted *The Washington Post* and the *Washington Star* to the thalidomide story and to the subcommittee's dossier which emphasized that thalidomide would have been marketed in the United States a year previously if it had not been for Dr. Frances Kelsey, who kept

15 Harris, *Real Voice,* p. 161.

insisting on further testing for the drug. As mentioned above, Morton Mintz of the *Post* acted on the story immediately and the *Post* gave the story front page coverage in the Sunday edition. It immediately became front page news throughout the country. The next day, Kefauver released the dossier on thalidomide to the press.

Two weeks later, the President declared that the Judiciary Committee bill, which he had previously approved, was inadequate and urged support for the administration bill introduced in the House by Oren Harris. It appeared as though the administration was seeking to embrace the proposed drug regulations as its own and to take the credit. Shortly afterward, the administration sent Eastland several proposed amendments to the committee bill.

Through two vigorous marking-up sessions, the Judiciary Committee bill was amended so as to bring it closer to the form in which Kefauver had originally introduced it, with a notable exception. The changes pertained only to regulation of drug safety. The patent and licensing provisions were not revived.

The committee reported the strengthened bill on August 21. Kefauver introduced his original patent amendment on the floor, but it was tabled on a 53–28 roll call vote. The Senate passed S. 1552 by a 78–0 roll call vote on August 23.

From August 20 through August 23, the House Interstate and Foreign Commerce Committee held hearings on the administration bill. The committee reported the bill on September 22. The major difference between the Senate and House committee versions concerned advertising. The Senate bill required that advertisements contain the generic name and information about side effects. The House version permitted advertisements to omit this information and substitute a statement that such information was freely available upon request. The difference was resolved by floor amendment largely in favor of the Senate version.

The bill passed the House on September 27 and was very similar to the Senate version. The House bill had a milder labeling requirement which was accepted by the Senate, and the House accepted the Senate requirement that drug manufacturers register with the Department of Health, Education, and Welfare.

The conference report was accepted by the Senate on October 3, and by the House on October 4. The legislation, which was popularly known as the Kefauver-Harris drug amendments of 1962, became PL 87–781 on October 10.

The most significant aspect of this legislative history is the manner in which the economic provisions were consistently scuttled at every opportunity. The original hearings and Kefauver's original report predominantly concerned drug costs, not safety. Yet, it was this aspect of the bill which was entirely eliminated. Although the presentation of profit figures sometimes exceeding 100 percent on individual products was certainly dramatic, it was the issue of drug safety which became the catalytic agent in strengthening the bill. After the thalidomide incident, the issue became entirely one of safety. The President's second round of proposals concerned safety, and the Senate Judiciary Committee revision was aimed at preventing a future episode similar to the thalidomide crisis. The economic issue was not even considered in the House. The toughest point of resistance was this economic issue. Once it was deleted, the bill could be passed.

Truth-in-Lending

The origins of this issue are generally credited to one man—former Senator Paul Douglas, Democrat of Illinois. His interest in consumer credit problems goes back to the days of the New Deal when Douglas was in the Consumers Division of the National Recovery Administration. After learning that many lenders were charging interest on the basis of the original amount rather than on the amount of the unpaid balance and the rate the lenders were quoting was therefore much less than the true annual rate the borrower was paying, Douglas proposed that interest rates be based on the unpaid balance. This proposal created considerable opposition and controversy, but like other consumer-oriented proposals in the NRA it was not implemented.

After serving several years in the Senate, Douglas renewed his interest in consumer credit and instructed his aide, Milton Semar, to begin work on a truth-in-lending bill in 1959. The bill was introduced in the spring of 1960. As originally introduced, the legislation required that the following information be disclosed to the borrower: the total cash price of the goods or service, the down payment, the difference between the down payment and the total cash price, all charges not directly resulting from the extension of credit, the *total* finance charges, and the finance costs expressed as a simple annual interest rate calculated on the basis of the unpaid balance of the debt through time.

It was this last proposal which was the heart of the matter and aroused the most opposition. The principal public argument against the legislation was that an annual interest rate was extremely difficult to calculate in that there was no agreed formula for arriving at it. It was argued that requiring such calculation would work a hardship on small retail merchants. A secondary argument was stated by Brooks Schumaker of the National Retail Merchants Association who argued that the bill:

> propagates fear, doubt, and distrust through junking . . . the well-understood monthly terms for monthly transactions and substitutes new and little understood simple annual rates for monthly transactions—requiring in turn a radical readjustment of the consumer mind —and particularly the female mind.[16]

Another retail merchants' spokesman argued that stating a 1½ percent monthly charge as 18 percent annually would "create an undesirable psychological effect on the American consumer's buying habits, resulting in a serious business lag."

There were three other basic objections. First, the bill would actually provide less information to consumers since credit costs could be hidden in the base cost of the merchandise. Second, the economic premises of the bill are wrong in that credit is not being used excessively. Finally, regulation should be left to the states.

Opponents of the bill included the Chamber of Commerce of the United States, loan companies, and retail merchants. Bankers initially opposed the bill, but later switched to a supporting role. The initial opposition of the banks is surprising. Since they offered the lowest interest rates, they stood to benefit from annual rate comparisons. A supporter of the legislation stated that he learned that bankers were profiting from kickbacks by retail establishments such as auto dealers who did their own financing. If the rates were to come down, the banks would no longer get the kickbacks.[17] Senator Douglas declined, however, to make this an issue in the campaign for the legislation.

The only financial institutions which supported the legislation throughout its history were the credit unions and the mutual savings

[16] *1962 Congressional Quarterly Almanac.*
[17] Personal interview which was not for attribution.

banks. Indeed they played an active role. The credit unions had a mass membership base which was an aware public. One of the mutual savings banks devised a simple device similar in design to a circular slide rule which could easily calculate the simple annual interest rate. This, of course, took a lot of air out of the principal opposition argument.

Other than the credit unions and mutual savings banks, the chief source of private group support was the large industrial unions, primarily the Industrial Union Department of the AFL-CIO, the International Ladies Garment Workers (ILGWU), and the Steelworkers.

The bill, in much the same form, was introduced by Douglas in every Congress from the 86th Congress in 1960, until his defeat in the 1966 senatorial election. After that, Senator William Proxmire of Wisconsin continued the campaign. The Production and Stabilization Subcommittee of the Senate Committee on Banking and Currency held hearings on the measure every year from 1960 to 1964 and in 1967.

In 1960, the subcommittee approved the bill, but it was not reported out by the full committee. The Eisenhower administration opposed the bill. It was reintroduced in the 87th Congress in 1961. In 1962, President Kennedy endorsed the measure in his first consumer message. This time, however, the bill did not even clear the subcommittee where it was defeated on a 4–5 vote with committee chairman A. Willis Robertson joining the Republican subcommittee minority who were unanimous in their opposition.

In the 88th Congress, Douglas introduced the bill as S. 750. In 1963 and 1964 hearings were held in Louisville, Boston, New York, and Pittsburgh in an attempt to generate grass roots support by getting better local press coverage. Louisville was elected largely because the support of the prestigious *Louisville Courier-Journal* was felt to be important as a means of enlisting support of some Southern senators. Whether this was an effective strategy in pursuit of the proponents' goals is not relevant. It is significant, however, that the mobilization of public awareness was perceived as leading to public support, and that the proponents systematically sought to use the press for that purpose. The subcommittee took no further action in 1963, but reported the bill to the full committee by a 5–4 vote on March 16. However, on June 23, the full committee by an 8–6 vote recommitted the bill to the subcommittee which killed it for that Congress.

Douglas reintroduced the bill (S. 2275) in the 89th Congress

(1965–66), but no action was taken by the Banking and Currency Committee. In 1966, senators Douglas and Robertson, the chief antagonists for and against the bill, were both defeated in their bids for reelection.

In 1967, truth-in-lending was introduced by Senator Proxmire with strong administration backing. Hearings were held in the Banking and Currency Committee's Financial Institutions Subcommittee, chaired by Proxmire. A compromise was made in the subcommittee on the administration bill in the form of amendments which largely exempted revolving charge accounts and contracts calling for less than a ten-dollar finance charge from the rate disclosure requirements. The bill unanimously cleared both the subcommittee and the committee in June, 1967, and was passed by the Senate 92–0 on July 11.

In the House, a group of Democrats led by Leonor Sullivan introduced a bill which was far more extensive than the bill passed by the Senate. It did not exempt revolving charge accounts, contained interest ceiling provisions, and banned wage garnishment. Hearings were held in the Consumer Affairs Subcommittee of the House Committee on Banking and Currency. The bill became deadlocked in subcommittee and a weakened version was reported out by the full committee on December 13, 1967. As in the Senate bill, the committee bill exempted revolving charge plans from the provisions of the bill.

Then an unusual phenomenon occurred on the House floor during the debate which took place from January 30, to February 1, 1968. Ushered through by floor manager Leonor Sullivan, the bill was strengthened by three major amendments which closed Senate loopholes and added new protection. The revolving charge account exemption was abolished after several large retail chains withdrew their support for that exemption. The ten-dollar minimum was dropped in the absence of any support for it in the House. Finally, by a 101–98 teller vote, the House passed a committee amendment restricting wage garnishment to ten percent of a person's income over thirty dollars. On February 1, the House passed the bill by a 384–4 roll call vote. By voice vote the House substituted the provisions of HR. 11601 for the weaker S. 5 and sent it to conference. The conference report maintaining the strong bill was issued on May 22, and the President signed the act on May 29, 1968.

Although the bill is commonly referred to as truth-in-lending, its official title is the Consumer Credit Protection Act. The title indicates the more comprehensive nature of the act as amended in the House. The truth-in-lending section (Title I) basically required disclosure of the total finance charges and the annual interest rate based on the declining balance. The second title imposed a twenty-five percent ceiling on the amount of a worker's take-home pay that can be garnished by a creditor with a flat 48-dollar weekly exemption. The third title made loan-sharking a federal offense. These last two titles were added in the House.

The above is the raw legislative history. For purposes of this study, the key questions are why it took so long and why it did finally pass. Most other consumer issues have gone through at a much faster rate. There are two principal factors behind the delay. The most important reason was the impossible situation in the Senate Banking and Currency Committee. Until 1967, Willis Robertson was chairman of the committee and a member of the Production and Stabilization Subcommittee. He was unalterably opposed to the legislation and usually aligned himself with the Republican minority on this and other committee business. One former staff member described Robertson's orientation as being rooted in a belief that that committee is best which legislates least. Until 1967, the only Republican on the committee who broke ranks and voted for the legislation was Jacob Javits.[18] The proponents always believed that the bill was home free if it could only reach the floor. Passage in 1967 seemed to vindicate that belief.

The situation in the committee was made more sticky by the personal situation of two members. In 1962, the president of the National Retail Merchants Association which vigorously opposed the bill was Harold H. Bennett, brother of Senator Wallace Bennett who was unsurpassed on the subcommittee in his vigorous opposition. In addition, Senator Bennett, at the time he was opposing the legislation, was coowner of a hardware store and owned a Ford automobile dealership, both of which handled credit transactions. Senator Edward Long, whose ethics were questioned by *Life* magazine with regard to other matters, opposed the bill in the full committee at the same time that he

---

[18] For a more detailed account of the conflict within the Banking and Currency Committee, see John F. Bibby, "Legislative Oversight of Administration: A Case Study of a Congressional Committee," Ph.D. diss., University of Wisconsin, 1963.

was president of a major Missouri small loan company and of two banks. Pro-legislation staff members attempted to persuade Long to at least abstain from voting on the matter because of his personal interest, but Long still voted against the legislation. It is an interesting comment on congressional ethics that the direct financial stake in the legislation of Bennett and Long was no secret. On his CBS national news program, Walter Cronkite pointed out their connections to the loan business in his report on the committee vote. Long and Bennett simply denied any conflict of interest. Senator Douglas never exploited this issue or the potential scandal of kickbacks to the banks. It is said that he considered such tactics ungentlemanly.

A second factor was the lack of support for consumer issues in general at that time. Douglas alone took the initiative and was joined by several of the other liberals who went in because it was Douglas's legislation. It was thus identified as a liberal piece of legislation although the ideological split broke down in 1967. But in general, the mood of the Senate was one of indifference. This indifference just couldn't overcome a well-organized and well-financed opposition.

Yet, in 1967, despite the seven-year delay, the legislation got through the Senate. In this bill, and in others, assigning causation is a hazardous undertaking. Nonetheless, several factors can validly be considered to be responsible for final passage. First is the absence from the committee of Willis Robertson who was defeated in his bid for reelection the previous year. Since the bill was reported unanimously, we can not analyze the passage simply in terms of a changed voting alignment. However, the loss of the uncompromising Robertson paved the way for bargaining which Proxmire was more willing to engage in than Douglas. Second, the issue now had strong presidential support to the extent that it was considered an "administration bill." Finally, there was simply a greater receptivity in Congress toward consumer bills. The ground had been broken by the automobile safety bill and this type of legislation had proven popular and fairly safe.

The new popularity of the issue partially explains Senate passage and the reporting of the Senate bill by the House committee. However, it is not a satisfactory explanation for the strengthening and transformation of the bill on the floor of the House. That explanation is found in the pattern of support for the three main changes: revolving credit, garnishment and loan-sharking.

Although nearly the entire credit industry was opposed to the general concept of a truth-in-lending law, once that law passed the Senate with an exemption for revolving credit, the united front began crumbling. The revolving credit exemption gave lenders using revolving credit a comparative advantage over lenders such as furniture retailers and small loan companies using fixed installment contracts. In effect, the former could deceive their customers while the latter could not. Consequently, after Senate passage and House committee reporting of the Senate bill, it became obvious that some bill would pass; the American Bankers Association, the Furniture Manufacturers Association and a number of small loan companies then came out in favor of eliminating the exemption. Thus, although all originally opposed any meaningful bill, they ended by supporting a tougher bill on the House floor.

One key staff aide working for the bill believes that the position of those opposed to the revolving credit exemption had a spill-over effect. They contacted their congressmen and urged them to support Congressman Sullivan's efforts to remove this loophole. Many congressmen translated support for Mrs. Sullivan on this issue to support on other issues because many of their constituents were not very specific as to which position taken by Mrs. Sullivan they favored. Apparently some congressmen assumed that their petitioners favored her total stance on the bill.

Important as the preceding factors were, the real breakthrough came when the big department store chains dropped their support of the exemption. The exemption was originally put in the bill at the instigation of major retail chains. Indeed, it was immediately called the "J. C. Penney Amendment." All the retail chains assumed it would exempt their charge plans. However, the staff of the House Banking and Currency Committee prepared a report defining the exemption. When this report was released and circulated, officials of Montgomery Ward were shocked to discover that their plan would not be exempted. The exemption applied only to charge plans calling for a payment of more than sixty percent of the balance in a year; the Montgomery Ward plan called for less than the sixty percent payment when the service charge was subtracted. Ward's initial reaction was to try to amend the exemption, but J. C. Penney was opposed to altering it. At the same time, Mrs. Sullivan had been doing her best to publicize the exemption as the "Ward, Sears, Penney Amendment," and this was a source of concern to Montgomery Ward. When it became apparent that the amendment would not be changed, the president of Montgomery Ward sent Mrs. Sullivan a telegram withdrawing Ward's support for the exemption. Mrs. Sullivan then called Sears which also agreed to withdraw its support and sent a telegram to that effect. After announcing the withdrawal of chain store support, the Penney amendment received only nineteen votes on the floor in an unrecorded vote. This was one of the first floor votes on the bill, and it was so resounding a victory that it greatly encouraged and emboldened proponents of a strong bill.

Mrs. Sullivan originally proposed a complete ban on garnishment, an idea which previously no one had taken seriously. The President took no position on that issue. Following the suggestions of other proponents of the bill, Mrs. Sullivan whittled down the garnishment section and proposed restrictions rather than an outright ban. This also passed on an unrecorded vote.

The loan-sharking amendment was originally offered by a Republican, Richard Poff of Virginia, and most of the other House Republicans rallied behind it. The amendment was so loosely drawn that it was probably unconstitutional and, if passed, would doom the whole bill. The Democrats in favor of the bill suspected a trap, yet they would have a difficult time explaining to their constituents why they voted against an amendment to make loan-sharking a federal offense. However, Mrs. Sullivan accepted the amendment in order to get the Democrats off the hook. She knew the bill would be rewritten in conference at which time the thrust of the loan-sharking amendment could be changed. The amendment passed easily.

The bill was stalled in conference for six weeks, but by then so much publicity surrounded the bill that the Senate conferees were in an increasingly untenable position. The bill cleared conference with most of the differences resolved in favor of the House version. Eight years after Senator Douglas began, the bill was passed.

Automobile Safety

Although the issue of auto safety did not burst into the public consciousness until 1966, consumer activists had long pursued the matter.[19] As noted in Chapter 1, from 1956 until 1964, Congressman Kenneth Roberts held auto safety hearings and Congress passed three piecemeal bills. The hearings, however, were little noted and received practically no publicity. This lack of publicity was probably due to Roberts' role in the House. He was an "inside" man who did not seek publicity and his witnesses were predominately engineers unfamiliar with the realities of congressional hearings.[20] Consequently, the public never learned that anyone in government was suggesting that the auto itself was a factor in traffic safety. Thus Roberts had no public constituency on this issue. In October, 1963, Ralph Nader wrote an article on auto safety critical of the industry. Still, nothing happened.

The matter stood there until February, 1965, when Senator Abraham Ribicoff, chairman of the Senate Governmental Operations Committee's Subcommittee on Executive Reorganization, announced that the subcommittee would hold hearings on traffic safety. The background to this announcement contains the seeds of the eventual passage of the bill. Ribicoff ascended to the chairmanship of this subcommittee in the fall of 1964. Ribicoff has a reputation of being not the least bit reticent in seeking publicity. He thus decided to use his subcommittee as a forum for an investigation of the federal role in automobile safety.[21] Senator Robert Kennedy joined the subcommittee upon his arrival in the Senate in 1965.

Although the hearings nominally involved a couple of bills intro-

---

[19] The issue here is the safety of automobiles themselves which is a part of the larger problem of traffic safety. It was the new focus on the automobile rather than on the other factors which gave the issue its controversy. The official line of the automobile companies, echoed by the President's Committee for Traffic Safety and the National Safety Council, was that traffic safety was a function of the driver and the highways. From this, it followed that responsibility for traffic safety should be lodged in state and local governments who were the natural candidates for undertaking stricter law enforcement, highway building, etc. It was this orientation that was being challenged by Ralph Nader and others.

[20] I am indebted for this interpretation to Professor Paul Halpern of UCLA whose Ph.D. dissertation (Harvard, 1971) is a comprehensive study of the automobile safety issue.

[21] Elizabeth Brenner Drew, "The Politics of Auto Safety," *Atlantic Monthly* 218 (October, 1966): 96. Donald Matthews also points out the relation between congressional behavior and the reaction anticipated from the press. *U.S. Senators and Their World* (New York: Vintage Books, 1960), pp. 203–206.

duced by Ribicoff, they were irrelevant to the notoriety achieved by the hearings. Robert Kennedy's very participation in the hearings was in itself newsworthy. But even beyond that, the situation was structured to achieve publicity. The top officials of the auto industry were invited to testify. Like sheep to the slaughter, they came. Given the potential for conflict between Ribicoff and Kennedy on the one hand and the automobile executives on the other, the hearings received heavy press and television coverage.[22] That potential was realized particularly in the following exchange:[23]

KENNEDY: What was the profit of General Motors last year?

ROCHE (G.M. president): I don't think that has anything to do—

KENNEDY: I would like to have that answer if I may. I think I am entitled to know that figure. I think it has been published. You spend $1¼ million, as I understand it, on this aspect of safety. I would like to know what the profit is.

DONNER (G.M. board chairman): The one aspect we are talking about is safety.

KENNEDY: What was the profit of General Motors last year?

DONNER: I will have to ask one of my associates.

KENNEDY: Could you please?

ROCHE: $1,700 million.

KENNEDY: What?

DONNER: About $1½ billion, I think.

KENNEDY: $1 billion?

DONNER: $1.7 billion.

KENNEDY: About $1½ billion?

DONNER: Yes.

KENNEDY: Or $1.7 billion. You made $1.7 billion last year?

DONNER: That is correct.

KENNEDY: And you spent $1 million on this?

DONNER: In this particular facet we are talking about.

KENNEDY: Just tell me what you spent on this whole program of safety.

Needless to say, this exchange and others that day received wide

[22] Bernard Cohen stresses that conflict or potential conflict is the standard of newsworthiness most frequently cited by correspondents. *The Press and Foreign Policy* (Princeton: Princeton University Press, 1963), p. 56.

[23] Drew, "The Politics of Auto Safety," p. 97.

publicity. G.M. later increased its estimate of safety research expenditures, but the damage was done and the later figure was suspect. The hearings adjourned that month.

In November, 1965, a book entitled *Unsafe at Any Speed* by Ralph Nader was published.[24] It identified the automobile itself as being a significant cause of traffic accidents and injuries. Despite the earlier flurry of publicity, the book's early sales were only moderate.

The White House publicly entered the picture with the 1966 state-of-the-union message which proposed a "highway safety act." Actually, the administration action had its roots in the secret task force which began work on the administration proposal shortly after the Ribicoff hearings.

However, the substance of the bill was in dispute within the administration. Secretary of Commerce Connor favored a bill which would allow the secretary of commerce to set safety standards after two years if voluntary action by industry was unsatisfactory. On the other hand, Charles Schultze, director of the Bureau of the Budget, favored a bill which would require the commerce secretary to set safety standards outright without delay. Connor's weaker proposal won in the administration, but this still was the strongest auto safety bill which had ever come before Congress.

Elizabeth Drew credits the period during which the administration bill was debated within the administration as being an extremely important fermentation time during which the advocates of auto safety could activate more public interest and during which they could press for an even stronger bill.[25] The administration bill soon took on the appearances of a base. The administration approach was leaked to the newspapers and Ralph Nader denounced the bill as a "no-law law." Ribicoff urged mandatory standards immediately.

The administration bill was introduced in both houses on March 2. The Senate Commerce Committee, chaired by Warren Magnuson, opened hearings on March 16 and Magnuson announced that he would introduce amendments to require immediate standards.

On March 24, the Commerce Committee reported out a stiff tire safety bill which had its roots in a 1965 bill introduced by Gaylord

24 (New York: Grossman, 1965).
25 Drew, "Politics of Auto Safety," p. 98.

Nelson. The bill required the secretary of commerce to set minimum safety standards for passenger car tires. By voice vote the Senate accepted a floor amendment by Nelson to establish uniform quality grading standards. The bill passed 79–0 on March 29, 1966. Although the spotlight was on auto safety, the importance of the tire bill cannot be overlooked. The Senate had unanimously passed a bill which would ultimately require the government to establish a grading system for a major manufacturing industry. The times were certainly changing.

About this time, Senator Ribicoff requested a complete list of auto defect warnings issued to dealers by the manufacturers since 1960. A few weeks later, Ribicoff released the information. There had been 426 recall campaigns involving eight million cars. The industry position was seriously weakened.

March was a busy month—the key month in the bill's history. On March 10, the *New York Times* reported that General Motors had admitted it had undertaken a "routine" investigation of Ralph Nader. Ribicoff, who was being edged out of the act by Magnuson and the Commerce Committee, jumped back in the picture with hearings on the possible harassment of a witness. It turned out that Nader was being followed, and his politics, sex life, drinking, finances, etc., were being investigated. Most observers credit the G.M. investigation and resultant adverse publicity with being the key factor in passage of a stiff bill.

Nader's book *Unsafe at Any Speed,* had been published the previous November. But sales had only totaled about 25,000 copies. All that changed. The publicity led to increased book sales and greater public awareness of Nader and his arguments. The industry was shown in an extremely unfavorable light. One senator who credits the bill's passage to this incident was reported to have said, "Everybody was so outraged that a great corporation was out to clobber a guy because he wrote critically about them. At that point, everybody said the hell with them."[26] In addition, the media began generating a second wave of stories by reporting the varied reactions to the G.M. incident.[27]

The Commerce Committee marked up the bill in constant consultation with Ralph Nader and Lloyd Cutler who became the in-

[26] Ibid., p. 99.

[27] Robert Bishop and Jane Kilburn, "Penny Whistle or Public's Advocate," *Public Relations Quarterly* 12 (Winter, 1968): 27–28.

dustry's chief lobbyist in April. On June 23, the committee reported a bill which was stronger than the administration bill in two main respects. Safety standards were to be mandatory and the reporting and notification of defects was to be more systematic and open. A group of liberal senators were central in strengthening the bill. These included Democrats Magnuson, Ribicoff, Kennedy, Hartke, Mondale, Nelson and Republican Javits. The bill was reported unanimously by the Commerce Committee.

The House Interstate and Foreign Commerce Committee, chaired by Harley Staggers, started hearings on March 15 and began with the administration bill as a mere skeleton upon which to build. The committee reported out a bill which combined automobile and tire safety provisions. It was tougher than the Senate bill in its scope (it included ICC-regulated trucks and buses and used cars) but weaker in enforcement provisions. These weaknesses were largely resolved by acceptance of a series of floor amendments offered by Staggers. The bill passed the House unanimously on August 17.

It should be noted that in both the Senate (14–62) and the House (15–120) floor amendments for criminal penalties were rejected. The Senate had a roll call vote while the House had an anonymous standing vote. Even accounting for House-Senate differences, it is significant that on a record vote a somewhat larger proportion of legislators voted for criminal penalties on a consumer issue. We can speculate that this indicates a congressional perception of a more militant consumer protection demand by the public.

Futher evidence for this speculation is found in the conference report which resolved all House-Senate differences regarding the auto industry in favor of the stronger provision. The addition of the tire provisions was also kept. The report was agreed to on August 31, and, on September 9, the President signed the National Traffic and Motor Vehicle Safety Act of 1966.

Several factors should be noted about the act. It was the first time that the automobile industry had succumbed to any regulation. The press was a crucial factor in passage of the bill. The administration was a very late entrant and a conservative one. Support for the bill sprang from the political maintenance needs of two senators—Ribicoff who had a new forum and Magnuson whose staff urged him to change his pro-industry image and broaden his base of support.

In a larger context, many observers consider this the breakthrough legislation. The impossible had been done. The feared auto industry turned out to be, in the words of Elizabeth Drew, "a paper hippopotamus." Ralph Nader became a popular figure and consumer legislation was to be a popular issue with good publicity value. Future bills would be easier.

The Case Studies
in Perspective

With full cognizance of the hazards implicit in generalizing from individual cases, the facts of the preceding cases can now be reviewed together to illustrate certain important features of consumer protection politics. Some of the features have already been pointed out in the context of each individual case. What remains is to make explicit three themes which emerge when these cases are taken together.

The first theme is the role, or lack of role, of a scandal or publicized crisis in passing legislation. The auto safety bill was preceded by G.M.'s bungling harassment of Ralph Nader, the drug bill was given an impetus by the thalidomide scandal, but there was no precipitating event of that type in the truth-in-lending bill. The truth-in-lending bill thus contradicts the conventional wisdom that such a crisis is needed to mobilize public awareness. Without comparative survey data, one can only speculate on the role of crisis in the interaction between public opinion and legislative action. The truth-in-lending bill had the longest legislative history of any of the consumer bills. There was no accompanying crisis, yet, in the opinion of the activists fighting for the bill, by the end of the process there was a preponderant public opinion in favor of the bill—a public opinion which forced the Senate conferees to accept most of the House version. Thus it can be hypothesized that a long and slow process of building public awareness can substitute for a crisis in mobilizing public opinion.

A related lesson in this theme of crisis and scandal is that such events usually do not simply happen spontaneously. The best kind of precipitating scandal is one whose timing and publicity have been managed. Thalidomide was made an issue at a key moment in the progress of the drug amendments. The G.M. investigation of Nader was magnified in importance when Senator Ribicoff held hearings specifically on that issue (attempted intimidation of a congressional witness). Similarly, there were scandalous elements in the activities of the opponents of truth-in-lending. However, Senator Douglas was unwilling to take the necessary next step of exploiting that situation. All three cases illustrate the importance of managing publicity resources.

The second theme is the importance of the particular configuration of forces within each committee. In two of the cases, the bills were nearly deadlocked because of opposition by persons in key committee positions. This observation is, of course, not new in describing congressional behavior.[28] However, it is important to note that this is a situation which does not necessarily arise from seniority or the tyranny of Southern chairmen representing regional forces. Rather it stems from the orientation of committee members and chairmen who are from a variety of regions of the country. This empathy with the industries which are the objects of legislative proposals is an attitude not at all confined to Southerners. However, the most usual pattern of obstruction finds Southern Democratic chairmen and committee members giving sympathy and voting support to the more active opposition of regionally dispersed conservative Republicans.

What is more interesting about the importance of the committee situation is the different perspective on lobbying shown in these cases. Both the model of government being manipulated by selfish private interests and the more sanguine view of Lester Milbrath, that lobbyists do not have much influence, seem irrelevant.[29] In fact, a frequent phenomenon of consumer legislation is the process of *internal* lobbying. Members of Congress have been the de facto representatives of particular industries.[30] Thus, in truth-in-lending, Senator Wallace Bennett was a far more important and effective representative for the small loan industry than their own trade association, which was, in fact, irrelevant. With senators Dirksen and Hruska on the scene, the phar-

[28] See, for example, Woodrow Wilson, *Congressional Government* (Boston: Houghton Mifflin, 1885).

[29] Lester Milbrath, *The Washington Lobbyists* (Chicago: Rand McNally, 1963).

[30] This is also suggested in Raymond Bauer, Ithiel de Sola Pool, and Lewis Anthony Dexter, *American Business and Public Policy* (New York: Atherton Press, 1963), pp. 436–437.

maceutical industry had hardly any need of their own trade association. While to many readers this may sound like a pejorative judgment, it is purely a statement of fact. Supporters of Bennett, Dirksen, and Hruska would admit that they represented the interests of certain industries in particular cases; but they would claim that such interests coincided precisely with the consumer interest. It is in this equation between the consumer interest and the business interest that conflict lies, and not over the fact that a number of senators function as representatives for those industries.

The third theme is the importance of unity of opposition to particular legislation. This was most evident with the truth-in-lending bill when the crumbling of a united front by the large chain stories paved the way for the strengthening of the bill. On the other hand, neither the "big three" auto manufacturers nor the drug firms faltered in their opposition to the legislation affecting them. But, as noted previously, these two cases were accompanied by well-publicized scandals.

There are two comments to be made about these differences. First, a common assumption about consumer protection is that programs are instituted only when a consumer interest coincides with a powerful producer interest as in the need for commodity standards in certain industries.[31] This was the case in truth-in-lending when the united front of the credit industry crumbled and several of the chain stores championed a consumer interest. But it was not true in the other two situations. Indeed, truth-in-lending is unique among all the recent legislation in having a splitting of the opposition. Therefore, that bit of conventional wisdom simply is no longer true.

Second, these case studies, taken together, demonstrate that there is no single sine qua non for the passage of consumer protection legislation. The most common assumptions are that a crisis is necessary for passage or that the consumer interest must coincide with the producer interest to be recognized. The three case studies are representative of other bills in showing that these factors are usually sufficient, but not necessary, for passage of legislation. In short, there are a variety of substitutive factors which may lead to the passage of legislation.

[31] See for example, Merle Fainsod, Lincoln Gordon, and Joseph Palamountain Jr., *Government and the American Economy,* 3rd ed. New York: W. W. Norton & Co., 1959), pp. 228–229.

Analysis and Conclusions

Although no case study can be said to be typical, the preceding ones reveal in a direct way some of the nuances which would be concealed by aggregate data. However, such data is itself revealing of the legislative patterns of consumer protection issues.

As in the beginning of the chapter, the first question revolves around partisanship and sectionalism. It has already been established from the voting records of the senators that consumer protection is a partisan issue with Northern Democrats supporting the legislation in disproportionate numbers. The next step is to break down that data into the component votes to determine which issues elicited the greatest partisan and regional division. Since the focus is on the issue rather than the members, the four House roll calls will also be included. To aid the reader in interpreting the results, a brief description of the issue involved in each vote and the shorthand label for the vote in the tables which follow is presented in Table 4–6. They are in chronological order.

Table 4–7 lists the issues in order of increasing index of likeness (decreasing partisanship) for the Senate and House separately. The Senate and House must be considered separately in this context since they voted on different issues. Rather than apply an arbitrary standard of partisanship, the data can be examined for a natural breaking point.

In the Senate, the first four issues, from Packaging 2 to Deceptive, group together naturally. The fifth issue is closer to those four than to the next one down the list and therefore will be grouped with them as the most partisan issues. It should be remembered that these are the most partisan by the results of roll call votes and not by any subjective factors. In the House, none of the roll calls was as partisan as in the Senate, but we can still use the grouping of results for a breaking point and consider Gas 1 and Meat 1 as the two partisan issues.

Two important results emerge from analysis of the preceding facts. First, it might be hypothesized that since consumer protection was a program under the wing of a Democratic President, both in the abstract and by specific messages, partisanship would be tied to whether or not the President took a position. However, this is not the case. Of the five most partisan issues in the Senate the President took no position on two (40 percent) of the votes, Auto 1 and Deceptive Sales. Indeed, the

Table 4–6   Congressional Roll Call Votes on Consumer Protection,
            1962–1968

Senate

DRUGS—Motion to table Kefauver amendment imposing strict licensing requirements for drug patent holders. Passed 53–28 (1962).

PACKAGING 1—Amendment to delete weight and quantity standardization sections. Truth-in-packaging bill. Rejected 32–53 (1966).

PACKAGING 2—Motion to table "fair trade" amendment to packaging bill. Passed 51–29 (1966).

PACKAGING 3—Motion to refer packaging bill to Judiciary Committee for further consideration. Rejected 190–64 (1966).

PACKAGING 4—Passage of Fair Labeling Act. Passed 72–9. (1966).

AUTO 1—Automobile safety bill. Amendment to eliminate the bill's requirement that patents, information, uses and processes developed with federal aid be fully and freely available to the general public. Rejected 35–43 (1966).

AUTO 2—Amendment for criminal penalties for violations of act. Rejected 14–62 (1966).

GAS 1—Natural gas pipeline safety bill. Amendment to include gas gathering lines in the group to be regulated by the secretary of transportation. Passed 37–32 (1967).

GAS 2—Amendment imposing criminal penalties. Rejected 31–44 (1967).

DECEPTIVE SALES—Amendment to delete the provision of the deceptive sales bill which would allow the FTC to seek temporary restraining orders to prevent fraudulent or deceptive practices. Passed 42–37 (1968).

POULTRY—Wholesome poultry bill. Amendment to eliminate committee language allowing poultry and meat processed under state inspection standards at least equal to federal standards to be shipped between states even though it had not been federally inspected. Passed 52–19 (1968).

House of Representatives

PRODUCT SAFETY—Resolution creating National Commission on Product Safety. Passed 206–102 (1967).

MEAT 1—Wholesome Meat Act. Motion to instruct House conferees to accept the Senate amendments (which were stronger than the House bill). Rejected 166–207 (1967).

MEAT 2—Adoption of conference report. Passed 336–28 (1967).

GAS 1—Adoption of committee amendments lessening the regulatory authority given the secretary of transportation under the bill passed by the Senate. Passed 247–125 (1968).

Table 4–7   Indices of Likeness in Order of Decreasing Partisanship

Senate

Packaging 2	20.7
Auto 1	25.1
Packaging 1	26.3
Deceptive	26.5
Packaging 3	35.6
Gas 2	49.4
Drugs	50.4
Packaging 4	66.9
Auto 2	73.0
Gas 1	81.0
Poultry	88.1

House

Gas 1	47.2
Meat 1	49.0
Product Safety	65.3
Meat 2	90.9

The index of likeness is a standard simple measure of voting differences between two legislative groups. The score is obtained by first subtracting the percentage voting yea in one group from the percentage voting yea in the other group and then subtracting the difference from one hundred. The index runs from zero (complete dissimilarity) to 100 (identical voting).

President failed to take a position on a total of only three votes, and two of those were among the most partisan.

Second, the most partisan Senate votes all involved economic issues rather than health and safety issues. Even though one of the votes was related to the auto safety controversy, that particular vote concerned patent rights and not safety per se. These issues were the classic sort of government-regulation-of-the-economy questions where one would expect to find Democrats and Republicans in opposition to each other. Furthermore, with the possible exception of Deceptive Sales, the Senate votes affected giant corporation segments of American industry.

The House votes were far less partisan. It is interesting to note that none of the record votes in the House concerned purely economic issues; all four were health and safety issues. Based on the results in the

Senate, this probably explains the lower degree of partisanship. Indeed, the differences in partisanship within the House lose all meaning when one realizes the two most partisan issues were the only ones where there was any sort of contest. There was never much doubt that the National Commission on Product Safety would be created, and Meat 2 was a nearly unanimous vote for final passage.

In consumer protection, as in other issue areas, the degree of partisanship is modified by the crosscutting effect of the "conservative coalition" of Republicans and Southern Democrats. The ratings of individual members on consumer index and scale scores place Southern Democrats in a position midway between Northern Democrats and Republicans.[32] The fact that they group together in the second scale category indicates that regionalism does have an effect. Table 4–8 shows the locus of that effect in both the Senate and the House. The

Table 4–8   Northern Democratic–Southern Democratic Split. Votes in order of increasing index of likeness*

Senate	
Poultry	31.3
Gas 2	33.0
Drugs	42.3
Deceptive	50.2
Gas 1	62.3
Packaging 1	71.1
Auto 1	75.4
Auto 2	82.7
Packaging 2	83.3
Packaging 3	90.0
Packaging 4	95.0
House	
Gas 1	23.0
Meat 1	28.8
Meat 2	68.4
Product Safety	68.4

* See Table 4–7.

[32] See Table 4–3.

question is which issues are the points of greatest contention between Northern and Southern Democrats? Taking the four lowest indices of likeness in the Senate, the breaking point follows Deceptive Sales. In the House, there is a wide gulf which divides the votes in half, and again there is a natural breaking point.

In analyzing the issue locus of sectional differences, the obvious factor to look for is the question of states' rights. While all the consumer legislation involves some accretion of federal power, this growth is of two types. In the first type the federal government is granted power which generally has not previously been held by any governmental jurisdiction in the United States. Furthermore, it is generally conceded that if such a power is to be exercised at all, it must be exercised at the federal level. Securities regulation is such an issue. The second type of accretion involves federal government assumption of a power which traditionally has been held by the states or which, in the case of a universally new power, a substantial number of state officials contend should be held by the states.

Going back to the data, it can be seen that consumer protection issues break the same way as other issues. The issues with the lowest intra-Democratic party index of likeness were those that involved a perceived states' rights issue. There is one exception to this—the 1962 drug amendments. The explanation is that the amendments were perceptually and in fact the project of Estes Kefauver who had earned the hatred and disdain of most of the other Southern senators. But the other votes with a regional split clearly involved states' rights issues. The natural gas pipeline safety bill was opposed by the National Association of (state) Regulatory Utility Commissioners who urged state rather than federal regulation and endorsed an alternative bill to that effect.[33] The poultry bill was squarely a question of federal versus state inspection. Deceptive Sales involved retail sales, an area traditionally within state policy powers. Gas 1 presents a slight problem of interpretation, but this is largely accounted for by the geographical configuration of gas gathering lines and the general closeness of the vote. The remaining issues, those on which there was little North-South split, did not involve any issue of states' rights since they dealt with the manufacture of internationally marketed goods.

[33] *1968 Congressional Quarterly Almanac,* p. 340.

The results are the same in the House of Representatives. Natural gas pipeline safety and the question of state versus federal inspection of meat were clearly the bills with the greatest regional split. While at first glance, it may appear tautological to announce the finding that states' rights issues elicited the largest regional split, such a finding is not without importance. The significance of the finding is twofold. First, it indicates that "public interest" issues are no different in sectional configuration than other issues. One might just as well have hypothesized that such issues would cut across sectional lines. Secondly, it demonstrates the depth of the sectional split. Even the new and popular consumer protection issue is not free from the traditional cleavage between Northern and Southern Democrats. It would seem that this cleavage, while it may have arisen over race, now transcends the racial question. Indeed, a recent study considering a variety of issues, confirms that the dissidence of Southern Democrats has increased in depth and scope since the time of V. O. Key's classic *Southern Politics*.[34]

The final topic in considering the patterns of consumer legislation is a consideration of the differences between the Senate and the House. Such distinctions traditionally have been made in studies of issue areas in Congress.[35] For purposes of this study, the important differences between House and Senate are those that reflect the institutional degree of support for consumer protection legislation. This is measured by the locus and frequency of strengthening and weakening moves in both houses, and by the initiation of action.

The initiation of legislation is a good indication of the locus of activism. Initiation is here defined as holding original hearings of either the publicity-generating or legislative type. Of the bills we have been considering, the Senate initiated seven, the House initiated four, and four were simultaneous or nearly so. In this issue area, the Senate is, by a small margin, the initiating body. When we go beyond the aggregate data to look at the individuals involved it is clear why the Senate is

---

[34] W. Wayne Shannon, *Party, Constituency, and Congressional Voting* (Baton Rouge: Louisiana State University Press, 1968), pp. 95–114.

[35] For example, Richard Fenno has pointed out the differences in the budgetary orientations of the Senate and the House in *The Power of the Purse: Appropriations Politics in Congress* (Boston: Little, Brown & Co., 1966), pp. 626–641.

more often the initiator. In the Senate with only a fourth as many members as the House, men with relatively low seniority are more often in a position to initiate action. Low seniority activitsts such as Ribicoff, Proxmire, and Nelson have subcommittee chairmanships from which they may take the initiative unfettered by their junior status.

In discussing the locus of strengthening action, it is first necessary to establish a concise and accurate definition of the term "strengthen" as used in this context. In this study, a bill is considered strengthened if the scope of activities under regulation is increased and/or if enforcement is made more certain and penalties for violation are increased. Weakening is the opposite of this process.

Unfortunately, there are not enough cases for a meaningful comparison of individual committees. Thus, Senate committees and House committees will each be considered as units of analysis. In considering whether a bill was weakened or strengthened, the reference point is the previous status of the legislation. Thus, if a committee *reports* out a bill that is wider in scope than the bill as originally introduced by its sponsors, the committee is said to have strengthened the bill regardless of what happens later in the legislative process.

The common wisdom holds that regulatory legislation is generally weakened in committee when it is out of the public eye. Table 4–9 tests the validity of that assumption. As can be seen, the assumption proves invalid in the case of Senate committees. Only two out of fifteen bills were weakened in the Senate. Although only a minority of bills were weakened in House committees, more were changed by weakening than were strengthened. Thus, in committee behavior the House conforms somewhat to the common assumptions about regulatory legislation.

Table 4–10 shows the legislative pattern on the floor of both chambers. Clearly, the pattern is the same for both chambers and con-

Table 4–9   Number of Enacted Consumer Protection Bills Changed by Congressional Committees 1962–1968

	Strengthen	Weaken	Both	Basically Unchanged
Senate	6	2	—	7
House	1	6	1	7

Table 4–10   Number of Consumer Protection Bills Changed on the Floor,
              1962–1968

	Strengthen	Weaken	Unchanged
Senate	2	1	12
House	3	1	11

forms to the usual norm of ratifying committee action. However, the
aggregate data should not blur the importance of the few changes which
did occur. Even though it is a nearly isolated case, the transformation
of the truth-in-lending bill on the floor of the House was of great significance as noted earlier. Thus, while the significance of the few
changes which occurred should not be overlooked, nonetheless the
changes were few, and the Senate and House demonstrate the same
pattern of floor action.

The final matter to consider is the last opportunity for major
changes in the Congress—the conference. If regulatory legislation is
going to be weakened, the conference committee with its invisible and
closed procedures is the ideal place. Of course, not all bills went to
conference. Where differences were minor, substitute bills were passed.
Considering both these procedures together, it is somewhat surprising
to note that only five of the fifteen bills emerged weaker than the
stronger of the two bills as separately passed by both houses. Four were
compromises that strengthened the bill. One was an even split of differences. Five were cases of similar or identical bills originally passed by
both houses. Thus, in the case of consumer protection legislation, the
image of a closed conference invisibly destroying the fruits of the open
legislative struggle does not generally apply.

Conclusion

Rather than attempting to recount the preceding discussion com-
prehensively, I will briefly present the salient conclusions which emerge
in this chapter.

First, the representation of the consumer interest in Congress depends on the activities of individual consumer activists rather than on
any sort of coalition within Congress or between Congress and the
Executive Branch. Any coalitions which do emerge are strictly ad hoc

and emerge late in the legislative history of a particular bill. Otherwise, there is little coordination among activists. These activists are specialists in consumer protection, but at various times they have other concerns of equal importance to them. Only staff members are full-time specialists in consumer protection.

Second, both the activists and the most consistent supporters of consumer protection are primarily liberal Democrats. Consumer protection is a partisan issue, although the states' rights factor is an important intervening variable.

Third, the championing of consumer protection is generally perceived to be "good politics," but consumer activists do not have any greater degree of electoral success than other Northern Democratic liberals.

Fourth, subcommittees which do not directly lead to the enactment of legislation are, nevertheless, important factors in expanding public awareness of particular issues and in gaining publicity and prestige for less senior consumer activists.

Fifth, there is no single requirement for the passage of consumer legislation. Two important factors are scandal and a divided producer interest. However, these may be sufficient but not necessary conditions.

Finally, the Senate rather than the House is the congressional locus of consumer activism and is more often the initiator of inquiry and legislation.

chapter 5

The Consumer Advocates

This chapter considers the representation and articulation of consumer interests by groups and individuals outside the federal government. Naturally, the focus is on those participants who are most deeply involved—the "consumer activists." There are three types of nongovernmental consumer activists who will be discussed. The first, which can be labeled as "traditional," consists of large organizations of long standing and/or those whose techniques of exerting influence are basically similar to the techniques used in previous eras of consumer activism—particularly in the 1930s. The second type are the "new" activists who are both recent in origin and employ techniques largely novel to the current consumer protection issue. Included in this category are Ralph Nader and the public-interest lawyers. Finally, the press will be considered as a third type of consumer advocate because of a variety of properties unique to the press. Although heterogeneous in many ways, these organizations all function as advocates of consumer interests and they represent those interests in the councils of government. Of course, different groups approach this broad goal in different ways, and it is this representational focus which is the ultimate concern of this chapter.

There are two broad representational roles played by interest groups. First is the agency role—acting as agents on behalf of the perceived beliefs or objective interests of a group or class of people. The Automobile Manufacturers Association acts on behalf of the automobile producers, the National Rifle Association acts on behalf of gun buffs, and so on. This role is directed primarily toward government policy makers. The second role is that of constituency expansion which is directed back to the people being represented. This role consists of expanding the constituency of an interest by increasing the awareness that people have of their own self-interest or to increase the number of people who perceive themselves as holding certain interests. For example, the Sierra Club seeks to increase knowledge about environmental problems and to increase the number of people who feel that they have a stake in dealing with those problems. These roles are broad tendencies rather than sharp distinctions. Nonetheless, organizations tend to emphasize one or the other. The utility of these roles in influencing policy depends on the nature of the policy being pursued. This chapter sets out to demonstrate that the influence and effectiveness of consumer groups varies with the representational aspect that they emphasize. Specifically, the hypothesis to be validated is that the consumer interest is most effectively represented by organizations whose strategy is to emphasize the second aspect—increasing awareness and increasing the size of the attentive constituency.

The early sections of the chapter describe the background, strategy, and activities of the various consumer advocates. Their relation to each other, to consumers generally, and to the government will be discussed. This discussion will ultimately lead to an analysis of their effectiveness as it relates to their representational role and their function in the political system.

The Traditional Consumer Advocates

Basically there are two types of political groups: private-interest groups and public-interest groups.[1] They are divided by the nature of the

---

[1] I am using the word "group" as a convenient shorthand term meaning a unit of action. Thus, I consider the press and Ralph Nader as "groups" although they are not customarily thought of as such in the group theory literature.

benefits they seek. The distinction is clearly drawn by E. E. Schatt-schneider:

> Is it possible to distinguish between the "interests" of the members of the National Association of Manufacturers and the members of the American League to Abolish Capital Punishment? The facts in the two cases are not identical. First, the members of the A.L.A.C.P. do not expect to be hanged. The membership of the A.L.A.C.P. is not restricted to persons under indictment for murder or in jeopardy of the extreme penalty. . . . Its members oppose capital punishment although they are not personally likely to benefit by the policy they advocate. The inference is therefore that the interest of the A.L.A. C.P. is not adverse, exclusive or special. It is not like the interest of the Petroleum Institute in depletion allowances.[2]

In short, "public-interest" groups seek collective or widely-shared benefits. "Private-interest" groups primarily seek exclusive benefits.

Of course, many private-interest groups seek some collective benefits, and herein lies the distinction to be made among consumer-oriented groups. Some few groups may be termed "primary consumer groups;" they are pure public-interest groups and seek only collective benefits for consumers. The second type are private-interest groups which seek collective benefits as an activity incidental to their normal function. This distinction is in accord with the "by-product" theory of large pressure groups posited by Mancur Olson:

> The common characteristic which distinguishes all of the large economic groups with significant lobbying organizations is that these powerful economic lobbies are in fact the by-product of organizations that obtain their strength and support because they perform some function in addition to lobbying for collective goods.[3]

For purposes of the present study, these by-product groups may be called "secondary" consumer groups.

The activities of the consumer groups will be examined shortly. But first it will be useful to discuss briefly the history and purposes of some of these groups so that their activities may be evaluated in light

---

[2] E. E. Schattschneider, *The Semisovereign People* (New York: Holt, Rinehart, and Winston, 1960), p. 26.

[3] Mancur Olson, *The Logic of Collective Action* (Cambridge: Harvard University Press, 1965), p. 132.

of this background. The most powerful secondary consumer groups are the labor unions, especially the AFL-CIO. Although the consumer activities of the unions will later be discussed in detail, the reader is probably already familiar with the history and organization of the unions as political participants, and this subject is extensively treated elsewhere.[4]

The oldest primary consumer group currently in existence is the National Consumers League which was founded in 1899. Actually, the original purpose of the league was not consumer protection as we think of it today, but to use the power of consumers to obtain better conditions for workers. Thus, it supported the then-novel concepts of minimum wages and social insurance. The organization, however, soon moved into the area of consumer protection and was an early supporter of the original pure food and drug legislation. It has continued to manifest a concern in both the areas of consumer protection and labor standards. Originally, the league included a number of state organizations, but nearly all of these state groups have left the league or dissolved. The organization is supported financially by its largely individual membership and works on a small budget. Its staff is composed of only the director and a secretary in a small Washington office. Although it is now overshadowed by other consumer groups, the league still engages in legislative lobbying.

The National Consumers League has recently become part of a new and larger organization, the Consumer Federation of America (CFA), which is composed of local and national consumer groups, both primary and secondary.

The need for an "umbrella" type consumer organization to bring together the scores of consumer-oriented groups had long been perceived and honored in the abstract. A previous effort at such a confederation during the New Deal failed, and in the intervening years the National Consumers League was left as the only national consumer organization.[5] With the increased concern for consumer protection in the 1960s and the growing activity of local consumer groups, it was

---

[4] E.g., see V. O. Key, *Politics, Parties, and Pressure Groups,* 5th ed. (New York: Thomas Y. Crowell Co., 1964), pp. 44–63; and J. David Greenstone, *Labor in American Politics* (New York: Alfred A. Knopf, 1969).

[5] See Chapter 1 above, pp. 19–20.

inevitable that the ideal of an umbrella organization would again be manifested.

The nucleus of the Consumer Federation originated with a nominal coalition of groups called the Consumer Clearing House. At the instigation of David Angevine of the Cooperative League of the United States, the Consumer Clearing House set up a consumer assembly in 1967, lasting two days and featuring various consumer activists in Congress such as senators Hart and Metcalf. It was judged a success by its participants and it was decided to make it an annual event.

With the experience of the first consumer assembly and the need of state organizations for a voice in Washington as impetus, a small group of consumer activists primarily from the labor unions, the President's Consumer Advisory Council, and Consumers Union met and decided to establish a consumer federation. The organization was set up in November, 1967. Its purpose was to inform its constituent organizations about pending legislative and administrative actions. Its intended function was to be an information and not a lobbying service. It was felt that if the local groups had the necessary information they could apply pressure in Congress themselves.

It is important to emphasize two points in connection with the establishment of the Consumer Federation. First, it came about late in 1967—well after consumer protection became a recognized issue in Congress and the Executive Branch. Second, it was set up by representatives of well-established organizations—especially the labor unions.

There are now approximately 140 member organizations in the Consumer Federation. Representative of the membership are such organizations as Consumers Union, the National Consumers League, Connecticut Consumer Association (and many other state consumer associations), the Communications Workers of America, and a number of consumer cooperatives. The CFA is based in Washington and is headed by an executive director who is assisted by one or two staff members and secretarial help. Compared to many other interest groups in Washington, its staff resources are small.

A third consumer group is Consumers Union. Surprisingly, it was a late entry into the ranks of primary consumer groups. It was always a primary group in the sense that its entire operation has been directed toward the consumer interests of its members and the users of its publication, *Consumer Reports.* However, Consumers Union is mainly a product testing organization and the advocacy of public policies benefiting consumers had been only a secondary by-product provided by the magazine. In September, 1969, Consumers Union opened a Washington office through which it is able to follow and be fully engaged in legislative and administrative affairs. Although Consumers Union had traditionally advocated public policies in its magazine, the establishment of the Washington office is a fundamental change which broadens the scope of its activities to benefit consumer interests.

Consumers Union is composed of individual *Consumer Reports* subscribers who merely have to indicate a desire to become members. Consumer Reports has approximately 1.3 million subscribers. At six dollars per subscription, the organization's financial resources are substantial.

Patterns of Participation:
Consumer Group Lobbying

In discussing lobbying, I use the term "lobbying" in the broad sense as defined by Lester Milbrath:

> Broadly defined . . . lobbying is the *stimulation and transmission* of a communication, by someone other than a citizen acting on his own behalf, directed to a governmental decision-maker with the hope of influencing his decision. (Emphasis added.)[6]

Legislative Lobbying

Legislative lobbying by consumer groups follows the broad patterns of other lobbying organizations except for variations which are differences of degree rather than of kind. A major function is to follow bills through their legislative history with an emphasis on guarding against weakening amendments—a hazard facing all social reform legislation. The first decision must be to determine the position the organization will take on a particular measure. Unlike some of the more

[6] Lester Milbrath, *The Washington Lobbyists* (Chicago: Rand McNally, 1963), p. 8.

esoteric tax and tariff measures studied by industry trade groups, there is seldom doubt among any of the consumer activists over what constitutes a pro-consumer bill or what amendments would weaken that bill. Indeed, most of the consumer bills followed by the CFA and the AFL-CIO until 1969 were those that had been endorsed by President Johnson.

Since there is usually not much doubt as to the position to be taken by the consumer groups, the process by which these positions are taken is quite flexible and the staff has a high degree of freedom. In the Consumer Federation of America, guidelines are drawn up at the annual membership meeting. These resolutions are quite broad leaving the executive director free to act as she deems appropriate.[7] The action usually consists of a favorable mention for a proposed bill in the association's newsletter and so there would really be no need for a more involved decision-making process.

It would be incorrect to assume, however, that all CFA positions are handled readily and superficially. The most prominent example of the handling of a very complex issue is the controversy over the Uniform Consumer Credit Code (UCCC). The UCCC was drafted by the National Conference of Commissioners on Uniform State Laws as a model law proposed for adoption by state legislatures. The Consumer Credit Protection Act enacted by Congress in 1968 contains a provision which allows states to be exempted from the truth-in-lending and garnishment section if they adopt credit cost disclosure and garnishment regulations of their own that are "substantially similar" to those in the federal law. Critics of the UCCC contend that it would emasculate the federal law since state enforcement tends to be more lax than federal enforcement. In addition, there are several other objections to the code, the technicalities of which need not concern us here. Suffice it to say that the code is lengthy and has highly complex legal and economic implications.

A preliminary draft of the UCCC was completed early in 1968. At the first CFA meeting in April, 1968, the delegates from the Pennsylvania consumer association who had been following the development

---

[7] As the CFA has grown and become more visible, the power of the executive director has been challenged. In the 1971 Consumer Assembly, several dissenters charged that executive director Erma Angevine was taking action without sufficient consultation with the membership.

of the code raised objections to it and alerted the meeting to the perceived threat. The result was that the meeting passed a resolution urging the National Conference of Commissioners on Uniform State Laws to delay further action on the code until the Federal Consumer Credit Protection Act went into effect in July, 1969. The conference did not reply to the CFA action until September at which time they assured CFA that consumer views were taken into account and reiterated that the conference would continue pressing for adoption of the code by state legislatures as soon as possible. It should be pointed out that Betty Furness had endorsed the code as an improvement over existing law. So consumer advocates by no means presented a united front.

It was at this point that CFA's ability to handle a complex issue was demonstrated. Much of the initial research was done by the research department of the AFL-CIO which pinpointed several objectionable features of the code. By September, 1968, the final draft of the code was completed and the general tenor of CFA objections to the code was clear. However, no detailed study of the code had yet been made by any consumer organization—a fact which constituted a major CFA objection to the process by which the code was drafted. Indeed, the Conference of Commissioners did not even reply to CFA until the final draft of the UCCC had been completed.

In November, 1968, representatives of the CFA met with staff members of the House and Senate Banking and Currency committees. At that time a task force of lawyers was established to make a detailed examination of the code. The task force was headed by Benny Kass, a former assistant counsel for the Senate Judiciary Committee. The task force originally consisted of four lawyers and an economist, but it soon became apparent that it was unmanageable at that size. Soon, all the work was being done by two lawyers, Anthony Roisman and Edward Berlin. By January, 1969, they had completed a preliminary section-by-section analysis of the UCCC. Shortly thereafter, the final analysis was completed and distributed to the state consumer groups who were urged to oppose the code in their state legislatures. During the time they were working on the code, Roisman, Berlin, and another attorney had formed a new law firm and they became the official counsel of the Consumer Federation. Thus, the analysis of the UCCC was eventually done by a legal firm being paid for its efforts. The firm of Berlin, Roisman and Kessler was subsequently retained as counsel for the CFA.

The most significant aspect of the fight over the Uniform Consumer Credit Code is that a consumer organization was able to utilize expertise equal to that of its opponents. The CFA has demonstrated its ability to handle issues of greater complexity than the national consumer bills it usually supports. This expertise enables state consumer associations to perform the information function necessary for lobbying success, particularly in state legislatures.

Legislative decision making in the AFL-CIO is more structured than it is in the CFA or National Consumers League, but the pattern is basically the same. The AFL-CIO has a subcommittee on consumer protection, consisting of representatives of about twenty member unions. It considers the merits of consumer bills which have been introduced and submits recommendations to the AFL-CIO legislative department regarding the position the AFL-CIO should take. The legislative department then forwards the recommendations to the executive committee. While this is a more formal and continuous process than occurs in the smaller groups, the result is much the same. There is rarely any doubt that the unions will support major consumer bills and the formal decision-making process is usually mere ratification of staff decisions. The important decisions for the unions are not whether to support particular consumer measures, but when to apply pressure and how much to apply—a subject which will be considered next.

Until 1970, there was no important issue on which the primary consumer groups and the unions were divided. Then the ever-recurring issue of tariffs arose as new tariff legislation came up in Congress. The legislation primarily centered on tariff relief for the textile industry which was suffering from foreign competition. The issue involved the interests of the union members who perceived their jobs as being at stake. At the same time, this put the traditional consumer groups, with their strong union support, in a ticklish situation. Tariffs have been traditionally harmful to consumers, depriving them of the benefits of lower-priced foreign goods. But for the textile unions this consideration paled in comparison to the threat to domestic jobs. In terms of their own self-interest they really had no choice other than going on record in favor of the tariff measures which were prejudicial to economic consumer interests. The Consumer Federation has been strikingly silent on the tariff issue—apparently out of willingness to give in on this issue to retain union support on other issues on which there are no conflicting interests.

The tariff issue illustrates the distinction between primary and secondary consumer groups and the problems of relying on secondary groups to support such low-level interests as the consumer interest. Lower prices and other consumer benefits are secondary concerns of the unions. When they conflict with the primary concerns of higher wages and job security for members, the secondary concerns are sacrificed. Inasmuch as primary groups rely on a labor constituency they are similarly restrained.

In summary, on most issues it is a simple matter to announce a position and to secure agreement between consumer groups. However, the collective facade of the traditional consumer groups cracks when the issue at hand pits the basic interests of the secondary groups against their secondary consumer interests.

Communicating with Legislators

Since communication is so central to the lobbying process, as Milbrath pointed out, it is surprising that the primary consumer groups have little direct communication with Congress. Partly this is a result of the fact that these organizations are not important providers of information to Congress as will be discussed later. There are also financial and legal obstacles. Consumers Union is a tax exempt organization and, while it is permitted to testify at hearings, may not engage directly in most other aspects of legislative lobbying. However, like most other such organizations in Washington, it does have occasional contact with friendly congressmen and congressional staff and has little difficulty making its views known both informally and formally. A more substantial limitation for the primary groups has to do with resources. All the traditional activist organizations have very limited financial resources and small staffs—none is larger than three people. This being the case, these organizations constitute a very small proportion of the total number of people involved in Washington-based consumer protection activities. Furthermore, the financial obstacles put limitations on the amount of activity the staffs can generate as well as on the number of staff members.

The main communications channel of these organizations consists of testimony at congressional hearings. This is the only lobbying function undertaken with any degree of regularity. The National Consumers League has testified in favor of nearly all consumer protection measures since the issue surfaced in the beginning of this decade. The CFA, the unions, and Consumers Union have made testimony a regular activity.

Testimony at congressional hearings is only one aspect of legislative lobbying, although a particularly important one for consumer groups. There are normally a variety of informal contacts between congressmen, staff members, and lobbyists. It has been found that lobbyists spend most of their time sending and receiving communications and most of this is done from the seclusion of their own offices.[8] Although the popular image of lobbying portrays lobbyists in the role of trying to convert reluctant congressmen to the lobbyist's point of view, this overstates the advocacy role of lobbyists. Recent research on Congress has found that congressmen predominantly hear from those lobbyists they agree with anyway.[9] The advocacy role of lobbyists therefore consists largely of reinforcing congressional predilections rather than swaying impartial minds. The pattern is similar for the primary consumer groups. Table 5–1 shows the results of the responses to the interview question, "Who in Congress do you work with most closely?" The respondents are consumer lobbyists. Clearly, the consumer groups work

Table 5–1   Number of Congressional Personnel (Staff and Members) With Whom Consumer Lobbyists Say They Work Closely

Consumer Federation of America	National Consumers League	AFL-CIO
7	10	8
Number of These Congressional Personnel Who Are Consistently Pro–Consumer		
6	10	7

[8] Milbrath, *Lobbyists,* p. 121.

[9] Lewis Anthony Dexter, "The Representative and His District," in *New Perspectives on the House of Representatives* ed. Robert L. Peabody and Nelson W. Polsby (Chicago: Rand McNally, 1963), pp. 11–14.

with those who agree with them. In the case of the two primary consumer groups, this is the total range of direct contacts. In the case of the AFL-CIO, whose lobbying operation will be discussed shortly, the close working relationships are only part of the range of direct contacts. The AFL-CIO touches base with a much larger number of congressional personnel, many of whom are not in agreement with union positions. So the primary consumer groups, but not necessarily the AFL-CIO, conform to the findings of Milbrath and Dexter that lobbyists see those with whom they agree.

A major function of lobbyists is to provide information. However, this is generally not the case with the consumer groups. The committees with whom they deal have greater resources and greater expertise at their disposal. In every major consumer bill of the past decade, the pro-consumer intelligence came from two sources—the bureaucracy and primarily from the committee staffs themselves. No congressional staff member who was interviewed for this study listed the traditional consumer groups as an important source of necessary information.

Consumer lobbying by the AFL-CIO more closely parallels the patterns of other lobbying activity described above.[10] This is to be expected since the AFL-CIO and its member unions are the largest lobby in Washington as measured by amount of expenditures and size of staff, and they handle consumer lobbying in much the same way as other issues are handled. It was roughly estimated that lobbying on consumer measures constituted five to ten percent of the total union lobbying effort in the 90th Congress. This proportion, of course, varies with time depending on whether consumer measures are near passage in committee or on the floor.

As stated above, the real decision in the AFL-CIO is not whether to support a consumer bill but when to apply leverage. This decision generally conforms to the adage that politics is the art of the possible. The actual lobbying leg work begins when the legislative department staff believes that a bill has a realistic chance of passage. Thus the unions officially supported truth-in-lending from the time that Senator Douglas introduced the bill. But it was only in the last two years of the

---

[10] Unless otherwise noted, this section on the AFL-CIO is based on personal interviews with AFL-CIO and United Auto Workers legislative staff members.

bill's legislative history that the AFL-CIO staff felt there was a good chance for passage. It was then that the real pressure was applied.

The leg work can be divided into two overlapping functions. First is the intelligence function. Like all good lobbyists, the legislative department staff closely follows the progress of bills, particularly as they are being marked up in committee and eventually in conference committee. Their information comes both from allied committee staff members and congressmen themselves with whom they may work very closely, as was the case with truth-in-lending. The result is that on bills they have decided to push, the union knows as well as the committee staff does, the exact status of bills in committee—the major points of contention, where the blockage points are, and the nature and purpose of amendments.

The second function is the application of pressure. There is overlap between that function and the information function both when the bill is in committee and when it is on the floor. The unions contact every member of the subcommittee with jurisdiction and eventually try to see every member of the full committee. These visits provide valuable intelligence about the progress of a bill. In the realm of the pressure function, such visits inform the union about each committee member's stand on the bill. This information is passed on to the local unions in each member's district if the bill is "hot."

When the bill reaches the floor an even more extensive lobbying operation begins. During the Johnson administration, the unions consulted with the President's legislative liaison men to compare estimates of the bill's chances and to seek agreement on positions to be taken. The membership of the House (or Senate) would be divided and responsibility for contacting members would be assigned to various component unions generally on the basis of strength in a congressman's district or state. Again, this procedure gathers information about how the vote will go and is a method of applying pressure for a favorable vote. Based on preliminary contacts with members, the AFL-CIO makes its "soft" nose count to see approximately where they stand. If a need is indicated, more pressure is applied. On occasion, delegations of union members might be brought in to apply additional pressure to their own congressmen. Finally the "hard" nose count is taken. This lists the members for or against the bill and those who are undecided, divided by the direction in which they are leaning. When a bill reaches the floor, the AFL-CIO estimate is generally accurate to within two or three votes. Simultaneously, the union staff consults with the majority leadership of the House where the vote is to be taken and discusses how to handle proposed amendments.

These procedures vary depending on how close the vote will be. When the vote looks close and the issue is important, other legislative department staff members not normally concerned with consumer bills will be called in to contact wavering members of Congress. With its large legislative department, the AFL-CIO consumer activists have unusually powerful resources from which to draw. Normally on consumer measures, such extensive canvassing is necessary only on amendments on the floor.

Two points should be made about this union lobbying operation. First, contrary to most other lobbying, union staff members do talk to many people who are opposed to the union position and urge them to change their minds. The greatest pressure is applied to committee members when it is learned (through contacts with other committee members) that they are wavering either in support or opposition. Second, the union lobbying staff provides a political intelligence service that is needed by congressmen. Nothing is left to the imagination; the congressman knows exactly how important a bill is to the union and how much opposition the union will try to generate in his district if he goes against the union position.

The use of electorally-based lobbying techniques is more typical of mass-based organizations. Part of the leverage of the AFL-CIO is the knowledge that the unions can and do tell their members who is voting "right" and who is voting "wrong." At the end of each session, the legislative department puts out a score sheet on Congress, listing each member and whether he voted right or wrong on a series of key votes—often on amendments.[11] Whether union members study the score sheet is unimportant. It serves as a guide to local union leaders who support or oppose particular candidates in particular districts where the local union is situated. The important point to be made is

---

[11] See, for example, the *AFL-CIO News*, October 5, 1968. This is the regular weekly AFL-CIO newspaper which devoted an entire edition to "The 90th Congress: A Report."

that the AFL-CIO utilizes a widespread internal publicity network ultimately directed toward congressional constituencies as a major resource in their lobbying operation. The primary consumer groups generally do not utilize this ad hominem electoral technique. Rather, they generally identify the committee chairman presiding over a bill and urge their members to write in support of the pending measure.

Political Parties

Milbrath found that lobbyists do not usually attempt to use political parties in their work.[12] This generalization certainly holds for consumer groups. In the case of consumer protection, there would really be no point in separately working with the political parties. The votes in Congress usually are partisan with Democrats being for and Republicans being against such legislation. Most of the major bills in the 89th and 90th Congresses were part of the program of the Democratic administration. Thus, the Democratic party was on record as being pro-consumer. The only approach to the parties per se came about during the 1968 presidential campaign when the Consumer Federation of America and the AFL-CIO separately urged both parties to adopt consumer protection planks in their platform. In addition, prior to the conventions the CFA directly solicited a statement from the candidates on consumer protection. Favorable responses were received from Hubert Humphrey, Eugene McCarthy, and George McGovern. Richard Nixon declined to make a statement and no response was received from George Wallace. As might be expected, the Democratic platform contained a separate consumer protection plank and the Republican platform made no mention of this issue. However, consumer protection was in no way an issue in the presidential campaign that followed.

Administrative Lobbying

Although the popular image of lobbying focuses on Congress, lobbyists' relations with the bureaucracy may be more important in terms of policy output. There are several categories of lobbyist inter-

[12] Milbrath, *Lobbyists,* p. 207.

vention in the administrative process. First is recruitment—groups
naturally seek the appointment of sympathetic administrators to positions that might affect their status. To achieve this end, they concentrate
their supplications on the appointing official and on congressmen in a
position to intervene. Conversely, business firms often recruit into their
own ranks individuals with past administrative experience as a means
of getting better access to executive agencies. Bauer, Poole, and Dexter
found that giant corporations are more likely than small companies to
have such people on their staffs. Thus, they will be more aware of the
techniques of seeking modification of existing legislation through the
steps of the administrative process. This administrative lobbying is
more attractive to big companies since it avoids publicity.[13]

Just as in Congress, the bulk of lobbyists' time with the bureaucracy is spent presenting the views of the represented organizations.
This is done both informally and through presentations at rule-making
hearings. Just as lobbyists tend to talk to congressmen who already
agree with them, they usually find a friendly reception at the agencies
when they represent clientele groups of the agencies. Indeed, the literature on regulatory agencies is nearly unanimous in charging that these
agencies are captured by the groups they are nominally supposed to
regulate.[14] The communications between lobbyists and administrators
are instrumental in creating that relationship.

Finally, lobbyists may apply what leverage they have in Congress
to gain a privileged position in the bureaucracy. The ability of certain
business groups to utilize the late Senator Everett Dirksen as their personal representative before regulatory agencies is a case in point.

Administrative lobbying is the weakest link in the traditional consumer groups' attempts to influence policy. There is practically no
effort to influence recruitment in the bureaucracy. This statement may
appear strange in light of the controversy surrounding President Nixon's
abortive attempt to appoint Miss Willie Mae Rogers as his Special
Assistant for Consumer Affairs.[15] However, the Willie Mae Rogers case

13 Raymond Bauer, Ithiel de Sola Pool, and Lewis A. Dexter, *American Business
and Public Policy* (New York: Atherton Press, 1963), p. 268.

14 See, for example, Marver Bernstein, *Regulating Business by Independent Commission* (Princeton: Princeton University Press, 1955).

15 See pp. 53–54.

is significant primarily because of the role the consumer groups did not play. Although the CFA and the AFL-CIO publicly had been urging that the President appoint someone as Special Assistant for Consumer Affairs, no specific candidate was pushed. When Miss Rogers was appointed to a watered-down version of that post, the opposition was centered in Congress, not the private groups. Indeed, the CFA did not even mention the affair in its newsletter put out on February 13—two days after the appointment had been made. The only private group significantly involved was the press which exercised its option of making the issue visible. Whether unpublicized congressional opposition would have been effective in this case is impossible to determine conclusively. It is clear that the attendant notoriety was a source of great annoyance to Miss Rogers and a source of considerable embarrassment to the administration—both of which contributed to the brevity of her career in government.

The inaction of consumer groups in the Rogers episode is typical of their lack of activity in the advocacy side of administrative recruitment. They do not involve themselves in the appointment process beyond occasional expressions of support or opposition to a particular appointee after he has been appointed. However, consumer activists have themselves been appointed to the various advisory commissions relating to consumer protection, especially the Consumer Advisory Council which is composed primarily of consumer activists and sympathetic academies. At various times, from one to four members of the board of directors of Consumers Union have been on the CAC. Ralph Nader is both on the board of directors of Consumers Union and on the National Motor Vehicle Safety Board as is the executive director of Consumers Union. The technical director of Consumers Union was on the National Commission on Product Safety. Thus, there is a great deal of overlap between the consumer groups and the advisory commissions. However, this overlap does not exist in the more important regulatory commissions. The well-known phenomenon of men going from industry to enforcement or regulatory agencies or vice versa has not been the case with consumer activists.

Although the traditional consumer groups regularly testify at congressional hearings, they rarely do so at administrative hearings. As noted in Chapter 3, a great variety of local and national consumer groups testified at the Federal Trade Commission hearings on consumer protection in November and December, 1968. However, consumer groups rarely appear at public hearings on industry guidelines. Not a single consumer group representative mentioned such appearances as one of their regular functions or as a part of their liaison with the Executive Branch. The result, of course, is that there is no genuine adversary procedure at these hearings. It should not be inferred from this that the consumer groups are unaware of the importance of the regulatory and administrative processes. It is primarily a matter of having insufficient staff to cover all the hearings. The director of CFA stated that the organization generally does not testify "unless there is something we are alerted to or feel keenly about." Thus, there is no systematic determination or set of guidelines used to decide when to expend the time and money necessary to prepare testimony. As might be expected, testimony covers diverse subjects. In the beginning of 1969, the CFA had filed a statement with the Federal Power Commission in connection with its hearings on whether private utility companies should be required to reveal the cost of their public relations activity. A second effort involved testimony at Agriculture Department hearings on cooked sausage standards.

Until around 1970, the lack of participation in administrative proceedings by the traditional consumer groups meant that this aspect of policy-making was virtually inaccessible to the presentation of consumer interests. However, since that time the new consumer activists have concentrated on consumer protection bureaucracies and sought active participation in this realm. Indeed, this is the major distinguishing factor between the new and traditional groups and will be discussed later in this chapter.

Although the national consumer organizations play a limited role in federal administrative rule making, state consumer associations which are members of CFA are much more active in this sphere. An examination of their activities as listed in CFA newsletters shows that attempts to influence state public utility commissions are the most frequent activity of local member organizations.

Unlike private interests, consumer groups do not try to influence the bureaucracy through the Congress. This is not due to a lack of skill but rather to a lack of necessity. The congressional consumer activists do not need to be urged to apply pressure to agencies with consumer protection responsibilities. They willingly do so on their own. For example, both Senator Abraham Ribicoff and Congressman Benjamin Rosenthal have used their positions on their respective Governmental Operations committees for this purpose.

Public Relations

A third major function of lobbying organizations is in the realm of public relations. Part of this function is directly related to administrative and legislative lobbying as indicated above. Campaigns to cultivate public opinion are primarily the domain of well-financed organizations since such endeavors are costly. V. O. Key classified these campaigns into two types: intensive short-term campaigns designed to stimulate public opposition to or support of a particular legislative measure, and long-term efforts to create "basic public attitudes toward support of a broad point of view or to create a favorable sentiment toward a particular corporation or industry."[16]

Propaganda campaigns are often designed not only to influence legislators but also for reasons internal to the organization. David Truman argued that internal publicity campaigns, ostensibly related to national issues, are also devices to maximize group cohesion and to preserve the existing organizational elite.[17] This is primarily the case with mass-based organizations, and its relevance to labor union consumer activity will be discussed later in the chapter. However, lobbyists for trade associations also spend some of their time convincing their clients of the efficacy of continued lobbying.

Interest in all the consumer group lobbying activities is the public relations function of lobbyists. The AFL-CIO lobbying effort involves direct appeals to congressional constituencies. There are two aspects to the consumer-oriented labor union public relations drive. The first aspect involves alerting the membership and local leaders to the existence of various consumer bills and directing pressure to urge favorable action on those bills. Secondly, there is the "scorecard" device— the traditional union listing of congressional friends and enemies. These two aspects can both be classified as short-run, "rifle" type campaigns.

[16] Key, *Politics, Parties,* p. 145.

[17] David Truman, *The Governmental Process* (New York: Alfred A. Knopf, 1951), p. 195.

Although union campaigns are typically directed toward particular bills and key congressmen, the cumulation of such campaigns actually constitutes a long-range effort. While there is no propaganda campaign aimed at the public at large, since 1966 the union membership has been notified that consumer protection is part of the governmental concerns of the unions. Thus, the unions have sought to build a favorable climate for this type of legislation.

Consumers Union already reaches an audience receptive to consumer protection.[18] *Consumer Reports* regularly has a feature article on proposed or enacted consumer legislation, regulatory agencies, or on selected consumer protection problems. In addition, there is a monthly partial summary of state, local and national administrative consumer protection action. Although the magazine usually takes a position on the merits of legislation discussed in an article, they do not specifically urge readers to write their congressmen or tell which congressmen to write to. The articles are designed more to provide information than to provoke action. However, this function should not be underrated. *Consumer Reports* provides the most comprehensive information and analysis of governmental consumer protection activities of any large circulation magazine or newspaper. Indeed, it is the only source of such information to reach a large public.

The primary consumer groups utilize newsletters as their primary public relations vehicle. The National Consumers League issues a semimonthly bulletin. The Consumer Federation was originally conceived of as a clearinghouse of consumer protection information. Its publicity techniques are thus central to its existence. The CFA sends weekly "memos" (newsletters) to officials of member organizations. In addition, each memo is usually accompanied by other material such as magazine article reprints, copies of speeches, and "fact sheets" on proposed legislation. There are also press releases which do not appear to be notably successful in actually getting newspaper space. In short, the CFA internal publicity operation is much the same as dozens of Washington-based trade associations. But there is one important difference: it is providing information about state and federal consumer action to groups which have not previously had the advantage of such informa-

18 Hugh W. Sargent, *Consumer-Product Rating Publications and Consumer Behavior* (Urbana: University of Illinois Press, 1959), pp. 44–46.

tion. And, as in the case of the Uniform Consumer Credit Code, the internal publicity system can be used to transmit highly sophisticated information necessary for state groups who oppose the UCCC.

An additional public relations activity is the annual Consumer Assembly held in Washington. Technically, it is not a CFA convention, but a meeting of representatives from a large number of local and national consumer-oriented groups organized by CFA. Although there are generally a few workshops, the assembly consists primarily of plenary sessions with speeches by government officials and consumer activists such as Senator Philip Hart, Senator Edmund Muskie, and Ralph Nader. In general, the consumer assemblies are more in the nature of rallies of the faithful than purposeful business meetings.

In this discussion of publicity techniques of consumer groups, the reader may have noted that the emphasis has been on internal communications. This reflects the greatest weakness of these publicity operations. None of the consumer groups has made any notable attempt to utilize the press to its own advantage. Of course, they eagerly cooperate with reporters and always grant interviews on request, but they do not furnish leads or attempt to get reporters to cover particular events. Their publicity network is directed toward people who already agree with them. In effect, then, its function is largely informational rather than persuasive. This is in contrast to their opposition which is successful in regularly planting editorials as news stories and using canned editorials. For example, the tobacco industry was able to place an article written by one of its public relations firms in *True* magazine. The article disputed the report of the surgeon general on the health hazards of smoking and was deceptively presented as an objective scientific report.[19] Another technique, unavailable to consumer groups, is the canned editorial. One firm, Industrial News Review, circulates about a dozen pro-business canned editorials each week. It is supported by large fees from the groups getting favorable mention in the editorials. These groups have included the American Medical Association, investor-owned utilities, the American Meat Institute, and other industry groups. The editorials appear in a variety of conservatively oriented

[19] For a detailed report on that article and its author's connection with the Tobacco Institute see "The Truth About *True*'s Article on Smoking," *Consumer Reports* 22 (June, 1968): 336–339.

newspapers under the guise of independently written editorials.[20] An examination of newspaper clippings kept by the staff of the President's Committee on Consumer Interest, reveals a large number of identical editorials criticizing government consumer protection activities. This is not to suggest that consumer groups should use the same methods, although the AFL-CIO does occasionally circulate canned stories with limited success. Rather, it should be pointed out that consumer groups are at a comparative disadvantage in the field of persuasive publicity.

The previous discussion has applied primarily to the "traditional" groups. The new consumer groups have different areas of emphasis and different techniques. But it should be noted that the division between them is not a mutually exclusive one and the difference is one of general mode of activity rather than a distinction between all activities. Both the similarities and difference between the traditional and the new can be seen in the emergence and development of Ralph Nader whose activities combine elements of both approaches.

The New Activists

The Consumer Crusader

Ralph Nader brought to his unorthodox crusade impeccable academic credentials having graduated from Princeton magna cum laude and from the Harvard Law School in 1958. Even during this early period of his formal education he displayed the reform impulse. At Princeton he unsuccessfully campaigned against the spraying of trees with DDT and for a reformed student disciplinary system. At Harvard, which he disdained for its emphasis on corporate law, Nader became interested in automobile accident cases. After law school and six months' service in the army, he began practicing law at Hartford, Connecticut. He continued his interest in automobile accident cases and became convinced that drivers were often falsely blamed when the real cause of accidents and injury was the automobile itself. He tried to interest the state legislatures of Connecticut and Massachusetts in automobile design safety, but made little progress.

There have been many efforts to explain the motives of Ralph

[20] U.S., Congress, Senate, *Remarks of Senator Lee Metcalf,* 89th Cong., 1st sess., April 5, 1965, *Congressional Record* III:6951–6957.

Nader. Suffice it to say that all available evidence confirms the impression that Nader is genuinely and deeply outraged at what he considers to be abuses and irresponsibility on the part of giant corporations. Among those who know him, it is agreed that Nader is driven by a keen sense of personal responsibility and the public interest. As one Washington political journalist put it, "Nader is not like you and me. Most of us tune out society's problems and concentrate on our own. Nader has chosen to make society's problems his problems and as a result he exists in a state of constant, barely controlled, outrage."[21] He simply takes it for granted that a lawyer should serve the public interest while realizing that he is one of the few who do. Thus, once he got interested in automobile safety, it was natural for him to go to Washington after discovering that state legislatures would do nothing about automobile design.

Nader came to Washington in 1964. He worked as a consultant with several congressional committees, but primarily he spent the next year working as a traffic safety consultant in the Labor Department under Daniel Patrick Moynihan, who was then assistant secretary for policy planning and research. Moynihan himself had previously written on automobile safety and was about to write a "muckraking" book on the subject when he was appointed to the Labor Department. He hoped to influence the Executive Branch from within and invited Ralph Nader to pursue this effort on a full-time basis. For the next year Nader tried, with little success, to enlist bureaucratic support for government action on automobile safety. During this time he also worked with the staff of Senator Ribicoff who was setting up hearings on the subject.

In early 1965, Nader felt that the inside influence strategy was not working and left the Labor Department to write his own book. During the time he was working on his book, Nader continued working with Senator Ribicoff's staff in preparation for the automobile safety hearings held that year by Ribicoff's Executive Reorganization Subcommittee of the Senate Governmental Operations Committee. Nader not only did research, but furnished questions to be asked by Senators Ribicoff and Robert Kennedy.[22]

[21] Patrick Anderson, "Ralph Nader, Crusader: Or, The Rise of a Self-Appointed Lobbyist," *New York Times Magazine,* October 29, 1967, p. 25.

[22] Elizabeth Drew, "The Politics of Auto Safety," *Atlantic Monthly,* October, 1966, p. 98.

In November, 1965, Nader began to get more widespread public attention with the publication of his book *Unsafe At Any Speed*. It was not until sometime after publication, however, that *Unsafe at Any Speed* became a best seller and Ralph Nader achieved "household word" status. It is generally agreed that the General Motors investigation of Nader was the single greatest factor in bringing both greater congressional and public acceptance. In January, 1966, Nader learned that he was being investigated by General Motors. In March, several news stories appeared about the investigation. General Motors issued a press release admitting that they had undertaken a "routine" investigation which purportedly related to Nader's possible connection with several Chevrolet Corvair liability suits pending against General Motors. Senator Ribicoff shifted the focus of his subcommittee hearings onto the investigation. It turned out that G.M. was conducting a full-scale investigation into all aspects of Nader's life; detectives constantly followed him and efforts had been made to get him in compromising situations. Nothing succeeds like martyrdom and Ralph Nader has had the rare opportunity to capitalize on his own martyrdom.[23] Having gained notice in the field of auto safety, it only remained for Nader to work on other subjects to become the nation's leading "consumer crusader." Two years and several bills later this title was finally accorded him by *Newsweek* in a cover story.[24] It is interesting to note that the *Newsweek* story made no mention of any other independent consumer advocates although various governmental consumer activists were discussed.

Nader's approach to consumer protection can be better understood by reference to his underlying philosophy of corporate life and government regulation. Basic to his activities is the belief that the great-

[23] Nader subsequently sued General Motors for invasion of privacy. After a technical ruling in Mr. Nader's favor by the New York Court of Appeals, G.M. settled out of court for $425,000 in August, 1970. After payment of legal fees and expenses, the money was used to further Nader's activities in consumer protection and corporate responsibility—including a continuous monitoring of General Motors itself.

[24] "Meet Ralph Nader, Everyman's Lobbyist and His Consumer Crusade," *Newsweek*, January 22, 1968, pp. 65–73. Apparently the title stayed with him for Nader reported with considerable amusement that sometimes he gets mail addressed to "Consumer Crusader, Washington, D.C." (Personal interview.)

est abuses against consumers are perpetrated not by "fly-by-night" operators, but by the largest corporations. These abuses are of two types: those that deprive the consumer of his income and those that inflict violence. He is concerned primarily with the violence caused by corporations. Nader alleges that major corporations are responsible for much of the violence in American life. This violence is of two types. There is first the instant violence accompanied by traumatic injury that is typical of automobile accidents, pipeline explosions, mine disasters, etc. The corporations are responsible for traumatic injury by neglecting the safety aspects of their products and practices. Secondly, there is the long-range violence of air and water pollution and other long-term environmental hazards. Such hazards are no less violent for being long-range in effect.[25]

At the heart of such violence is a system of corporate decision-making in which, consciously or subconsciously, executives place a price on human life by deciding how much additional cost they will absorb to make products safer. Nader believes that the violence and the decision-making system which underwrites it continues largely because of the insulation of corporate executives from the effects of their actions. This insulation is both personal and legal. Executives are rarely confronted personally by the public and rarely challenged to account for the social costs of their activities. Likewise, they are not personally legally accountable for those activities.[26] Thus, Nader urges that corporation presidents and not trade association representatives be forced to testify before congressional committees. In the automobile safety bill, he strongly advocated criminal penalties.

With regard to the representational responsibilities of the government, Nader holds that it is irrelevant whether or not the consumer cares about being protected from product hazards. No one deserves to be harmed or cheated, and government has the delegated function of protecting consumers. Nader views the role of government in terms of setting minimum safety and performance standards for potentially

[25] U.S., Congress, Senate, Committee on Government Operations, Testimony of Ralph Nader, *Establish a Department of Consumers. Hearings before the Subcommittee on Executive Reorganization,* 91st Cong., 1st sess., 1969, pp. 365–390.
[26] National Educational Television Network, Interview with Ralph Nader, February 27, 1968.

hazardous products. Again, the chief executive officers of corporations should be held legally responsible for compliance with those standards.[27]

Having summarized Ralph Nader's background and philosophy, the question remains, what does a "consumer crusader" do? In analyzing Nader's activities, a communications model is the most appropriate frame of reference. Basically, his effectiveness stems from the manner in which he receives and disseminates information.

Ralph Nader is the focal point of a fluctuating informational network. He receives information basically from three types of sources. First, he receives a large amount of mail from average citizens. These letters are primarily complaints relating to bad experiences people have had with particular products or services. These are frequently extensively detailed with copies of correspondence, receipts, bills, etc., and they can provide valuable resource material. These detailed complaints can be used to illustrate in human terms the nature of the problem that Nader is campaigning against. Included in mail from the public, are letters from people with expertise in technical areas alerting Nader to particular hazards he may have been previously unaware of. Thus, there is a constant flow of information reciting the details of old abuses and alerting him to new ones.[28]

In receiving citizen complaints, Nader, of course, is not alone. He is one recipient among many—including congressmen, the President's special assistant for consumer affairs, and the regulatory agencies. But it is significant that many individuals contact Nader in addition to or even instead of contacting the government. It is not clear whether they think he can help them, but it is clear that they may help him by occasionally furnishing good leads and dramatic examples for testimony, speeches and articles. It was such a source that got Nader into the natural gas pipeline safety issue. An engineering professor contacted Nader at an engineering conference early in 1966 and urged him to look into the subject. The professor outlined the basic details of the safety problem and gave Nader a few names. From there Nader did his own research and was able to make a speech on the subject by June,

---

[27] Ibid.

[28] This paragraph and the subsequent ones on Mr. Nader's operation are drawn primarily from personal interviews with Mr. Nader (March, 1969) and others. In keeping with promises made to some respondents, direct attribution to particular interviews will generally not be used in this section.

1966. He was a witness before the Senate Commerce Committee hearing on proposed legislation on August 1, 1967.[29]

The second source of information originates from within industry and takes the form of secret phone calls or letters disclosing certain practices or data that a corporation would rather not reveal. A typical episode occurred in March, 1969, when Nader revealed in a congressional hearing that the modern Hormel meat packing plant in California was selling substandard meat to supermarkets, with the markets' knowledge, and was selling substandard meat to school districts without their knowledge. He related other fraudulent and dangerous practices indulged in by Hormel. The information came from a secret source in the corporation who provided detailed information including copies of memoranda and invoices documenting the accusations. The whole matter has been referred to the Department of Justice.[30] There is no discernible pattern in this communications flow. Informants come from all levels of the corporate hierarchy, and there is no network of regular informants.

His third source is within the bureaucracy, and this source is similar to industry sources in that there is no sharply defined network of informants. Nader has received "leaks" from almost all levels of the bureaucracy. However, he recalled that he did not get information from the very bottom of the bureaucratic hierarchy—the secretaries and clerks. Generally this information consists of reports which either through inertia or deliberate suppression have not been acted on or even made public. Occasionally the information can be explosive. One example occurred when Nader was alerted to the existence of a Department of Agriculture survey of intrastate meat packing plants, then not subject to federal regulation. The report was a catalogue of horrors listing a host of unsanitary practices. He transmitted the report of Nick Kotz, a reporter for the Cowles Publications, who then wrote extensive articles based on the report for which he received the Pulitzer Prize. There is general agreement among other consumer activists that this publicity provided the impetus for the passage of the Wholesome Meat Act.

In addition to being alerted to official reports, governmental

[29] Anderson, "Ralph Nader," p. 104.
[30] See testimony of Ralph Nader, *Establish A Department of Consumers: Hearings.*

sources give Nader information regarding their agencies' action or inaction in discharging official responsibilities. Thus, Nader received detailed information regarding the Interstate Commerce Commission's pattern of accommodation to motor carriers which eventually culminated in a major study of the ICC.[31]

Although the leaking of a previously repressed report complete with shocking revelations is the most dramatic contribution of Nader's governmental sources, it is not the most usual. Generally, the information is not secret, but just generally unknown. As anyone who has waded through government documents knows, a tremendous amount of information is already in the public record. By steering Nader to the right documents, his governmental sources provide an important informational function. This function provides one of the elements of the other aspect of Nader's intake of information—research.

Nader obtains his information not only from what is given to him by outside sources, but mainly through research. Useful information has to be pulled out of piles of documents and reluctant officials, reports must be summarized and beliefs must be documented. Nader stated, "It's amazing how much is printed, but no one reads it." Nader reads it, pulls out useful facts, and summarizes reports. Not all of the work involves the laborious perusal of government or industry documents. Nader's well-publicized revelation that the United Mine Workers had a 75 percent interest in the National Bank of Washington which cooperates with nonunion coal operators originated in an article he had read in the *Wall Street Journal*. Similarly, after his leads on gas pipeline safety by his initial engineering contact and contacts in the Federal Power Commission, Nader dug most of his information out of technical journals. From there he went to the people involved for any elaboration that was needed. Soon he had the equivalent of a complete legal brief on the issue.[32]

Although Nader no longer works alone as he did until 1968, he is still very much on top of the activities of his staff and associates. Because the amount of attention which can be given to problems is always far less than the problems potentially demanding attention, choices

[31] Robert Fellmeth, *The Interstate Commerce Omission* (New York: Grossman, 1970).

[32] Anderson, "Ralph Nader," p. 104.

have to be made and they must be made well if he is to be effective. In deciding which areas to pursue he has three criteria. First, it must be an urgent problem. Second, no one else is effectively working toward a solution. And finally, it must be an area in which he feels he can make a contribution.

When the research has been completed, Nader's information dissemination function begins. Having been the point of input of information from the sources listed, he assumes the role of "output point" and channels information to new points of input. In a sense, Nader performs a representation function for his sources of information. They bring to his attention problems they are concerned about in the hope that he can contribute to the solution of those problems. These sources are, in effect, his constituency. He has no direct remedial power to aid that constituency. His only power rests in his ability to communicate information in such a way that new opinion will be created. It is this newly created opinion that is the impetus for direct governmental action. Thus, going back to the example of the Wholesome Meat Act, there existed a prevailing public opinion that all meat was reasonably wholesome. Nader caused the creation of a new opinion that some meat might be dangerous. And it was this new opinion which supplied the pressure for a meat inspection bill. So the key point is that the communications put out by Nader are not ends in themselves but are directed toward utilizing whatever power there is in public opinion.

Nader's information output is disseminated primarily through two channels. The first of these is the press. Nader himself writes occasional magazine articles and these may contain dramatic revelations. Indeed, his original auto safety criticism appeared in *The Nation* magazine. In general, though, Nader's information is printed through intermediaries. He has excellent contacts and an excellent working relationship with the press—both newspaper and television reporters. However, there is no real pattern of contacts. There is no steady group of reporters in contact with Nader since they cover different problems within the general area of consumer protection. Among the same reporters, there is no pattern in the direction of contact. That is, sometimes Nader initially contacts individual reporters and other times they may contact him.

One aspect of Nader's relationship with the press is similar to that of other newsmakers. Nader will do or say something that is newsworthy and reporters will approach him to get additional information on that particular issue. His initial newsworthy activity is often testimony before Congress or a letter made public. Nader feels that he has no trouble reaching the public through the media when he has something of substance to say. The other aspect is when he acts as a covert conduit for "leaks." This was the case in the meat inspection controversy. Also, most of the late Drew Pearson's revelations regarding consumer protection were said to originate with Ralph Nader.

The second channel of Nader's information output is the Congress. Although he disseminates information through public testimony at hearings several times a year, he primarily communicates through intermediaries. Nader stated, "If I can stay on the sidelines and get three senators to say something, that's better than if I said it myself. I don't need any more enemies."[33] Most of his work with Congress occurs at the staff level in preparing reports, submitting exhibits and preparing for hearings. Nader has worked with the staffs of the Senate Commerce Committee, the Subcommittee on Executive Reorganization of the Senate Government Operations Committee (Ribicoff's subcommittee) and the Subcommittee on Monopoly of the Senate Select Committee on Small Business. In short, a significant part of his communication output has the effect of emanating from the more authoritative source of congressional hearings and reports.

In 1968, a new element was added to Nader's communication functions. In the summer of that year, he brought together in Washington a small group of law students to do a study of the Federal Trade Commission.[34] The resulting report was a severe attack on the FTC.[35] It was originally issued on January 6, 1969, in the form of a long press release, was extensively reported in the media, and was the subject of a feature presentation on NET's Public Broadcast Laboratory immediately after being released. Two sessions of the 1969 Ribicoff hearings on consumer protection were devoted to the charges made in the report. Although Nader did not participate in the actual preparation of the report, he was active in the initial stages by providing leads and helping the students gain access to their contacts.

[33] *Newsweek,* "Meet Ralph Nader," p. 66.

[34] See Chapter 3.

[35] Edward Cox, Robert Fellmeth, and John Schultz, *The "Nader Report" on the Federal Trade Commission* (New York: Baron, 1969).

The ranks of "Nader's Raiders" multiplied the following summer with over one hundred students of law, economics, and medicine involved in separate studies of government agencies including the Interstate Commerce Commission, the Food and Drug Administration, and others. By the summer of 1970, almost two hundred students were involved in teams studying a variety of institutions including not only governmental agencies but specific corporations and law firms. This voluntary activity has gone beyond Washington and beyond the summer months. The students of some universities have voted to devote a portion of their student activity fees to public interest causes and Nader envisions this as a potentially great resource. At the other end of the generation gap, Nader and his aides have been behind the organization of local groups of middle-aged and senior citizens to deal with a variety of consumer and environmental problems such as the inequitable property tax structure of many localities.

The activity of Nader's Raiders was given an institutional base in 1969 with the establishment of the Center for the Study of Responsive Law, which extends the investigative activity beyond the summer months. The center has a small full-time staff which heads the major investigative projects and follows them to completion. In addition to the original FTC study, the center has produced books on the Interstate Commerce Commission, the Food and Drug Administration, and the federal agencies nominally charged with the control of air pollution.[36]

In addition, Nader provided the impetus behind the formation of two other groups: the Center for Auto Safety which seeks to light a fire under government and industry officials to require safer automobiles, and the Project for Corporate Responsibility which seeks to effect greater accountability to the public by corporations.

To a large extent it is correct to agree with Nader's own assessment that the Center for the Study of Responsive Law and related activities are not an institutionalization of Ralph Nader, but rather an amplification. Nader is managing trustee of the center and its activities are very reflective of his own interest and philosophy. Most of the center's investigations originate with problems that Nader himself has become aware of through the sources mentioned above. Having

---

[36] Robert Fellmeth, *The Interstate Commerce Omission;* James S. Turner, *The Chemical Feast;* John Esposito, *Vanishing Air* (all New York: Grossman, 1970).

a staff bolstered by hundreds of student volunteers, Nader is able to focus attention (or have attention focused) on a far larger number of areas than he could alone.

The center and the summer projects have two basic political purposes which reflect the evolution of Nader's own style and his conception of his own role. The first is to directly influence governmental elites by providing a larger window on agency decision-making practices. Nader and the center staff members believe explicitly that the establishment of an ongoing investigative effort is an important pressure tactic to achieve more conscientious administration just as regular bank audits are conducive to the rectitude of bankers. Thus, the communications model must be amended to include potential communications output—a potential which manifests itself as fear of publicity. A second purpose is to build a public constituency for reform by making explicit the failing of government officials who should themselves be spearheading the reforms instead of being the objects of reformers' efforts.

In evaluating groups seeking to make an input into policy formation, it is relevant to know something of their resources as an indication of their ability to be effective. Nader himself originally operated only with the support of royalties from *Unsafe at Any Speed* and fees from articles and speaking engagements. Although the royalties from the first book have long since run out, Nader is still easily able to support himself by lecturing and writing. In 1970, additional support was supplied by, ironically, General Motors in a $425,000 settlement of Nader's invasion of privacy suit against G.M. A large portion of the income from these sources is channeled into other activities such as the Public Interest Law Group to be discussed shortly. The center has been the recipient of grants from several small foundations and is partially self-supporting through the royalties of the books produced under its auspices. To a large extent the operations of Nader and his full-time associates depend on the continued willingness of bright and dedicated people to work for far less money than they could receive in private law firms or businesses. Whether the present trend for bright young lawyers to commit themselves to a period of public-interest work will continue is an open question. However, limited resources make that commitment essential to the continuation of Nader's activities at their present level.

The Public-Interest Lawyers

The most recent entrants into the ranks of consumer groups are the public-interest lawyers. With due regard for the complexity of the concept of the "public interest," we may still utilize this label since it is the term widely used to describe a small group of lawyers who work full time practicing both traditional and novel conceptions of *pro bono publico* activity. Indeed, these lawyers have a distinctive and explicit conception of their own orientation toward the law and consider themselves members of a small and informal "public-interest bar." While such pro bono work as defending indigents or political dissidents has been around for many years, the term public-interest law refers to a new phenomenon—novel in its approaches to traditional pro bono work and novel in types of cases.[37] It is this novelty of legal work which is of interest in considering the public-interest bar as a consumer group.

Basically, the activities of the public-interest lawyers rest on the assumption that in many areas the need is not for new laws but for vigorous enforcement of existing laws. There would be a policy change in either case, but the public-interest lawyers approach the change in policy as one that is or should be required of governmental participants. Thus, they are not seeking to persuade government officials to establish new policies but rather to prohibit them from engaging in what they regard as the subversion of old policies.

As it relates to the formation of consumer protection policy, the public-interest bar is a small group based in Washington consisting of a few law "groups."[38] Their relation to more orthodox law firms and to other consumer activists can be seen by examples illustrating the major forms of activity of these groups: investigation, litigation, and representation. Most groups engage in all three activities but have different emphases.

The most investigatively oriented of the groups is Ralph Nader's

---

[37] For a comprehensive study of the varieties of public-interest law see, "The New Public Interest Lawyers," *Yale Law Journal* 79 (May, 1970): 1069–1152.

[38] Bar association rules prevent these organizations from calling themselves law "firms" unless they are titled by the names of the major partners. Most of the public-interest lawyers consciously do not want to personalize their organizations in this manner.

Center for the Study of Responsive Law. While the center does no litigation, it is valid to consider it among the public interest law groups since its goal is very explicitly to investigate regulatory agencies and other organizations with the aim of making legal institutions more responsive to a broader public. Thus the organization's name was chosen deliberately and does connote its concern with the administration of legal procedures to gain a more advantageous position for consumer interest in the policy process.

The center has a more explicit and consciously directed philosophy of its role in the policy process than most of the other consumer activists. Its criteria for getting involved in an issue are much like Nader's own. After making an initial assessment of a problem area the two key questions are whether anyone else is effectively involved in working on the problem (conversely, whether the center's involvement would be superfluous) and whether their involvement would have an impact on the problem's solution. The initial identification of potentially profitable area of investigation usually originates with Nader, and the center is thus an additional intermediate step in Nader's communication flow.

While, as noted earlier, the center is publicity oriented in the same sense that Nader is, our concern with it in the context of public interest law is in other aspects of its activity. The revelations uncovered by task force investigations not only provide material for public scrutiny but provide information which forms the basis for litigation by other lawyers. Also, based on investigative findings, individual staff members may become parties to suits against government agencies.

Typical of the litigative type of public-interest law group is another of Ralph Nader's projects, the Public Interest Research Group. Although there is no formal link between the two groups tied to Nader, the Public Interest Research Group is one of the major recipients of information from the center in regard to areas susceptible to litigation. The group was officially formed in July, 1970, and represents the culmination of a long standing goal of Nader's. Its origins go back several months earlier when two lawyers were financed by Nader to take some legal actions against government agencies. The organization does not generally have specific clients. Rather, the lawyers bring action on behalf of the "public" in an attempt to force government agencies to establish what Nader considers a better public policy. As examples of the kind of work done by the Public Interest Research Group, in 1970, a suit was initiated to require the Food and Drug Administration to require a more cautionary and explicit health warning on patients' packages of birth control pills. Another suit in 1970 sought to prevent the Department of Transportation from waiving certain safety requirements for taxicabs manufactured by the Checker Corporation. In addition to litigation, the firm acts on its own in participating in administrative rule-making hearings. Indeed, the establishment of a "public" voice in these hearings is a main goal of most public-interest lawyers.

Nader's group even in its infancy was one of the two largest public-interest operations. The other is the Center for Law and Social Policy. In its actual legal work the center is similar to the Public Interest Research Group. For example center lawyers, joined by the firm of Arnold and Porter as co-counsel, successfully filed suit on behalf of Ralph Nader, the Center for Auto Safety, and Physicians for Automobile Safety to require the Department of Transportation to withdraw from certain aspects of a settlement with General Motors in regard to safety-related defects on trucks. This is typical of a general approach which seeks to monitor voluntary settlements between government agencies and regulated industries and introduce a greater degree of outside (i.e., "public" participation). Thus, like most of the other public-interest law groups, the center first encourages and ultimately seeks to force this goal on government agencies through litigation.

One unique aspect of the center is that it has an auxiliary educational function for law students who receive credit from their own law schools while they intern at the center for periods of six months. The students fully participate in the public-interest legal activities of the center in addition to attending seminars and other more orthodox vestiges of legal study. It is important to note the educational program because it does have public policy implications. Inasmuch as the center constitutes an important part of the students' education and imparts a knowledge of and a commitment to public-interest law, it is making an investment in the future and is generating new resources in the form of an increased pool of talent and expertise. Other groups have established such programs for law students and the goal again is a very explicit investment in the future.

Many of the public-interest groups have broken away from the traditional legal mold of lawyer-client relationships and have instituted legal action in which the client is completely incidental to the larger policy goals. In many cases a client is named only when *someone's* name has to appear on legal paper. Some other groups are more client oriented. Thus the firm of Berlin, Roisman, and Kessler is retained and paid by the Consumer Federation of America to serve in the capacity of general counsel rendering legal services and advice including testifying on the organization's behalf in Congress. Thus, such an organization seeks its policy goals not only through legal means but also through new legislation like more traditional consumer groups. As noted before in the case of the Union Consumer Credit Code, they add an important element of professional expertise to the policy inputs of other participants.

The legal approach of these groups is closely related to their method of obtaining financial resources. Apart from their pattern of activity, there are basically three organizational modes of public-interest lawyers. First are groups like the Public Interest Research Group and the Stern Community Law Firm supported by foundations and thus independent of clients. Others such as Berlin, Roisman, and Kessler are supported by clients—usually public-interest consumer and environmental groups and thus more dependent and responsive to the demands of those client groups. A third type of public-interest law emerges from the traditional law firms which allow some of their lawyers to devote a proportion of their time to public-interest work or which have separate public-interest subsidiaries. The largest and most notable of these is the "establishment" firm of Arnold and Porter.

The public-interest lawyers are unique also in maintaining what might be called "cohesive diversity." As is common among the purveyors of a new and exciting enterprise there is a feeling of comaraderie among the public-interest lawyers who consider themselves alternatively as members of a small public-interest bar and as a shadow government existing in Republican Washington of the early 1970s. There is cooperation through periodic meetings and the sharing of information. However, the liaison that exists is directed not toward concentrated work in a particular area but toward the avoidance of overlapping efforts. As one lawyer put it, "One way we work with [other public-interest lawyers] is by not working with them. You see what they are doing and you try to avoid duplicating. Why should there be two people on the same issue when there are thousands of untouched issues?" All the public-interest lawyers who were interviewed put forth this criterion and the need for it in a world of scarce resources. In general, the whole pattern of relationships within the public-interest bar exhibited a greater degree of cooperation than was previously the case with consumer activists.

The goals of the various public-interest firms are very explicit and surprisingly similar in broad form. Apart from the objective in specific cases, all the public-interest lawyers expressed a desire to open up the decision-making process of the agencies charged with administering existing and new law. The essence of this goal was concisely stated by one public-interest lawyer:

. . . the public interest firm seeks representation or litigation for the public in forums where the public wasn't previously represented. For example, in construction and highways only recently has anyone cared what the public wanted. Previously only the builders were consulted.

This goal is pursued through a combination of three means. They seek greater public participation and the consideration of a wider range of views in rule-making procedures. Thus, every petition or suit to obtain such participation also seeks to establish the precedent of wider participation in such proceedings. Secondly, they challenge the validity or legality of bureaucratic actions which seem to them to fall short of the government's responsibility in the particular case. Finally, by the Freedom of Information Act (or threat of it) they seek to prevent the withholding of information (such as product testing results) from the public. Beyond seeking specific objectives, the public-interest lawyers also seek to establish the precedent of wider public participation which each successful action brings. Thus, they differ from other activists in that the target of their efforts is usually the bureaucracy which they approach either directly or through the courts if the direct approach is not fruitful. They alone among the consumer activists focus on the implementation of policy after its enactment.

The Press

The press and its relation to the process of government has become a subject of increasing concern to both political scientists and journalists.

It can and has been the subject of separate full-length studies. However, this section examines various aspects of the press-government relationship only as they relate to one central concern—the manner in which the press represents the consumer interest. As a representative institution, the press fulfills the constituency expansion role described at the beginning of this chapter. It provides feedback to consumers—who can be considered the "constituency" of the press. By providing feedback, the press gives direction to public (consumer) opinion and expands the attentive constituency. The representative function of the press is therefore analogous to the feedback function of lobbyists. Just as lobbyists inform their clients of what the government is doing and what they themselves are doing to further the clients' interest, the press informs the consumer constituency about governmental actions and the actions of private advocates of their interests. The justification for viewing the press as a consumer advocate thus rests in its performance of a representational function which is undertaken by most interest groups.

The press as a whole is generally considered to include purveyors of both the written and spoken word. It includes not only reporters, but editors and publishers as well.[39] While all of these have some bearing on all news coverage and transmission, including, of course, consumer protection news, the particular group being discussed is much smaller. The members of the press who can be thought of as constituting a consumer group are a very small group of reporters—only three or four reporters have consumer affairs as their regular "beat." Beyond them, there is a larger group of reporters who occasionally cover consumer protection issues or who have consumer affairs as one of their beats.

There are two further limitations on the size of the press group. First, no reporter has "consumer protection" as his beat. All the reporters covering consumer protection—even those who do so only occasionally—specialize in some issue area within this broad category such as drug safety. Secondly, this is a group with a constantly changing membership. Few reporters are permanently specialized and they often

---

[39] E.g., Bernard Cohen stresses the importance of the newspaper editing process and particularly wire service editing as it relates to the final newspaper output. *The Press and Foreign Policy* (Princeton: Princeton University Press, 1963), pp. 105–132.

move on to entirely different policy areas. In short, there is no "consumer press" as such. For purposes of discussion and brevity, however, the term "consumer press" will be used to denote a small group of reporters, most of whom have other assignments, who cover consumer protection issues.

The essence of the role of the press in representing the consumer interest is the transmission of information to the public. For purposes of this study, there are two important elements in this process—the choice of the story and the sources used to obtain that story.

The literature on the press indicates that there is no systematic process by which reporters decide which events to report, and there is no universally accepted definition of what is "news."[40] Some students of the press, however, have pointed out implicit criteria for newsworthiness. These include the events of the day, the judgment of other reporters, the interest of news organizations or what the reporter perceives as the interest of his news organization, and his relations with his sources.[41] One generally accepted criterion of newsworthiness is conflict. Physical or verbal combat between important groups of people is always good copy.[42]

The vagueness of criteria for news is no different among the consumer reporters. None of the reporters interviewed claimed to have any systematic method of consumer protection coverage. One prominent consumer protection specialist affirmed that

> There is no science in the newspaper business. . . . A reporter believes certain areas are important. You get a reputation in that area and people give you leads. This business is not rational or comprehensive.

The few consumer affairs regulars pick topics within their range of interests, and they keep abreast of congressional hearings and administrative actions which may be occurring simultaneously. When events do occur simultaneously, choices must be made and there simply is no

---

[40] For example, Bernard Cohen notes, "The implicit nature of conceptions of news may be expressed by references to 'the news-values inherent in the stories,' or in the tautology that 'a story is what is interesting, what is important.' " *Press and Foreign Policy*, p. 54.

[41] Delmer Dunn, *Public Officials and The Press* (Reading, Mass.: Addison-Wesley, 1969), pp. 26–36.

[42] Ibid., pp. 59–85; Cohen, *Press and Foreign Policy*, p. 56.

systematic way to describe this choice process. Similarly, among the larger group of reporters who occasionally cover consumer affairs, they must choose which events to cover. Sometimes the choice may be a consumer topic when that topic falls within their own instinct for what is news.

The sources which reporters use are not independent of their choice of story. Indeed the source may be the story itself as it is in the case of a congressional hearing when a reporter does not go beyond the events occurring at that hearing. Furthermore, as Delmar Dunn points out, the choice of story may be dependent on the source since reporters often do a story because they have better access to a particular source or one source might be inherently easier to cover such as a press conference.[43] In short, the sources, as much as choice of story, influence greatly the ultimate news output of the reporter. This holds true for our consumer press group as much as for reporters in any other area.

The most dramatic source, and the one generally in the public mind, is the "leak." The nature of leaks has already been discussed with reference to Ralph Nader, and the process is much the same with reporters. Leaks involve secrets and scandal only occasionally. In spite of its infrequency, however, the scandal-filled leak can be a more important and exciting source. During the years when George Larrick was commissioner of the Food and Drug Administration, Morton Mintz, a superb *Washington Post* consumer specialist, had a small group of informants within the agency. Based on these sources, Mintz was able to piece together stories of malfeasance and nonfeasance of duties within FDA which he eventually utilized in his book, *Therapeutic Nightmare*. More commonly, however, the leak can be better described as a "tip." Informants may steer reporters to public, but previously unknown, written sources of information. One reporter confessed that his technique was to go to congressional committee staff members he knew and get into a friendly argument. This greatly facilitated getting tips since the committee staffers would pull out industry trade sheets or governmental documents in support of their own position. The reporters could then utilize these documents in his own story.

Generally, consumer reporters have no difficulty in soliciting information from the staffs of committees handling consumer legislation.

[43] Dunn, *Public Officials and Press*, pp. 26–36.

Staff members who are committed to consumer legislation consider such reporters as Morton Mintz, David Vienna of the *Washington Post,* and John Morris of the *New York Times* as allies who can provide a valuable publicity service. Hence, cooperation is usually given. Again, this cooperation is usually in the form of merely alerting the reporter to particular documents, letters, statistics, etc., which the committee staff has accumulated. These written sources blur over into the next category of sources—the public record.

·Even a reporter like Morton Mintz who has as many contacts among the consumer activists as anyone, relies on the public record for over 90 percent of his material.[44] Other consumer reporters agreed that the public record was their most frequent source. In the case of consumer reporters, the public record usually involves Congress, particularly the record of congressional hearings. In addition to being a voluminous fount of information, congressional hearings have the advantage of being a safe source for attribution. There is no danger of libel suits or other challenges if a story says that "Congressman Jones charged that . . . ." Naturally, this gives consumer reporters much greater freedom than if they had to report the results of congressional staff investigations themselves before those results had been placed in the public record.

The few reporters who regularly cover consumer protection are at a greater advantage in the sources they are free to tap. They build up close contacts among the congressional committee staffs and with congressmen and senators themselves. Of even greater importance for investigative reporting, they establish contacts with professional people outside the government who can make them aware of further source material within the professional literature. This source is particularly advantageous to reporters who cover areas of technical complexity. The net effect is that the consumer protection regulars have a greater flexibility of sources which facilitates investigative reporting. While all reporters, at least in consumer affairs, draw heavily on the public record, the few regulars have a wider scope of the record upon which to draw.

The contacts between governmental consumer activists, particularly committee staff, and reporters have already been mentioned. There

[44] Personal interview with Morton Mintz.

is a thin line between such contacts as sources for stories and the participation of reporters in the shaping of public policy. Inasmuch as reporters do participate, they more actively represent the consumer interest. The importance of the press in the process of government has long been noted. Its particular function in the system as it relates to consumer protection will be considered in detail later in the chapter when the discussion will turn to the particular niche filled by each of the groups previously examined. For the present, the discussion will be confined to patterns of participation by consumer reporters in the consumer protection policy process.

Members of the press have traditionally played an important role in policy making. In the context of this study, the most celebrated example is that of the muckrakers discussed in Chapter 1. The example is particularly relevant in that the policy-making role of the muckrakers parallels the role played by their colleagues fifty years later. The most obvious aspect of their policy-making role was the influence they had through the disclosures they made, such as those in *The Jungle* which led to the Pure Food and Drug Act and the Meat Inspection Act of 1906. However, exposure was but one aspect of the dual nature of the muckraker's work. The other involved following through on the impact of disclosure and giving a nudge to other reformers.

This second aspect—participation by the press in policy making beyond the influence of the stories themselves—has increased in importance since the time of the muckrakers. The Fourth Estate has become "a *de facto,* quasi-official fourth branch of government," according to Douglass Cater who also noted the new position of the Washington correspondent:

> The reporter is the recorder of government but he is also a participant. He operates in a system in which power is divided. He as much as anyone, and more than a great many, helps to shape the course of government. He is the indispensable broker and middleman among the sub-governments in Washington.[45]

In his study of the Senate, Donald Matthews also testified to the influence of the press. He found that a law of anticipated reactions was

[45] Cater, *The Fourth Branch of Government* (Boston: Houghton Mifflin Co., 1959), p. 7.

present in the relations between the press and the Senate. Senatorial behavior is affected by the senators' desire to make news. Reporters may play a more direct role in influencing policy by being informal advisors to senators, by pressuring senatorial action and by providing external and internal communication for senators.[46]

Both aspects of reporters' influence depend on their relations with other participants in their subject areas. Because of this dependence, it is useful to begin the examination of the policy participation role of the consumer press with an analysis of its relation to other consumer activists. As it pertains to the other private activists discussed in this chapter, the analysis is, of necessity, brief. The nature of the relationship between Ralph Nader and the press has already been covered.[47] With the exception of Nader, no consumer group utilizes the mass circulation press as part of its strategy. None even has continuing contact with the same group of reporters. None of the reporters interviewed mentioned consumer groups as a source of information. The consumer group representatives interviewed confirmed this fact and none was attempting to establish regular contacts with the press. Of course the result of this lack of communication is that insofar as consumer reporters participate in policy making, they do so independent of other nongovernmental consumer activists—with the exception of Ralph Nader.

There is more contact within the bureaucracy, but very little activity beyond normal coverage of events that reporters covering those beats consider newsworthy. The pattern of coverage is very little different from that involving any of the other federal bureaucracies. The three agencies examined—the Federal Trade Commission, the Food and Drug Administration, and the President's Committee on Consumer Interest—all have press offices which hand out the usual flow of press releases. Reporters follow up on these releases only when they involve a "newsworthy" announcement of agency action or a speech by an agency representative. FTC pronouncements on cigarette smoking received major coverage; a recent pronouncement prohibiting discriminatory payment of promotional allowances between competing purchasers of Chinese foods did not.

---

[46] Matthews, *U.S. Senators and Their World* (New York: Vintage Books, 1960), pp. 203–206.

[47] Supra, pp. 183–184.

Of course, in following up or even anticipating press releases, reporters rely on contacts with the bureaucracies they cover. It has been observed that bureaucrats frequently utilize the press to promote particular policies or accrue some advantage to their agencies.[48] The large departments, particularly State and Defense, are covered by reporters who have them as their beats. In these cases, reporters build up a large network of contacts. This is not the case with the consumer reporters. As of 1970, the only consumer agencies regularly covered by a reporter specializing in their subject areas were the Food and Drug Administration covered by Morton Mintz and the Federal Trade Commission covered by David Vienna, both of the *Washington Post*.[49] During the tenure of Commissioner Larrick, Mintz had secret contacts with a small group of lower-ranking officials who provided him with information that the higher echelons within FDA preferred not be released.[50] Thus, he participated in policy making by altering the normal information flow out of the agency. During the regimes of commissioners Goddard and Ley, Mintz's contacts were less surreptitious, but he is still one of only two or three consumer reporters who has a regular network of contacts within a single agency. Generally these contacts are used only incidental to the normal business of writing news stories, but in the past they have given Mintz a policy-making role and the potential is always there for a resumption of that role.

The principal point of contact for the consumer press is Congress, especially the committee staffs. Consumer reporters have close and continuing contacts with the staffs of committees and congressmen involved in consumer legislation. Communication in particular instances is initiated by either side depending on circumstances. The most common event involving staff-initiated communication is the press release relating to a speech made by a congressman or a letter sent by the congressman to an agency in the Executive Branch. Congressional staff

[48] See Francis E. Rourke, *Secrecy and Publicity* (Baltimore: Johns Hopkins Press, 1961), pp. 183–207.

[49] This discussion includes only reporters for the mass media. The activities of the regulatory agencies are closely covered by the trade press such as the *Pink Sheet* for the drug industry.

[50] Morton Mintz, *By Prescription Only* (Boston: Houghton Mifflin Co., 1967), p. xxxvi.

members generally have a list of reporters who will be interested in particular areas covered by these releases and these reporters are personally contacted.

The better reporters never rely on press releases alone. Following up on the releases is one avenue of press-initiated contacts. A common technique is to interview the congressman involved for elaboration on the prepared release or to interview other governmental participants for their reactions to the release. Another avenue of press-initiated contacts is the follow-up of "leads" obtained elsewhere. A reporter might hear a rumor concerning pending administrative action and go to the relevant congressional committee staff for reaction to that rumor. A rumor is only one of many types of leads that causes the enterprising reporter to scurry over to his congressional contacts for reaction or amplification. Others include events which become generally known such as announcements by the administration or by an industry. In such cases, it is just a matter of timing as to who initiates the contact. Congressmen are just as eager to make a statement as reporters are to receive it.

A third point of press-Congress contacts occurs at congressional hearings. Hearings are covered as a routine matter and the amount of coverage depends on the vague criteria of newsworthiness discussed earlier. Just as in the case of press releases, the good reporters solicit further statements from the participants in those hearings.

Lest the reader wonder what bearing this brief discourse about press-Congress communications has on policy, it should be pointed out that such contacts are both preliminary to and an integral part of one type of participation by the press in congressional policy making—providing a communications service for Congress. Congress is the principal point of contact for consumer protection reporters because of the convergence of needs among reporters and congressmen—a convergence which puts reporters in a participatory role. Congressmen (directly or through staff members) need the press to promote legislation they are sponsoring and to get personal publicity for themselves. At the same time, reporters need the news stories generated by Congress. A truly symbiotic relationship is at work.[51] The participation of

---

[51] See Matthews, *U.S. Senators*, pp. 212–217. Matthews points out that in spite of the many opportunities for conflict, reporters and senators fall into a pattern of mutual back-scratching which is much more profitable to both sides.

reporters in policy making is inherent in these relationships and can be seen in what reporters give to and get from Congress.

Reporters provide two types of communications services for Congress. They deliver information to congressmen and staff members and they enable Congress to provide information to the public.[52] While this informational function is not as great in the small world of consumer protection as in such large, unwieldy areas as foreign affairs, it does exist and was mentioned by congressional interview respondents. The information conveyed is not limited to the finished news stories. A significant point is that by the very process by which they obtain news, reporters may participate in policy. In soliciting reactions as they follow through on stories, reporters make the participants they are interviewing aware of what other participants are doing. They create greater awareness and interest in the activities of other participants.

This provision of internal communication is not purely a case of reporters giving a service. It is in reality, only one side of a coin. The other side is the information the reporters receive in turn—information which is essential to their professional performance. This analogy also applies to their provision of external communications. The stories they write provide exposure for congressmen and legislative proposals. Staff members repeatedly stress the importance of press coverage of consumer issues. In this context, it is extremely significant to note that the consumer reporters (for the mass circulation media) are uniformly in favor of the legislation being pushed by the consumer activists in Congress. Thus, they provide publicity which is always favorable. This is not only, or even primarily a result of their own biases but is the result also of the inevitable public response to the issues. As one staff member pointed out, "Who isn't in favor of clean meat?" The other side of the coin is that the service provided to the congressional consumer activists is also a service to the reporter—it is what he is paid to do and it enhances his own professional reputation.[53] This process of mutual benefit

[52] Recent studies have shown that the press is the primary source of information for congressmen. See Cohen, *Press and Foreign Policy,* pp. 214–218, and Matthews, *U.S. Senators,* pp. 205–206.

[53] This was also true of the muckrakers who built up their reputations and the circulation of their magazines by their exposures. See C. C. Regier, *The Era of the Muckrakers* (Chapel Hill: University of North Carolina Press, 1932) pp. 10–26.

is especially evident in the granting of exclusive stories. For example, during the early period of the fight over the truth-in-lending bill, the Senate Banking and Currency staff gave Robert Novak, then of the *Wall Street Journal,* exclusive information enabling him to write feature stories which publicized the hearings. A staff member of another consumer-oriented committee noted, "When a reporter gives us a lead, and we pursue it, we'll try to give him first crack at what we come up with. We'll try to give him a byline story."

Although reporters participate in the legislative process by aiding congressional advocates of consumer protection in the manner discussed above, those interviewed did not perceive of themselves as advocates of a cause. Indeed, there was no instance in consumer protection legislation where reporters worked with committee staff members to map publicity strategy or otherwise perform as active partisans. Although they all favor consumer legislation, they do not fear that their biases will interfere with objective reporting. They realize that publicity is beneficial to consumer protection legislation, but they try to present the facts objectively, and feel very constrained to be accurate. Their attitude is best summed up by one reporter who stated:

> No one is objective. I see my function as enlightening the public and acting in the public interest. The facts are objective, but of course I have feelings about this. I can't divorce myself from those feelings. But I try to serve the public interest in my way just as Ralph [Nader] does in his way and [Senator] Ribicoff in his way.

Thus, the representation of the consumer interest by reporters is incidental to their normal work. It results from the process by which they gather stories and from the stories themselves.

Although the discussion so far has been limited to the activities of consumer group reporters, the total process of consumer representation in the press goes beyond the activities of these few reporters. When the analysis is extended to the press as a whole, it is evident that there are restraints on the representation of the consumer interest in the presence of conflicting interests.

A major restraint in some segments of the media has been advertising pressure or editorial solicitude to advertisers in anticipation of such pressure. In that consumer protection policy generally affects heavily advertised products and services, conflict is inevitable between consumer activists and advertisers whose products would be affected. Just as the consumer activists cultivate their allies in the press, so do the affected industries. At times this has placed constraints on the presentation of the views of the consumer activists. These constraints are not new and in comparison to previous times they are more subtle and milder. Except for a few muckraking magazines, the popular press bowed to the pressure of patent medicine manufacturers in 1906 to suppress unfavorable information. Indeed, some advertising contracts with newspapers bound the papers to editorially support the position of the patent medicine makers.[54] The situation was even worse in the 1930s with the absence of the muckraking magazines. Both because of advertising pressure and because of publishers' opposition to the original advertising provisions in the Tugwell food and drug bill, there was almost a complete blackout of coverage of the legislation.[55]

The classic recent example of such constraints occurred during the controversy over the truth-in-packaging bill. In November, 1962, Paul Willis, then chairman of the Grocery Manufacturers of America, gave a speech before the Television Bureau of Advertising's annual convention in which he commented on a meeting he had had with sixteen top executives of national magazines. The purpose of the meeting was to discuss "the facts of life covering advertiser-media relationships." Willis stated:

> We suggested to the publishers that the day was here when their editorial department and business department might better understand their interdependency relationships as they affect the operating results of their company; and as their operations may affect the advertiser— their bread and butter.[56]

Whether in response to Willis's reminder or not, a number of mass circulation magazines acted in a way that was very solicitous of the

---

[54] Louis Filler, *The Muckrakers: Crusaders for American Liberalism* (Yellow Springs, Ohio: Antioch Press, 1964), p. 151.

[55] Arthur Schlesinger, Jr., *The Coming of the New Deal* (Boston: Houghton Mifflin Co., 1958), p. 359.

[56] Reprinted in U.S., Congress, Senate, Committee on Judiciary, *Packaging and Labeling Legislation: Hearings before a Subcommittee of the Committee on Judiciary on S. 387,* 88th Cong., 1st sess., 1963, pp. 481–482.

interests of their advertisers. For example *Look Magazine* (January 26, 1965) featured an article by the General Foods chairman, Charles Mortimer, entitled, "Let's Keep Politics Out of the Pantry." The article contained a broad attack on the proposed truth-in-packaging bill and other consumer legislation. Senator Philip Hart, the bill's sponsor, offered to write an article replying to Mortimer's charges, but *Look* declined the offer on the grounds that there was insufficient interest in consumer protection. In addition, *Look* did not publish a single letter critical of Mortimer's article. Senator Hart expressed the belief that this was typical of a purposeful suppression of articles favorable to truth-in-packaging in the public press.[57]

A recent study of Arthur Rowse,[58] who now publishes an independent consumer newsletter, confirms Senator Hart's suspicion. Rowse asserts that certain consumer topics are blacklisted—in fact, if not formally. The press will avoid an issue dealing with an important advertiser as long as possible. News about automobile safety moved off the "verboten list" not because of a surge of social conscience on the part of the editors, but because the issue had become too explosive to ignore. However, in 1966, Bell-McClure Syndicate offered serialization of Nader's *Unsafe at Any Speed* to 700 newspapers, but no paper bought the rights. When the issue can be avoided, it will be. By April, 1967, no major news outlet carried the information that eight major automobile tires failed to pass the minimum safety standards of the Rubber Manufacturers Association.[59]

In addition to suppression of news unfavorable to advertisers, several magazines perform services of a more positive nature. For example, during the supermarket boycotts in 1966, *Good Houskeeping* took out a full-page advertisement in the *New York Times* to present "an open letter to Mrs. America" praising the food industry and urging women to use "intelligence and fair play" before joining the boycott. In the same vein, *Good Housekeeping* columnist Charlotte Montgomery

[57] Senator Philip A. Hart, "Can Federal Legislation Affecting Consumers' Economic Interests be Enacted?" *Michigan Law Review* 64 (May, 1966): 1261.

[58] Arthur E. Rowse, "Consumer News: A Mixed Report," *Columbia Journalism Review* 6 (Spring, 1967): 27–33.

[59] Ibid., p. 30.

wrote a brochure opposing truth-in-packaging circulated by General Foods.[60]

However, this type of overly eager solicitude of advertisers by elements of the press is declining for two reasons. First, consumer protection issues are much more newsworthy than they were in the pre-Nader days. Secondly, the tactics of overt opposition sometimes backfired. In the opinion of staff members connected with the truth-in-packaging issue, the opposition kept the issue alive by publicizing it— even with unfavorable publicity. One staff member noted, "The opposition really kept the issue alive. Every time interest would die down, they would do something like Charlie Mortimer's article in *Look* and people would hear about truth-in-packaging. It was a simple issue, and the kind of thing people could see. . . . It was an easy thing to keep alive."

There are other, less venal, restraints on consumer representation by the press. Cater notes that there is a congressional bias to Washington news reporting.[61] Congress is both easier to cover and more newsworthy because of the ever-present conflict there. While legislative controversies over consumer issues may be covered, the progress of the consumer interest in the bureaucracy is much less frequently covered. The effect is that the press does not represent the consumer interest in the routine process of enforcing consumer protection regulations. Similarly, the criteria of newsworthiness reflected in many news stories may not be congruent with the important consumer interests at stake. There was a good deal of coverage of the release of the "Nader's Raiders" report on the FTC. However, most of the coverage focused on the report's charges of political partisanship, cronyism, and alcoholism. The detailed analysis of the FTC's failure to effectively represent the consumer interest was overshadowed by those more spectacular, and newsworthy charges. This problem of journalistic Gresham's law is not peculiar to consumer protection coverage.[62] However, it still lessens the useful feedback available to consumers and had the net effect of weakening the representative performance of the press.

---

[60] Ibid., p. 32.

[61] Cater, *Fourth Branch,* p. 47.

[62] E.g., Cater notes that "the net effect of . . . publicity brouhahas has been to divert the public's attention from the underlying ills in government which need legislative attention." *The Fourth Branch,* p. 64.

Function of the Private Sector
in the Representational Process

At this point, we turn from a separate examination of the activities of the various nongovernmental consumer activists and consider them as elements of a system. Viewing consumer representation as a system, the question is what is the role of each element in the total system. In order to delineate their roles, it is first necessary to assess their performance—the effectiveness with which they influence policy.

Effectiveness

For purposes of comparison, a brief look at the effectiveness of private-interest group lobbyists is instructive. Milbrath found that lobbyists judged their own success quite highly.[63] However, the two most detailed recent empirical studies of lobbyists take issue with the lobbyists' perception of their contribution and with the popular stereotype of lobbyists successfully manipulating the levers of government. In his assessment of the influence of lobbyists Milbrath concludes:

> The weight of the evidence . . . suggests that there is relatively little influence or power in lobbying *per se*. There are many forces in addition to lobbying which influence public policy; in most cases these other forces clearly outweigh the impact of lobbying. Voters set the broad trends of public policy which all the other influences on policy must follow.[64]

In a brilliant study of the politics of foreign trade, Bauer, Pool, and Dexter reach a similar assessment of the power of lobbying:

> [Our study] tends to cast doubt on the stereotype of pressure politics, of special interests effectively expressing themselves and forcing politicians either to bow to their dictates or to fight back vigorously. Our presentation of the Congressman as one who is part of a transactional process, who can himself signal what communications he wants, and who has a good deal of latitude in those which he heeds is not precisely in accord with the stereotyped picture.[65]

[63] Milbrath, *Lobbyists,* p. 138.

[64] Ibid., p. 354.

[65] Bauer, Pool, and Dexter, *Business and Public Policy,* p. 484.

The effectiveness of consumer groups was judged by their reputation among governmental consumer activists as elicited in open-ended interviews. While this reputational method of assessing influence in policy is subject to criticism by political scientists,[66] I would argue that such an approach is appropriate here. As noted throughout the preceding pages, we are dealing with a small universe whose actors are well known to each other. The assessments of influence were made not by third parties but by participants whose behavior the consumer groups sought to influence. Furthermore, being allies they would have no reason to underrate the relative influence of other consumer activists. In any case, no pretention is made of an absolutely precise measure of influence. Within the bounds of practicality and available information, however, reasonably accurate assessments of influence can be made.

The primary consumer groups were judged as quite ineffective until recently, and they are now considered moderately useful to legislative consumer activists. This usefulness rests in their ability to reach a wide audience of consumer-oriented local groups and to generate mail directed toward Congress. This is not to suggest that they can direct anywhere near the volume of mail mounted by organizations such as the National Rifle Association or the American Medical Association, but where there was previously no supporting mail, now at least there is some. Consumer activists do not regard this as crucial, but useful. While they have some externally based influence, the primary groups lack the internal influence to affect the shape of legislation or administrative actions.

Labor unions are more influential, and this influence is based on perceptions of their power in electoral politics. However, since the AFL-CIO generally does not get onto a consumer bill until it is already moving through the legislative mill, their influence is in the nature of adding to the sum total of political "clout" applied and is usually not in the shaping of policy.

It must be remembered that this judgment is made by consumer activists involved in federal legislation and applies only to the effectiveness of consumer groups in influencing federal policy. Since the Consumer Federation of America was designed to service state organiza-

66 See Nelson Polsby, *Community Power and Political Theory* (New Haven: Yale University Press, 1963).

tions and not actively lobby in Congress, its lack of effectiveness does not represent a failure to achieve organizational goals. Furthermore, no judgment is made regarding the CFA's effectiveness in the state and local scene—a subject which is beyond the scope of this study.

In the Executive Branch, most of the respondents interviewed were not themselves pursuing new programs or policy changes. Their function was not one which lends itself to a judgment of the effectiveness of groups. However, those bureaucrats in higher policy-making positions tended to share the assessment of the congressional consumer activists—consumer groups have little if any effectiveness in influencing policy.

An entirely different picture emerges in considering Ralph Nader's effectiveness. Among all respondents who had contact with Nader or who worked in policy areas in which he was involved, there was unanimous agreement that he did have an influence on policy. His effectiveness is based primarily on two factors. First is the publicity he brings to bear on an issue. He is influential because he creates public awareness. Secondly, even before an issue is publicized, Nader's involvement creates a situation which other participants expect to be publicized. His potential for publicity is thus a factor in his influence. Particularly on bills involving safety, Nader's involvement has "put the heat" on other participants, forcing them to act favorably on the measures in question when they otherwise might not have done so. Usually, it was not so blunt a situation. There are degrees of support, and Nader's involvement was frequently cited as a reason why a particular measure received high priority. This was true both in Congress and in the bureaucracy.

Generally, it is easier to make a clear assessment of influence in Congress and the legislative aspect of policy formation than in the bureaucracy. The legislative process culminates in the passage of legislation in which the gains and losses of the participants can easily be seen. Administration is a continuing process in which few decisions are final and where decisions are more numerous and less visible. Thus, an overall evaluation of the effectiveness of the public-interest lawyers whose target is the bureaucracy is both difficult and, more importantly, premature. Not until several years after this book appears can a realistic "score card" of the impact of these activists be drawn. For the present, the best preliminary indications of their influence is the success of specific efforts in court which indicate a high degree of initial success. In *Wilderness Society* v. *Hickel,* lawyers from the Center for Law and Social Policy sued in federal district court to enjoin the secretary of the interior from issuing permits for the construction of the Trans-Alaskan Pipeline System and obtained a preliminary injunction based on the National Environmental Policy Act of 1969. The center scored a major victory in *Environmental Defense Fund et al.* v. *Hardin* in which the center on behalf of the Environmental Defense Fund, the Sierra Club, the National Audubon Society, and others filed a petition with the secretary of agriculture urging him to suspend the use of DDT in the United States. The secretary of agriculture took action which was substantially less limiting than this and the center lawyers filed a petition for review in the circuit court of appeals. The government filed a motion to dismiss on jurisdictional grounds. In May, 1970, the court decided all the jurisdictional points in favor of the environmental groups and recognized their standing to bring suit. The opinion establishes the right of greater citizen participation in federal pesticide regulation. In *Nader* v. *Volpe,* mentioned earlier, a center lawyer representing Ralph Nader and others filed a motion for a preliminary injunction to require the Department of Transportation to reopen a proceeding in which General Motors agreed to replace only 50,000 of 200,000 allegedly defective truck wheels. The court rejected the government's contention that the matter was left to administrative discretion and held that the consumer plaintiffs did have standing. The case was remanded back to the National Highway Safety Bureau.

These cases are significant not only as examples of success in specific substantive issues but more so because of the precedents they established. The primary administrative objective of all the public-interest lawyers is to open administrative actions to greater public participation and to require that the views of citizens outside the regulated industry be heard in the exercise of administrative discretion. This is the real importance of *Environmental Defense Fund* v. *Hardin.* Thus, the real measure of success is not wins and losses in court but permanently changed administrative procedures. It is still too early to measure that, but the trend appears to be in favor of the goals sought by the public-interest lawyers.

The press was unanimously considered effective. The most influential consumer reporters were considered to be the late Drew

Pearson and Morton Mintz. While there is a wide chasm between the reputations of the two men for veracity, nonetheless everyone read Drew Pearson and they believed that he was read by the "folks back home." It is sometimes difficult to separate the influence of the press from that of Nader because as noted earlier, Nader works largely through the press. Congressional activists especially stress the importance of publicity in consumer protection matters. Those who work on less "sexy" issues such as antitrust policy bemoan the lack of news coverage and partially attribute their lack of success to the dearth of publicity.

A typical example of the way in which the press has effectively influenced policy is the passage of the Wholesome Poultry Act (PL 90–492). After the House had passed the administration's poultry inspection bill in June, 1968, the Senate Agriculture Committee held hearings on four poultry bills. Senator Spessard Holland succeeded in getting through committee an amendment to exempt from federal inspection meat and poultry in *inter*state commerce which was produced in states which had inspection standards equal to federal standards. Since an Agriculture Department study had already shown state enforcement procedures to be extremely lax, this was a weakening amendment of the grossest sort. When the amended bill reached the floor, Morton Mintz and Nick Kotz gave the legislative fight extensive press coverage. Once the amendment had been publicized as one which threatened to release millions of pounds of diseased meat and poultry into commerce, the amendment became totally untenable. It was eliminated on the floor by a 52–19 roll call vote.

In this as in other instances of press influence, it cannot be said that the press "caused" a particular result, both because causation cannot be so precisely assigned and because other participants were actively seeking the same result. However, influence does not require absolute power to obtain a result different from what otherwise would have occurred. Rather, the press as one among several groups of participants made its unique contribution. The contribution consisted of the arousal of public opinion and it was one of the important elements leading to the defeat of the amendment.

Although the press is regarded as effective, it is also regarded as falling far short of its potential effectiveness. There is simply an insufficient amount of coverage—coverage which does not match the magnitude of the problem. This is a judgment made not only by students of the press,[67] but shared uniformly by consumer activists.

In assessing the influence of Ralph Nader and the press, consumer activists implicitly assume that there is power in public opinion and that Nader and the press can alter public opinion. Whether these assumptions are true or not is beside the point. Inasmuch as the behavior of participants is affected by these assumptions, they have the effect of being true. Furthermore, the judgment these participants have of the effectiveness of other participants is extremely significant because their own behavior is, by admission, altered by those judgments. It is thus a reinforcing cycle. The political resources of Ralph Nader and the press include their past effectiveness—or the belief that they have been effective in the past. The more they use their political resources effectively the greater these resources become. Similarly, the odds are weighed against the consumer groups because of their lack of effective influence in the past.

Function in the System

We come now to a consideration of the roles played by the nongovernmental participants in the total process of representing the consumer interest. We are concerned here with the particular niche filled by each group based on its activities and interrelationships.

Having determined that primary consumer groups are not effective by their own actions, can it be said that they are therefore useless? Far from it. These groups provide a legitimating function which is particularly important in the case of a diffuse interest. Their support bolsters the claims of others to be acting on behalf of the consumer interest. For example, in an argument against the Uniform Consumer Credit Code, House Banking and Currency Committee Chairman Wright Patman wrote, "Contrary to the implication of your editorial, I do not know of a single consumer organization that is supporting the Uniform Code. None has contacted me. And I do know that large consumer organizations, like the Consumer Federation of America, are adamantly opposed."[68]

---

[67] Rowse, "Consumer News," pp. 29–30.

[68] Letter to the Editor, *Washington Post,* March 23, 1969.

Insofar as the labor unions are effective, they provide a resource-mobilizing function. They add to the overall political "clout" of the other participants. The primary consumer groups add finesse to that "clout" by cloaking other activists with the mantle of the public interest. Their function is thus analogous to that of blue ribbon advisory commissions. They have no real power in the conventional sense, but their existence adds legitimacy to the rhetoric of other participants.[69]

Ralph Nader's function is not so clear-cut or one-dimensional. He is a central contact point for a variety of people including consumer activists, the press, and citizens. More than anyone else, he is at the center of a shifting coalition of consumer activists seeking consumer protection through governmental action. A second role is as amplifier of issues. He takes phenomena defined as problems and lifts them to the point where they become political issues—a larger public becomes aware of the problems and governmental participants feel pressures to take action on the problem. These two functions are not wholly unique to Nader. They are the result of activities in which he is more successful than others. Basically these functions emerge from the same approach to the policy process taken by the traditional consumer groups. They were Nader's original orientation and the path toward success. However, more recently Nader has assumed a third function which is more divergent from the general mode of activity of the traditional groups. The third function is direct participation in the policy process.

Direct participation is also the primary function of the public-interest lawyers and, therefore, they and Ralph Nader can be considered together in this regard. Where the traditional groups relied on political means to *persuade* governmental participants to take particular actions, the direct-action lawyers utilize legal means to *compel* them to take those actions. The functions performed by the traditional groups and Nader's traditional functions are all political functions or functions necessary for the indirect exercise of influence. Instead of creating and mobilizing resources from outside the network of decision-making elites (e.g., public opinion), the new consumer groups manipulate resources within this network in ways which compel the decision makers to take certain actions. Their function is perceived to be necessary largely be-

[69] See, for example, Michael Lipsky and David J. Olson, "The Politics of Riot Commissions," *Trans-action* 6 (July, 1969): 8–21.

cause if left alone the decision makers would not be sufficiently responsive to the consumer constituency represented by the direct-action consumer groups. Thus there are two aspects to their direct participation function. First, they act as direct representatives and participants in the policy process. While they cannot legally compel an offending corporation to take specific action, they can, through the courts, compel a government agency to compel that corporation to take the desired action. A second, closely related, aspect is that of auxiliary (and usually unwanted) law enforcement. They act to fill the consumer interest side of the adversary process when they perceive that nominally responsible government officials are not discharging that responsibility.

Two qualifications must be added before concluding this assessment of the new consumer groups. First, the division of functions between the traditional and the new activists is not as sharp as is suggested by the requirements of orderly analysis. Indeed, increasingly the traditional groups are themselves plaintiffs in legal actions in which they are represented by the new public-interest lawyers. Second, the new groups have not disregarded the importance of outside political support and do not work in a vacuum. Persuading officials and appealing to public opinion are perceived as being necessary but not sufficient conditions for representing the consumer interest. Their function as direct participants is simply perceived as a more effective means of representing consumer interests in one area of the policy process where public support already exists.

Returning to the traditional indirect and persuasive techniques, the most important and extensive function is reserved for the press. In examining the activities of the press as discussed above, it can be seen that the press plays three roles in the representational system. First, it is the transmitter of the public record. The public's knowledge of government hearings and reports comes not from any perusal of those awesome tomes, but from reports in the media. And it is the public record which comprises most press reports. Consequently, the determination of which parts of the public record are truly public is made primarily by the press.

Secondly, the press is the creator and exploiter of scandal. As the thalidomide episode shows, crises in consumer protection do not just appear spontaneously. They nearly always require the initiative of the press. These crises or scandals do not exist in a vacuum; rather, they are indicative of larger problems. The deeper aspect of this second role is the press's function of giving symbolic meaning to an extensive consumer problem via the explosive crises. Thus, the callousness of the automobile manufacturers was symbolized by General Motors' harrassment of Ralph Nader.

The third role stems from the sources used in gathering the news. This function is "ventilator" of the bureaucracy. The press serves as the conduit through which some bureaucrats release information suppressed by other bureaucrats. In so doing the press fulfills its cherished role as "public defender" by keeping the bureaucracy honest and diligent.[70] As a result, the normal hierarchical power relationships are short circuited. Bureaucrats whose policy preferences are vetoed by their superiors can by-pass those superiors through the press and appeal directly to the public. By bringing information to the public which forces a policy change, the lower-ranking bureaucrats exhibit more power than their superiors who would have preferred the status quo. The press thus functions as transposer of power relationships within the bureaucracy.

The three roles of the press combine to form its essential function in representing the consumer interest. A key blockage point to consumers perceiving and pursuing their own interests are the information costs involved. Both Anthony Downs and Mancur Olson demonstrate that it is irrational for consumers to invest the energy necessary to obtain the information necessary to influence policy relating to their role as consumers. Only in their role as producers, be it as businessmen or laborers, can the payoff make the investment be worthwhile.[71] However, the press overcomes this blockage point in certain instances by functioning as a "wholesaler" of information costs. Even though their criteria may be questioned, reporters, as part of their producer function, select a small amount of information from the mountains of data available, and present it in digested form to the public (in their role as

[70] David Broder, "Political Reporters in Presidential Politics," *Washington Monthly,* February, 1969, pp. 32–33. Broder points out that one of reporters' favorite self-images is that of public defender.

[71] Anthony Downs, *An Economic Theory of Democracy* (New York: Harper & Row, 1961), pp. 238–256; Mancur Olson, *The Logic of Collective Action* (Cambridge: Harvard University Press, 1965).

consumers) who have then invested only minimal information costs. Having had the information costs invested for them, the public is free to proceed from there and attempt to influence policy. The press can thus activate a potential constituency into an active one. Vague dissatisfactions can become activated as an issue gains saliency through news stories.

Furthermore, because of the way the press operates, the presentation of issues in the press is likely to prompt public response. Although the criteria of newsworthiness are vague, reporters try to sense what the public will find most interesting in a situation, and they tend to report dramatic issues. Thus, the same factors which make a story newsworthy make it likely that consumers will respond. Whether they do so or not is another question. The important point is that the press helps to eliminate an important obstacle which previously limited the influence of consumers on public policy.

In assessing the function of the nongovernmental sector as a whole, it is useful to carry forth Schattschneider's distinction between private-interest groups and public-interest groups, and, considering consumer groups as a species of the latter, contrast the function of the two types. There is a common thread which runs throughout the studies of private-interest groups. The basic function of these groups is to inform the government of their policy preferences and the intensity and extensiveness of those preferences. Indeed, Charles Lindblom bases his analysis of democracy on the argument that only through competing interests can proper weight be assigned to differing interests.[72] The private-interest groups know their interests and seek governmental action favorable to those interests.[73] Being aware themselves, they set out to make the government aware. Furthermore, they seek to limit entry to the decision-making arena. As was pointed out by Bachrach and Baratz, private-interest groups with claims currently being recognized by the government suffer losses when competing claims are even put

[72] Charles Lindblom, *The Intelligence of Democracy* (New York: Free Press, 1965).

[73] While Bauer, Pool, and Dexter found that businessmen did not always correctly assess their self-interest, it is nonetheless true that they were generally aware that the foreign trade issue would affect their economic interest in some way and most of them did indeed act in congruence with their self-interest. *Business and Public Policy*, p. 129.

on the agenda for government decision.[74] Opening the decision-making arena can only reduce the impact of their own claims and increase the probability that competing claims will produce a result less favorable to one's own claims.

The public-interest groups (and all groups pursuing public interests) also perform an informational function but the direction is different. Instead of informing the government, they inform the public. They seek to create awareness in the public of the public's self-interest. Let us return to the distinction drawn between the two aspects of representation presented at the beginning of this chapter—the agency role and the constituency expansion role. These can be represented as polar tendencies at each end of a continuum. The representational focus of various groups can be depicted along this continuum as is done in Figure 1.

Figure 1

	Trade Associations	Consumer Groups	Press	
Agency (Represent Known Interests				**Constituency Expansion** (Create New Interests)

It can be seen that all consumer-oriented groups tend toward the constituency expansion end of the continuum. Drawing on the material presented earlier in the chapter, Figure 2 places the consumer groups themselves on such a continuum in greater detail.

Figure 2

	Traditional Consumer Groups	Labor Unions	Public Interest Law	Ralph Nader et al.	Press	
Agency (Represent Known Interests)						**Constituency Expansion** (Create New Interests)

[74] Peter Bachrach and Morton Baratz, "Two Faces of Power," *American Political Science Review* LVI (December, 1962): 947–952.

Recalling the evidence presented a few pages earlier, the reader should notice that the position of consumer groups on this representational continuum corresponds to their perceived effectiveness. The ones who are most effective (in influencing policy) are those on the opinion creation end of the continuum as was suggested at the outset of this chapter.

The reasons for the effectiveness of the opinion-creating consumer activists do not lie in abstract notions about the necessity in a democracy of an informed citizenry. Information is only a means toward an end. In this case, the end is the widening of the scope of conflict. The importance of the scope of conflict was concisely stated by E. E. Schattschneider and forms the basis of his theory of political conflict.[75] Schattschneider posits two propositions:

> The first proposition is that the outcome of every conflict is determined by the extent to which the audience becomes involved in it. That is, the outcome of all conflict is determined by the scope of its contagion. The number of people involved in any conflict determines what happens; every change in the number of participants, every increase or reduction in the number of participants affects the result. . . .
>
> The second proposition is a consequence of the first. The most important strategy of politics is concerned with the scope of conflict.[76]

The position taken by contestants on the scope of conflict depends on their relative position. The most powerful "special interests" want private settlements involving a limited number of participants. The weaker interests seek outside intervention in the hope that a wider scope of conflict will redress the balance and alleviate their previous lack of power.

> In the school yard it is not the bully, but the defenseless smaller boys who "tell the teacher." When the teacher intervenes the balance of power in the school yard is apt to change drastically. It is in the function of public authority to *modify private power relations by enlarging the scope of conflict*. (Emphasis in the original.)[77]

[75] E. E. Schattschneider, *The Semisovereign People,* especially pp. 1–46.

[76] Ibid., pp. 2–3.

[77] Ibid., p. 40. Also see, Grant McConnell, *Private Power and American Democracy* (New York: Alfred A. Knopf, 1967). McConnell argues that limited constituencies permit the existence of a series of elite-based power structures.

A good example of this function in consumer protection is the automobile safety case. Until 1965, decisions relating to automobile design were made by a relatively small group of people. Considerations of passenger and pedestrian safety could, with impunity, be treated lightly. In both industry and government there was a small tightly-knit automobile safety "establishment" that effectively insulated automobile design from being considered a safety hazard. Occasional critics of automobile design in and out of the industry were unable to have any influence under those circumstances.[78] The situation was changed only when Ralph Nader was successful in widening the arena of controversy. In doing so, he made a large number of people aware that there was a controversy. The number of people concerned about automobile design increased from a handful to a large segment of the public. The controversy took an entirely different shape. The widened scope was then institutionalized with the enactment of legislation and the permanent interjection of public authority.

So far the discussion has centered on public opinion and has seemingly not included the new tactics of direct participation. But a review of the new consumer activists reveals that they have the same constituency-broadening function and simply a different means of executing that function. In approaching government agencies as direct participants, they seek to open a channel for public (consumer interests or environmental interests) input. As public-interest groups, they seek collective benefits extending far beyond the welfare of the individual participants. Similarly, the participation they seek in agency proceedings is not for themselves as individuals but as representatives of a wider public. Behind every substantive action the precedent of independent representation of the "public interest" in that policy area is sought as an equal benefit. The public-interest lawyers interviewed were unanimous in stating that their ultimate long-range objective was to increase public participation in the administration of public policy.

Just as the traditional groups widen the scope of conflict by making private issues into public ones, so the direct-action groups achieve the same result. That is, when a regulatory agency is "captured" or at least is highly solicitous of the regulated industry, the dealings between

---

[78] Ralph Nader, *Unsafe at Any Speed* (New York: Grossman, Pocket Books, 1965), pp. 175–221.

regulator and regulated become, in effect, private dealings. Rather than public enforcement of the law, public policy is the result of a series of quid pro quo arrangements shielded from outside scrutiny. The new consumer groups seek to widen the scope of conflict and create a public constituency for these agencies. Thus it is probable that public policy outcomes will change by increasing the number of participants and the number of options with which decision makers must deal.

We can now restate the principal representational function of nongovernmental consumer activists. The function is to affect consumer opinion so as to widen the arena in which decisions affecting consumer welfare are made. Consumers are large numerically but inherently weak in each of the whole range of product and service areas. The consumer activists widen the scope temporarily by making consumers aware of conflicts which potentially affect them and widen the scope permanently by creating government regulation where none existed previously and by making public those regulatory proceedings that would otherwise be private.

chapter 6

Consumer Protection: Costs and Benefits

In the preceding chapters, consumer protection was presented as an issue which differed only according to the goods and services to which particular policies applied. In analyzing the activities of consumer activists, other aspects of consumer protection policy were held constant. However, viewing consumer protection from a different perspective, it is clear that consumer issues differ along another dimension —the scope of interests which are involved in particular consumer issues. Some consumer issues deal with collective values—aspects of consumption in which every person in the country has a nearly equal interest. These are primarily the health and safety issues which affect citizens at every income level nearly equally. While the poor may eat more food of the type that is amenable to food poisoning, both rich and poor are equally sick when they get food poisoning. While auto safety may seem to apply more to upper income families with more cars, a lower income person is just as likely to be the pedestrian fatality of faulty auto brakes. In short, this type of consumer issue deals with defects in the marketplace which affect all consumers in approximately the same way.

The second type of consumer issue involves widely shared values but deals with abuses whose impact varies with income. Basically, these issues revolve around the cruel irony that "the poor pay more."[1] Lower income people are more susceptible to fraud, are more likely to be defrauded, and can least afford it. Indeed, abuses against consumers in low-income areas are not only a symptom of poverty but actually intensify that poverty by causing wasted expenditures of income. It is not only outright fraud which disproportionately affects lower income people. Any consumer problem which results in artificially higher prices does the most harm to the poor and can be termed a differential problem.

The distinction between consumer issues can be seen by the example of the continuing controversy surrounding regulation of prescription drugs. Drug safety is a completely collective issue affecting all income levels equally. On the other hand, high drug prices represent a comparatively small problem above a certain income level; however, the bite of those prices is differential and increases as income level decreases.

Having stated the dimension on which consumer issues differ, the next step is to go beyond the categorization of issues to examine the implications of this dichotomy in terms of both government process and policy. Specifically, the remainder of this chapter will examine the relation of the type of consumer policy to the allocation of costs and benefits of policy and also to the intensity of opposition.

The Allocation of
Costs and Benefits

The dichotomy of consumer problems leads directly to the same dichotomy in consumer protection policy—a dichotomy based on the benefits conferred upon consumers by the policy. Policies which seek to correct collective problems are policies with collective benefits and policies which deal with problems which affect consumers unequally are differential benefit policies. In the example of prescription drugs,

---

[1] See David Caplowitz, *The Poor Pay More: Consumer Practices of Low Income Families* (New York: Free Press, 1963). In this classic study, Caplowitz found that the poor paid more not only proportionately but in absolute amount for credit and merchandise.

drug safety legislation is a collective benefit policy whereas antitrust action aimed at reducing costs is a policy which confers widely shared, but differential benefits.

As noted above, collective benefit policy deals primarily with health and safety problems. In terms of specific policy, this generally takes the form of regulatory legislation which requires the licensing and supervision of certain activities (such as operating clinical laboratories), the inspection of certain facilities and products (meat inspection), or prescribing safety standards for a variety of manufactured products (automobiles, textiles). In general, this legislation places specific restraints on businesses and expands the participation of the government in private economic life.

Regulatory legislation, however, does not exhaust the possibilities of collective benefit legislation. Some policies may be termed "self-regulatory" in which the group nominally being regulated is more benefited than restrained by its own system of control.[2] Consumers receive fewer benefits from this system of regulation, and those benefits are usually collective. Thus, self-imposed safety standards for products benefit all consumers while at the same time benefiting producers by alleviating the threat of more rigid and protective governmental standards. The benefits are still collective; they are simply on a lesser order. Other collective benefit policies may confer few, if any, benefits on anyone. These are policies representing deferred decisions—primarily the establishment of government study commissions. No restraints are placed on anybody and consumers receive no direct benefits. Everybody is equally unaffected, although consumers may assume they are receiving governmental benefits.[3]

Differential benefit policy can be primarily of two kinds. The first is aimed at specific abuses which fall with disproportionate weight upon those with low incomes. This can range all the way from requiring true disclosure of credit costs (truth-in-lending) to making certain kinds of frauds into federal felonies.

---

[2] Robert H. Salisbury, "The Analysis of Public Policy: A Search for Theories and Roles," in *Political Science and Public Policy,* ed. Austin Ranney (Chicago: Markham, 1968), p. 158.

[3] Murray Edelman, *The Symbolic Uses of Politics* (Urbana: University of Illinois Press, 1964), pp. 23–29.

The second kind of policy aims at the more generalized abuses stemming from conditions which create artificially higher costs for retail goods and services across entire industries. These abuses result from anti-competitive tendencies in the economy and the policy typically put forth to curb these forces is antitrust policy. Such policy is differential to the extent that monopoly and (more typically) oligopoly result in higher prices which disproportionately disadvantages those with low incomes.[4] Furthermore, such policy at the present time would not simply prevent differential abuses, but would confer differential benefits. This is not inherent in the nature of antitrust policy; rather, it is due to the fact that such policy at the present time is not designed to *maintain* competition—it is too late for that—but to *restore* competition. This study takes it as axiomatic that the corporate marketplace is far less competitive than official corporate ideology and pronouncements state. While there are degrees of competition running from free market through oligopoly to monopoly, if one had to state only whether or not the present economy was competitive in the classical sense (competition by price and quality), one would certainly say that the market was not competitive. To develop and prove this assertion would occupy a separate volume. For the skeptical reader, I can only cite sources which develop this theme in greater detail than is possible here.[5] By restoring competition, antitrust policy would adversely affect oligopolists by depriving them of the benefits they received from the condition of oligopoly. Conversely, it would redistribute those benefits to the victims of oligopoly—the consumers.

Having related policy types to policy benefits, we can proceed to

---

[4] For a concise analysis of monopoly and antitrust policy, see Paul A. Samuelson, *Economics,* 8th ed. (New York: McGraw-Hill, 1970), pp. 459–509.

[5] The most comprehensive recent source material on the decline of competition is U.S., Congress, Senate, Select Committee on Small Business, *Planning, Regulation and Competition: Automobile Industry: 1968. Hearings before Subcommittees of The Select Committee on Small Business, on The Question: Are Planning and Regulation Replacing Competition in the American Economy? (The Automobile Industry as a Case Study),* 90th Cong., 2nd sess., 1968. A shorter and more readable treatment of the same subject is Senator Estes Kefauver, *In A Few Hands: Monopoly Power in America* (Baltimore: Pantheon, 1965). Also see John Kenneth Galbraith, *The New Industrial State* (New York: Houghton Mifflin Co., 1967), and Samuelson, *Economics.*

relate these two together to policy success and then to intensity of opposition. Policy success is shown in Table 6–1 which lists the enacted legislation by policy type. The chart tells a rather unmistakable story. Nearly all the legislation confers collective benefits. This does not mean, of course, that much of this legislation is unimportant or that it does not correct major abuses. It is not the worth of the legislation that is at issue here. Rather, this pattern is significant because of three points it demonstrates about power relationships and the economy.

Table 6–1   New Consumer Protection Legislation 1960–1970

Collective Benefit	Differential Benefit
Postal Fraud	Consumer Credit Protection
Flammable Fabrics	Fair Labeling (truth-in-packaging)
Wholesome Meat	Interstate Land Sales
Clinical Laboratories Licensing	Federal Deposit Insurance Act
Poultry Inspection	Amendment (unsolicited credit
Radiation Control	card prohibition and credit bureau
Automobile Safety	regulation)
Natural Gas Pipeline Safety	
1962 Drug Amendments	
Food Marketing Commission	
Automobile Insurance Study	
Fire Safety Research	
National Commission on	
Product Safety	
Poison Prevention Packaging	
Toy Safety	

First, lower-income people have a greater total need for consumer protection than higher-income people. While these lower-income people benefit equally from collective benefit policy, they have a greater need for a differential benefit policy. However, the actual policy outcome is, from this point of view, regressive. The citizens with the greatest needs are granted relief only to the extent that such relief is equally beneficial to all citizens. The benefit is distributed regressively. Furthermore, inasmuch as the costs of collective consumer protection benefits are passed on to consumers, lower-income consumers are paying a regressive (i.e., uniform) "tax" for the benefit when the costs are assessed equally.

Consumer protection policy as a whole always had the potential of having spill-over benefits to affect the "War on Poverty." In fact, it fell far short of that potential and manifested itself as an entirely different policy type. In general, income-related consumer problems were given short shrift in favor of problems of secondary importance to those to whom economic survival is the first concern.

Secondly, although this legislation was billed as heralding a new era of consumerism, it actually did nothing of the kind. It increased the obligations of sellers to buyers, but did not substantially alter preexisting power relationships between corporations and consumers. The legislation placed minimal restraints on sellers. Although the collective benefit legislation which was enacted requires either government specification of product standards or inspection of manufacturing processes, it merely alters the conditions in which business is done without altering the advantages of the seller over the buyer. For example, it can not be seriously argued that requiring automobile manufacturers to install specified safety devices imposes any greater burden on them than is imposed by their own voluntary nonfunctional style changes which necessitate a retooling anyway. As of this writing, no legislation has yet been passed which changes the nearly powerless position of the purchaser of a "lemon" vis a vis General Motors.[6] He is safer, but G.M. has not suffered any loss of economic power. Furthermore, part of the pattern of restraints is the system of sanctions used to maintain those restraints. Proposals to enforce consumer protection laws with criminal penalties have generally failed. While such penalties may not have concretely benefited consumers, they would represent a significant reallocation of societal sanctions and deference values by treating corporate executives who break the law in the same manner as we common folk are treated. Viewed from this perspective, the total pattern of restraints which actually were established was quite mild.

The importance of the collective benefit policy which was passed can be seen not only by the type of policy it is, but by the type it is not. Differential benefit policies usually tend to alter economic power rela-

---

[6] For practical advice on this problem, see Ralph Nader, Lowell Dodge, and Ralf Hotchkiss, *What To Do With Your Bad Car* (New York: Grossman, 1971).

tionships. This occurs because the perpetrator of the economic abuse being corrected had previously been able to extract a higher economic toll from those who could least afford it and who were least prepared to defend themselves. A differential benefit policy alters this power relationship by using the power of the state to compensate for this weakness of the economically disadvantaged. In the case of fraudulent sales practices, government intervention disadvantages the fraudulent operator at the same time that such intervention confers benefits on the potential victim. Even in the case of large industries whose revenues are not dependent on exploiting the poor, a policy which confers economic benefits, such as preventing artificially higher prices, also increases the economic power of the poor by decreasing the chances that they will suffer the modern serfdom attendant upon such practices as garnishment, repossession, and eviction.

Of all differential consumer protection policies, antitrust policies would furnish the most comprehensive alteration of power by restoring competition to the marketplace and thus providing a self-regulating system of protection for consumers. Such policies, however, have not been forthcoming. To the extent that collective benefit policies rather than differential benefit policies are enacted, the fundamental imbalance of power between consumers and producers is maintained. The balance of power as a means of reducing uncertainty is an important consideration for corporations, and it has been argued that its maintenance is the prime objective of corporate management.[7] Thus, corporate management has not suffered impairment of its prime objective as a result of "consumerism."

Thirdly, and finally, although nearly all of this legislation was opposed by the industries it affects, almost none of it costs these industries any reduction of earnings or profits. Because it is mostly regulatory, costs of improved standards of performance are imposed across an entire industry. The costs are generally not great in the first instance, and these marginal costs can readily be passed on to consumers. An illustration of both the low cost and the ease of shifting these costs to the consumer is afforded by the case of the automobile industry. According to the Bureau of Labor Statistics the average retail price of a 1969 automobile increased by $41.00 over the previous model year.

[7] Galbraith, *New Industrial State*, pp. 166–179.

Quality improvements were worth $24.00 (but reduction in warranties cut the net improvement value to $1.00). Of this amount, only $4.00 was for changes in response to new or modified federal safety standards. An additional $10.00 in cost was for other safety changes in anticipation of future requirements or which were deemed desirable.[8] Thus, existing safety regulations cost only $4.00 per unit and total safety-related quality improvements were $14.00 per unit—costs which are passed on directly as part of a general price increase which far exceeds the net cost of improvements to the manufacturer.

Ironically, in spite of initial industry foreboding, consumer protection legislation may result in greater earnings. One example of this is the tire industry. As a result of a new safety consciousness among purchasers of replacement tires, premium tire sales increased while the sales of low-priced replacements dropped, with a resultant five percent increase in the median price of replacement tires in 1966.[9] Clearly, the consumer protection issue may not only be a negligible cost to producers, but may be a positive benefit instead.

Consumer protection legislation, like any regulatory legislation, may impose various "psychic costs" on newly regulated businessmen as Robert Lane pointed out,[10] but these costs are more easily borne when the realization sets in that the legislation will not be adversely reflected in the next earnings report. Furthermore, since material costs are generally shared by all members of an industry, passing them on not only prevents an absolute deprivation to the producer, but prevents any comparative disadvantage as well.[11]

---

[8] U.S. Department of Labor, Bureau of Labor Statistics, *Preliminary Report on Prices of New Passenger Cars,* Washington, D.C., October 7, 1968.

[9] *Wall Street Journal,* October 10, 1966, p. 6.

[10] Robert Lane, *The Regulation of Businessmen: Social Conditions of Government Economic Control* (New Haven: Yale University Press, 1954).

[11] There are two instances when regulation can impose substantial costs. First, if demand is highly elastic a price rise might reduce demand enough to adversely affect profits. Second, small firms may be unable to comply with fixed cost regulation and still remain competitive. In the first case, consumer legislation has not affected products where the demand was sufficiently elastic to reflect relatively minor price increases. Such elasticity is not a trait of oligopolistic industries anyway. In the second instance, it appears that only a few marginal meat packing plants have been economically unable to comply with new regulations.

Only in the case of differential benefit legislation are any costs borne by producers. The only consumer legislation of this nature might be the Consumer Credit Protection Act. Inasmuch as it requires uniform and truthful disclosure of annual interest rates (the truth-in-lending section), it should tend to impose costs on those elements of the installment credit and small loan industry which had previously enjoyed a comparative advantage to the extent that they engaged in misleading advertising and false statements of their interest charges. It is still too early to tell whether the legislation has increased competition and lowered costs in the consumer credit industry to the benefit of consumers. However, a story of similar legislation in Massachusetts suggests that this effect is not probable.[12] Nonetheless, the legislation effects a genuine alteration of economic and legal power relationships by limiting the garnishment of wages. It is the only consumer protection legislation which definitely contains so important a differential benefit.

The Locus of Opposition

It was stated earlier in this chapter that the policy outcome would be related to the intensity of the opposition. At this point, that assertion should be modified to mean successful intensity of opposition. So far we have only Galbraith's argument and the content of enacted legislation as evidence that the producers were successful in maintaining their prime goals intact. It remains to be seen whether this was indeed their actual objective and reflected the intensity of opposition. To that problem we now turn.

There are two ways to demonstrate that the relatively conservative legislative outcome of consumer protection reflected the intensity and power of industry opposition. The first is to look at a series of decisions and to examine original goals and the ultimate success in achieving those goals. This is basically the pluralist analysis of power—an analysis which requires that assessments of power be tied to specific decisions

[12] Robert Pullen, *The Impact of Truth-in-Lending Legislation* (Boston: Federal Reserve Bank of Boston, 1968).

affecting individuals or groups.[13] A novel alternative to this conception was offered by Peter Bachrach and Morton Baratz. According to their conception, power is not to be measured solely in terms of positive action toward one's objectives by victory in a controversy but also by one's ability to keep that controversy from surfacing in the first place. Achieving a "non-decision" in an area where Participant Smith has an interest in maintaining the status quo is as much a demonstration of power as if Smith had fought in a public controversy and won. Indeed it may indicate greater power. In the first instance, the danger was avoided completely. In the second, the issue was at least placed on the public agenda—already a result disquieting to those preferring the status quo.[14]

In the community power debate, these two approaches to power have been stated in opposition to each other. In the present context, however, they are complementary and lead to the same conclusion. First, the total policy outcome testifies to the power of non-decision. The enacted legislation on the whole does not even concern itself with the intensely opposed policies which sought to restore market competition. Indeed, proposed legislation which has not yet been passed follows the same pattern. It is not even considered. Thus, out of 94 separate consumer related proposals introduced but not passed in the 91st Congress, only one, providing for independent consumer class action law suits, proposed a direct alteration of economic power relationships between producers and consumers.[15] Furthermore, policy such as Ralph Nader's proposal that General Motors be broken up into its component divisions does not even reach the official policy-making agenda. Thus, in the Bachrach and Baratz model there is preliminary evidence for the successful exercise of power by producers. Indeed, this evidence is so pervasive it allows little room for viewing specific decisions—so few of them get on the agenda. However, two proposed differential policies

[13] See Robert Dahl, "The Concept of Power," *Behavioral Science,* 1957, pp. 201–215; and Nelson Polsby, *Community Power and Political Theory* (New Haven: Yale University Press, 1963).

[14] Peter Bachrach and Morton Baratz, "Two Faces of Power," *American Political Science Review* 56 (December, 1962): 947–952.

[15] A complete list may be found in the *Consumer Legislative Monthly Report* (Washington, D.C.: President's Committee on Consumer Interests, October 1, 1970).

which did get on the agenda demonstrate the same point while satisfy-ing the pluralist conception of power. The mutual reinforcement of the theories is seen even more vividly in the fact that these are the only additional times that policies to restore price competition reached the agenda.

The most important and persuasive of these cases is the Kefauver-Harris drug amendments of 1962. This case has already been discussed in Chapter 4, but there are two important points which should be re-stated in the present context. First, the general approach of the bill was shifted from drug prices to drug safety. The bill which originally would have been strongly redistributive by focusing on drug prices and would have conferred differential benefits weighted in favor of lower-income consumers was changed to a regulatory measure conferring collective benefits. Furthermore, this was not simply a coincidence. The economic provisions of the original bill were the sections most intensely opposed by the drug industry and their representatives in the Senate.[16]

A second bill which suffered a similar fate was the truth-in-packaging bill (S. 985) first introduced by Senator Philip Hart in 1962. As originally conceived and introduced, the purpose of the bill was to facilitate price and quantity comparison of retail grocery items by shoppers—in short, to introduce price competition in the supermarket. It was to accomplish these objectives by package size standardization which would allow a simple price comparison. This provision was eliminated from the bill and the substitute version merely allowed for voluntary limitation of a number of package sizes plus such minor features as prohibiting the use of qualifying adjectives before statements of quantity (e.g., ten jumbo ounces). Again, the result reflected the intensity of industry opposition. By general agreement on both sides, the standardization proposals were at the heart of the controversy and were the chief target of industry lobbyists.

The preceding examples have pointed out the focus and success of opposition on two particular measures. These examples are congruent with the general pattern of restraint in consumer protection. This can be seen in Table 6–2 which indicates the locus of congressional opposi-tion to consumer protection policy in terms of the percentage of mem-bers voting against the "pro-consumer" position on the twelve Senate

16 Richard Harris, *The Real Voice* (New York: Macmillan Co., 1964), p. 148. This book is an excellent case study of the 1962 drug legislation.

and four House nonunanimous roll call votes from 1962 through 1970.[17] Table 6–2 shows that opposition increases in proportion to

Table 6–2   Congressional Opposition to Consumer Protection Policy

Vote	"Anti-consumer" percentage
Senate	
AUTOMOBILE SAFETY—Amendment to have criminal penalties for violations of the proposed Traffic and Motor Vehicle Safety Act. Rejected 14–62 (1966).	82%
CONSUMER AGENCY—Amendment to strengthen the independence of the proposed Consumer Protection Agency. Rejected 24–51 (1970).	68
DRUGS—Motion to table Kefauver amendment imposing strict licensing requirements for drug patent holders. Passed 53–28 (1962).	65
GAS PIPELINE SAFETY—Amendment imposing criminal penalties for violations of proposed Natural Gas Pipeline Safety Act. Rejected 31–44 (1967).	59
DECEPTIVE SALES—Amendment to delete the provisions of the proposed Deceptive Sales Act which would allow the FTC to seek temporary restraining orders to prevent fraud. Passed 42–37 (1968).	53
GAS PIPELINE SAFETY—Amendment to proposed Natural Gas Pipeline Act to include gas gathering lines in the group to be regulated by the Department of Transportation. Passed 37–32 (1937).	46
AUTOMOBILE SAFETY—Amendment to eliminate the requirement of the proposed Traffic and Motor Vehicle Safety Act that patents and technology developed with federal aid by fully and freely available to the public. Rejected 35–43 (1966).	45

[17] The "pro-consumer" position is the one favored by congressional consumer activists who initially sponsored the legislation. Votes with at least 95 percent voting on one side are considered unanimous and therefore not included in this analysis.

Table 6–2—*Continued*

Vote	*"Anti-consumer"* percentage
PACKAGING—Amendment to delete voluntary weight and quantity standardization sections from the proposed Fair Labeling (truth-in-packaging) Act. Rejected 32–53 (1966).	38
PACKAGING—Motion to table "fair trade" amendment to Fair Labeling Act. Passed 51–29 (1966).	37
POULTRY—Amendment to Wholesome Poultry Act to eliminate committee language allowing poultry and meat processed under state inspection standards at least equal to federal standards to be shipped between states even though it had not been federally inspected. Passed 52–19 (1968).	27
PACKAGING—Motion to refer fair labeling bill to Judiciary Committee for further consideration. Rejected 19–64 (1966).	23
PACKAGING—Passage of Fair Labeling Act. Passed 72–9. (1966).	11

House

GAS PIPELINE SAFETY—Adoption of committee amendments lessening the regulatory authority given the Department of Transportation under the Senate-passed Natural Gas Pipeline Safety Act. Passed 247–125 (1968).	77
MEAT INSPECTION—Motion to instruct the House conferees to accept the Senate amendments to the Wholesome Meat Act (which were stronger than the House bill). Rejected 166–207 (1967).	56
PRODUCT SAFETY—Passage of resolution creating a National Commission on Product Safety. Passed 206–102 (1967).	33
MEAT INSPECTION—Adoption of conference report on Wholesome Meat Act. Passed 336–28 (1967).	7

the intensity and scope of the pro-consumer measure. The five Senate votes in which the anti-consumer percentage was greater than 50 percent were the most differential and the most restraining for business of all the issues being voted on. The differential benefits of the truth-in-packaging bill which received less opposition are of such a minimal amount and the bill as enacted was so innocuous that it makes no difference either in perception or implementation whether those benefits are differential.[18] In the House, the two most opposed votes were on proposals which would have increased governmental regulatory authority. Thus, the general pattern of opposition was one in which the most extensively opposed measures were those which were most limiting on the affected industry's freedom of action or which would have imposed real costs which could not be readily passed on to consumers.

Summary

Both a pattern of restraint in policy and a pattern of power have been shown in this chapter. The restraint is demonstrated by the pattern of policy which emerges—predominantly low restraint-collective benefit. The pattern of power is seen in the fact that, first, this policy is the least costly of the alternatives. Second, other alternatives were vigorously and successfully opposed. Third, this is confirmed by the opposition on congressional votes. Thus, both by the decisions that were made and by those that were not made, it can be seen that consumer protection legislation has been unsuccessful in challenging prevailing patterns of economic and political power. While policy need not be zero-sum to benefit consumers, in the cases when a zero-sum game was played (e.g., drug prices and truth-in-packaging) it is instructive to note that consumers lost. To date, these are the limits of consumer protection policy.

[18] See, for example, "What's Happened to Truth In Packaging?" *Consumer Reports* 24 (January, 1969): 40–43.

chapter 7

Representation and the Consumer Interest

The concept of representation has long been a concern of political theory. While it may be true that, "There does not even seem to be any remotely satisfactory agreement on what representation is or means,"[1] there is still a major theme uniting most of the work on representation —a theme which is at the center of debate. That theme is the relationship between the representative and the represented. The classic concern is whether a representative should cast his vote in faithful reflection of the opinions of his constituents or whether he should exercise his own judgment independently of those opinions. Professor Pitkin calls this concern the "mandate-independence controversy."[2] A variety of other formulations have developed such as how close a resemblance between representative and represented is required, e.g.,

[1] Hanna Pitkin, "The Concept of Representation," in *Representation,* ed. Hanna Pitkin (New York: Atherton Press, 1969), p. 7.

[2] Like many problems of political theory, this dichotomy has been illuminated by modern research which shows that in fact the representative is a relatively free agent who has trouble even knowing what his constituents want him to do. See, for example, Lewis Anthony Dexter, "The Representative and His District" in *New Perspectives on the House of Representatives,* ed. Robert Peabody, and Nelson Polsby (Chicago: Rand McNally, 1963), pp. 3–29.

should a legislature mirror the religious and racial composition of the total constituency. However, almost all analyses of the concept and practice of representation have revolved around the theme of the role of the representative vis a vis his constituents. The discussion has thus proceeded upon the implicit assumption that the representational function is carried on in a similar way in all policy areas. Even recent research has rested upon this assumption.[3]

An important exception to this trend was the study by Warren Miller and Donald Stokes of constituency influence in Congress.[4] They found differences in the congruence of roll call votes and constituency attitudes in the three policy areas they investigated: foreign affairs, social welfare, and civil rights. The most important predictive factor in a congressman's vote was his perception of constituency attitudes. The study is an important departure in that the representational role varies among policy areas. But the departure is still in keeping with the main theme of representation theory since it focuses on the behavior relationship between representative and represented.

Implicit in this study is an analysis of representation which borders on the Miller and Stokes study. While they differentiate between one policy area and another, they do not analyze the factors which account for the congruence or lack of congruence they find. Furthermore, their study proceeds in the context of concrete issues and policy areas. And, as noted above, the major theme is the relationship between representative and represented. This study is similar to their conceptual framework in recognizing the differences in policy areas, but it goes a step beyond by considering only the type of issue and passing over the relationship between representative and constituency. That is, the focus has been on the manner in which an interest of all citizens has been represented rather than on the manner in which particular groups of citizens have had all their interests represented.

---

[3] For example, Wahlke et al. differentiate representational roles (delegate, trustee, politico) according to party and constituency characteristics without reference to issue differences. John Wahlke, Heinz Eulau, William Buchanan, and LeRoy Ferguson, *The Legislative System: Explorations in Legislative Behavior* (New York: John Wiley & Sons, 1962).

[4] Warren Miller and Donald Stokes, "Constituency Influence in Congress," *American Political Science Review* 57 (1963): pp. 45–56.

In the preceding chapters we have already analyzed the actions of selected governmental and nongovernmental participants with the concept of representation being an implicit theme. The purpose of this concluding chapter is to make that theme explicit by reviewing the findings of the preceding chapters in the context of the concept of representation of a particular type of interest in the formation of public policy.

General Problems of the Consumer Interest

Diffusion

The first feature of the consumer interest is its diffusiveness. The consumer interest is an objective interest of the entire public; it is a widely shared or collective value depending on the benefits it confers. It is a public interest or a part of the public interest depending on one's conception of the term. Thus, it is similar to other diffuse interests and these general features of the consumer interest are largely applicable to other public interests (e.g., environmental quality).

Intensity

The second important feature of the consumer interest which leads to problems of representation is the variable intensity of the interest. All people are consumers, but their self-awareness as consumers is generally lower than their awareness of their other roles. Consequently, their interests as consumers are at a lower intensity than their other interests. This means, of course, that the representative seeking to reflect the consumer interest is dealing with an issue that most people do not care very much about. Representation in this context has several implications.

First, the intensity of this issue, like others, depends on the public's perception of the importance of the issue and of the action being taken on it. Unlike other issues, however, this perception is more shifting and less stable. Given the lower intensity of the issue, simply to create any perception of the issue's existence is a primary task of representation.

Second, the low intensity of the interest gives added importance to symbolic and psychological factors. As a subject becomes more important to a person he is less likely to be swayed by extraneous and ephemeral considerations. The relatively unimportant choice between makes of cars can be influenced by various kinds of emotional appeals. The much more important choice of a house is more generally grounded in rational factors. Similarly, in consumer protection a citizen is likely to be misled by "the symbolic uses of politics."[5] As the interest is less intense, the citizen is more likely to assume contentedly that the government must be doing something about it. But this cuts the other way also. In the meat inspection controversy, the stripping away of the symbolic assurance that all meat was inspected led to a greatly increased intensity in consumer concern about the issue.

Finally, the issue's generally low intensity magnifies the importance of the press as an aid to those representing the consumer interest. Low intensity is another way of saying low visibility and this gives the press a major role in increasing visibility and hence intensity.

Objective and Perceived Needs

With an interest of low intensity such as the consumer interest there are likely to be instances when the perceived needs of the public differ from its objective needs. The public may be moved to respond to the most dramatic and sudden problems while professional observers feel that the long-range problems present the most difficulty. It will be recalled that the priority system of the Food and Drug Administration accorded the greatest weight to immediate and obvious public health hazards at least partly because of public perceptions rather than the judgment of experts.[6] The point here is that such differences in perception may exist, not that they are common.

In terms of the "mandate-independence" controversy, the usual mode is that the representative of the consumer interest is an independent agent. This is particularly true if we include bureaucrats as representatives. In low-level issues, the public has only the vaguest notions of what its welfare requires. While at first blush this may sound like an

---

[5] See Murray Edelman, *The Symbolic Uses of Politics* (Urbana: University of Illinois Press, 1964).

[6] See Chapter 3.

elitist notion, it is hardly anti-democratic to note that the public is not likely to be able to judge what measures should be taken to prevent salmonella poisoning. Indeed, only the smallest fraction of the citizenry has any conception of salmonella. Thus, inasmuch as intensity of interest and knowledge are low in matters of this sort, the representative must, of necessity, establish broad matters of policy, as well as details, with little reference to public opinion. There is likely to be no expressed public opinion anyway.

There is no clean break between mandate and independence. Rather, there is a continuum. At one end are issues like public education where professionals representing the public have (decreasingly) little role in defining the educational interest of students. At the other end are such low intensity issues as consumer protection where representatives are not faced by many public demands or needs perceived by the public.

Difficulty of Definition

As a result of all three of the above factors, the consumer interest is extraordinarily difficult to define. The definition of an interest is inextricably bound up with the conception of what constitutes the protection of that interest. Thus, Governor Ronald Reagan of California proposed a state department of consumer affairs. Yet it is obvious that his conservative conception of consumer protection is far removed from that of Ralph Nader. When an interest is so widely held, nearly everyone can claim to represent it. Indeed, even a Bureau of the Budget representative from an administration favorably disposed toward consumer protection stated, ". . . I think the consumer interest is important, and permanent, but I don't think it is separable in terms of most types of programs that go into the consideration of the public interest."[7] Obviously, this vagueness carries over to a variety of public interest questions.

This theme was sounded in Chapter 3 where the main implication

---

[7] Testimony of Harold Seidman, in U.S., Congress, House, Committee on Government Operations. *Creating a Department of Consumers. Hearings before a subcommittee of the Committee Operations on H.R. 7179*, 89th Cong., 2nd sess., 1966, p. 250.

of this feature of the consumer interest was discussed—the bandwagon effect. There are two aspects to the bandwagon effect. First, agencies and groups with only the most tangential consumer protection responsibilities claim to be in the mainstream of the advancement of the consumer interest. Second, groups with nearly opposite approaches to the problem can all claim to be the true and worthiest representatives of consumers.[8]

A further implication is that ultimately it is the government that defines the consumer interest. The interests of special groups such as the American Trucking Association are always articulated by themselves and pressed upon the government in the form in which they are articulated. The resulting governmental policy may be at variance with the group's definition of its own interests, but few doubt that the self-interest of the group's members has been originally defined by the group itself. On the other hand, a variety of governmental and nongovernmental consumer activists may attempt to define the consumer interest, but the difficulty of definition of a diffuse interest of this type gives other governmental actors equal claim on positing a definition while the authority and visibility of the government gives legitimacy to its own definition. Thus, in his first consumer message, President Kennedy stated the "Rights of Consumers." In doing so he did not reflect previously demanded rights. As the chief representative of the federal government he defined those rights himself.

On Representing the Consumer Interest

The representation of non-intense diffuse interests is a theme in recent political theory although it is not a major concern and is usually expressed almost as an afterthought. Usually such interests are treated as interests which are left over and the theory seeks to account for what happens to the leftovers. While the preceding chapters have dealt

---

[8] Thus, Governor Reagan's consumer advisor could, with a straight face, advise consumers to rely on a National Association of Manufacturers handbook rather than *Consumer Reports* to guide their purchasing. Quoted in *Consumer Reports* 35 (January, 1970): 6.

specifically with consumer interest, we can now look at the problem in broader perspective by briefly assessing the findings of the previous chapters in relation to more broadly based theory. There are two theoretical constructs which are particularly profitable to examine in this regard: pluralist theory and economic models of politics.

One of the most cogent statements of pluralist theory is that of Charles Lindblom.[9] Consumer interests are examples of what Lindblom terms widely shared values or, in some cases, collective values. These values are synonomous with most conceptions of the public interest. Then the question becomes, "Is the public interest given weight in the policy process?" Lindblom answers in the affirmative in the following way: He conceives of the total decision-making process as one of "partisan mutual adjustment" in which each participant pursues only his own immediate goals without considering all the consequences of his demands and without unilaterally changing demands in response to some notion of the "public interest." Lindblom argues, nonetheless, that the public interest (widely shared values) is not neglected in such a system. First, there are powerful incentives toward agreement in partisan mutual adjustment. These incentives lead to the mutual acceptance of shared values. Second, those participants who have as their responsibility the pursuit of widely shared values have special authority and powers. Finally, some important participants seek shared values as their principal goal.

There are several problems with this interpretation of the representation of widely shared values. First is the problem of definition demonstrated earlier. A value may be defined so broadly that agreement on it is meaningless since controversy centers around narrower grounds. In the present case, all participants agree that the consumer should be protected. The producers contend that protection rests in the marketplace with a minimum of tampering from the government. The consumer activists seek to make formal public policy the prime protector of consumer interests. The widely shared value that the consumer should be protected is thus almost meaningless. Industry would not act differently even if it did not espouse this widely shared value. Nonetheless, a portion of Lindblom's analysis can be incorporated within

[9] Charles Lindblom, *The Intelligence of Democracy* (New York: Free Press, 1965).

the framework of this study as will be demonstrated shortly. First, however, we turn to the economic theories of democracy.

The economist Mancur Olson presents a theory of groups which is at odds with pluralist thinking.[10] Olson maintains that there is a qualitative as well as a quantitative difference between large and small groups. In a large group seeking benefits for a large number of members, it is in every member's interest for everyone to contribute resources to the organization to obtain collective benefits. However, there are so many members that any voluntary contribution by the member will likely be greater than the benefit he might gain. Furthermore, there are so many other members it is unlikely that his contribution will make any difference. Thus there is no rational incentive for the individual to contribute voluntarily. He cannot affect the outcome any more than an individual firm in a perfectly competitive market can affect the total profit of any industry by restricting its own output. In each case, the individual actor loses more than he gains. However, the situation differs in small groups. Just as in the cast of oligopoly, such a group is small enough for an individual effort to affect the total outcome. An individual's contribution might well be less than the collective benefits which result from his effort. In such a case it is rational for him to make the effort even if no one else contributes.

In a similar perspective, Anthony Downs demonstrates the irrationality (and hence improbability) of consumer influence.[11] Influence requires costs, particularly information costs. People will only invest those costs when the return is likely to offset the investment. Since people consume in many areas, but produce in only one, they will concentrate their influence in the area of their production (as businessmen, laborers, professors, etc.) rather than in their many areas as consumers. Therefore, producers will have more influence than consumers.

The problem with the ingenious analyses of Olson and Downs is that consumer protection legislation has been passed, albeit in limited form. Nevertheless, their theory would seem to allow no possibility of even limited success. In short, while Lindblom may be accused of being

10 Mancur Olson, *The Logic of Collective Action* (Cambridge: Harvard University Press, 1965).

11 Anthony Downs, *An Economic Theory of Democracy* (New York: Harper & Row, 1961), pp. 238–256.

too optimistic about the success of widely shared values, the economists appear to be unduly pessimistic. The contrast between the theories and their apparent inconsistency with empirical observation may be resolved if we look at the policy-making process in consumer protection in terms of "professional consumers."

Professional Consumers

Downs specifically argued that the consumer interest is usually unable to be translated into policy because people are more interested and involved in their role as income earners rather than as consumers. However, the preceding chapters have shown that the consumer interest is represented by specialists. A plausible model would be that the consumer interest is furthered through part-time concern by a large number of governmental officials. However, this study has demonstrated the validity of an alternate hypothesis—effective representation results from the independent action of a small number of specialists. Consumer protection is their income-earning role. While, as Downs and Olson assert, it may be irrational and improbable that the public devote the necessary costs to exert influence as consumers, it is entirely rational for consumer protection specialists to do so since they are, in effect, professional consumers.

This notion of the full-time public-interest specialists was also utilized by Lindblom as part of his assertion that collective values will not go unrepresented. This study thus corroborates that part of Lindblom's theory by confirming that there are indeed a group of men whose career orientations lead them to pursue collective values as their primary goals. This is not to say that I have confirmed or even accept the totality of the Lindblom argument about the success of collective values—only that small part of it just discussed.

The Greater Representativeness of Congress

It is often assumed that the President is more representative of the public (diffuse, widely shared) interest than the Congress since the President is the only nationally elected official in the country and must have a broader base of support than senators or representatives. At the very least, the Presidency is taken to be the institution most

representative of urban industrial America—and hence the majority of
the population—while the distribution of power in Congress makes it
the mirror image of the Presidency representing rural small town
America.[12]

However, in the case of consumer protection the generalized expectation does not hold, and, as will be seen, that expectation may be
theoretically weak in overlooking an important feature of the congressional process. First, the specific case of consumer protection.

Although it is often difficult to pinpoint the origin of ideas there
is solid indication that the Congress rather than the Executive Branch
has been the initiator of most recent consumer protection legislation.
Of the seventeen consumer protection acts passed from 1962 through
1968, nine were introduced independently and prior to their being
embraced by the Democratic administration. Three were proposed first
by the administration, and five were either introduced nearly simultaneously or their point of origin is doubtful. Clearly, the Executive
Branch has been the follower rather than the leader in consumer protection contrary to the trend toward Executive leadership in legislation
in other areas.

Two questions can be raised about the above finding. First, it may
be objected that initiation of an issue does not necessarily mean that
the initiator is the participant who is more vigorous in pressing that
issue—only that he is first. Second, consumer protection may well be
a completely isolated case. These two objections are stated together
because the theoretical importance of the result compels a response to
both objections in combination.

First, while it is true that initiation does not necessarily prove
vigor, it is indeed the case in consumer protection that individual members of Congress have attempted to press the consumer interest faster
and farther than even the Democratic administration. Several examples
demonstrate the point: the truth-in-lending bill did not receive presidential endorsement until 1962 although first introduced in 1959. More
importantly, it did not receive active support until 1967. The Kennedy
administration supported a far weaker prescription drug bill than that
introduced by Senator Kefauver. The Johnson administration at first
sponsored a weaker meat inspection bill than that ultimately passed by

---

[12] For example, see James MacGregor Burns, *The Deadlock of Democracy,
Four-Party Politics in America* (Englewood Cliffs, N.J.: Prentice-Hall, 1963).

the Senate. In these examples, and in general, the congressional consumer activists have been more aggressive in promoting the consumer interest.

The greater aggressiveness of Congress, is not the result of greater virtue on the part of congressmen. Rather, it resulted from the very process by which the diffuse consumer interest is represented. Since the activists are identified with the consumer issue, there is no advantage to be gained from caution or moderation beyond that required to get a compromise on legislation. Even a President on record as being favorable to an active consumer protection program must be more restrained than activists who maintain an identity with consumer protection as one of their primary public issues.

Beyond the President himself, it can be seen that Congress has certain advantages over the Executive Branch in promoting public interest issues. If the chief ranking official of an executive agency acts against the consumer interest or promotes policies with that effect, the agency can aid the consumer only insofar as lower ranking officials are willing to do so surreptitiously—by leaking information to Congress and the press. Although the chain of command is routinely bypassed in the Executive Branch it still imposes a barrier of sorts and may prevent an entire agency with consumer protection responsibilities from discharging its duty. No such constraint exists in Congress—particularly in the Senate. Indeed, the reason that the Senate is more consumer-oriented than the House[13] is the same reason that the Congress is more active than the Executive agencies. The senatorial activists have subcommittees of their own and have no effective opposition which prevents them from surfacing issues. In short, issues which may be buried in the Executive Branch can more readily be brought forth in Congress. Inasmuch as such activity is a vital part of representing the consumer interest, the Congress is thus a more vigorous advocate of that interest.

The Conditions of Success

The discussion of the preceding pages still leaves open the question of why the activists have been successful when they have been successful. The answer is elaborated in Chapter 5. Basically, successful activism was undertaken by those who relied considerably on widening the

[13] See Chapter 4.

"scope of conflict" of consumer protection, primarily by appealing to and altering public opinion. The most successful activists have been certain members of Congress, Ralph Nader, and a few consumer-oriented reporters. Their success lay in their ability first to reach and then to arouse some measure of public opinion. The extent to which the public even perceived the issues is unknown. But of greater importance, a variety of decision makers themselves perceived public pressure and acted as though that public pressure dictated action.

The question concerning the conditions of success is particularly interesting in light of the theories of Downs and Olson. The dilemma of their models was that theoretically consumer or other diffuse interest legislation should not be passed, while in fact it is sometimes successful. In the Downs model in particular the dilemma arose from the improbability that consumers would incur the information costs necessary to exert effective influence. Although the activity of "professional" consumers demonstrates that certain people will incur those costs, the dilemma still remains for consumers at large. The conditions of success just reviewed, however, can lead to a resolution of that dilemma also. The activists incur the information costs themselves and "stockpile" that information. It is the press that becomes the key link in the policy by screening information and presenting it in condensed form. In effect the press cuts information costs and may be conceived of as a "wholesaler" of information.

Remember that a problem of consumer issues is their normally low intensity. This problem will not be resolved if consumers themselves must incur the necessary information costs to remedy their political problems. But the "cut-rate" information presented by the press acts to raise the level of intensity of the interest. By their very nature, consumer protection measures have inherent appeal once they are presented since they benefit nearly everyone. Therefore, the single most important common condition of success is increasing public awareness of pending consumer issues.

Representation and Policy

The fact that the success of activists generally depends on raising the intensity of the particular consumer interest they are representing has implications which go beyond simply explaining that success. The importance of this need to shift intensity is that the most dramatic issues come to the fore. Dramatic and immediate problems like meat purity and drug safety are more rapidly and easily perceived by the public than long-range technical problems such as antitrust policy. Since these dramatic issues are also more newsworthy, they are more likely to be featured by the news media. This reinforces their appeal to the public at large.

This reinforcing cycle is closely related to the problem of objective and perceived interests discussed earlier. These interests do not necessarily coincide and it is frequently the case that the dramatic issue is symptomatic of more deeply rooted and longer-range problems. The interest perceived by the public would be the solution of the immediate and visible problem while a knowledgeable observer would realize that a more comprehensive solution necessitates tackling the problem itself rather than its symptoms. For example, it could be argued that the problems of auto safety, automobile-related pollution, and resistance to mass transportation are really manifestations of the lack of corporate responsibility (to public and stockholders alike) and the uncompetitive nature of the automobile industry. However, the symptomatic problems are more readily attacked and more visible and comprehensive to the public.

Furthermore, even apart from symptoms and ultimate causes of consumer problems, the most dramatic problems and those perceived as most urgent are not necessarily the most important objectivity. Undramatic but very important legislation such as truth-in-lending must struggle through the legislative mill for years before any appreciable number of people are even aware of its existence. The same is true to an even greater extent of antitrust legislation or amendments which chronically fail to pass. This is an unfortunate side effect of the nature of diffuse public interest issues and the manner in which they have been successfully represented.

There is, however, an emerging way out of this problem. In diffuse issues of this type, changing public opinion is an essential first step in influencing policy, but once the issue is firmly on the agenda and there is a supportive public, other means of widening the scope of conflict can greatly add to the effectiveness with which an interest is represented. Just as consumer protection "professionals" can cut the information costs of a wider public and widen the public constituency, they can take direct action to widen the attentive constituency confronting policy makers—particularly in the bureaucracy. This is primarily the province of the public-interest lawyers who force policy makers in the bureaucracy to consider a wider range of policy alternatives than they might otherwise do.

The importance of this can be seen by recalling the conclusions drawn in Chapter 3. It was found that important policy-making centers within the bureaucracy did not respond to increased public concern with consumer protection. The perceptions of public opinion which were so important in the Congress were not translated into policy changes in the bureaucracies dealing with consumer affairs. Conversely, most bureaucracies have traditionally been more insulated from public view than legislatures.

In the case of consumer protection, a basic problem has been that bureaucracies have mainly dealt with and responded to business interests simply because consumer interests were not as directly pressed upon them. They have responded to the only attentive clientele they had—business groups. In most cases, periodic public outcry has been insufficient to affect bureaucracies from the outside. By 1970, however, the politics of consumer protection had matured to the point where not only was there widespread public support for consumer advocates, but the consumer position was being pursued in the more insulated reaches of the bureaucracy. This is not to say that the bureaucracy suddenly became more responsive to consumer interests in the early 1970s (although the Federal Trade Commission certainly seems to have done so), but at least there is now more direct pressure for them to be responsive.

The importance of forcefully presenting consumer interests in the bureaucracy can also be seen in the efforts to establish an independent consumer agency which would act as an advocate of consumer interests before other government agencies—particularly the regulatory agencies.[14] This would provide formal recognition of the necessity of having

[14] The Senate, on December 1, 1970, passed legislation to establish an independent Consumer Protection Agency. A similar bill had been reported out by the House Committee on Government Operations, but it died in the House Rules Committee by a 7–7 tie vote the day after Senate passage. Nonetheless, this proposal has emerged again as one of the major consumer issues in the 92nd Congress.

consumer advocacy before the agencies and would provide the means for achieving that advocacy on a more permanent and comprehensive basis than is now possible through the public-interest bar.

In summary, just as the scope of conflict has been widened by creating awareness among mass publics, so too has the next stage of consumer protection politics centered on widening the scope of conflict in more insulated centers in the bureaucracy. It is this ability to increase the size of a constituency which is the most important element in government policy in behalf of diffuse interests such as consumer protection.

For Further Reference

This bibliography lists sources which pertain primarily to the political or potentially political aspects of consumer problems. It does not, however, include the much larger body of literature on the whole range of consumer problems, consumer behavior, or consumer economics. Excellent bibliographies of a more comprehensive nature may be found in President's Committee on Consumer Interests, *Consumer Education Bibliography* (Washington, D.C.: U.S. Government Printing Office, 1969) and David A. Aaker and George S. Day, eds., *Consumerism: Search for the Consumer Interest* (New York: Free Press, 1971). The latter volume has a useful collection of articles on a variety of consumer problems.

Books and Articles

Anderson, Oscar E., Jr. *The Health of a Nation.* Chicago: University of Chicago Press, 1958.

Armstrong, Richard. "The Passion That Rules Ralph Nader." *Fortune,* May, 1971, p. 144.

Bauer, Raymond A., Ithiel de Sola Pool, and Lewis Anthony Dexter. *American Business and Public Policy.* New York: Atherton Press, 1963.

Baum, Daniel Jay. "The Federal Trade Commission and the War on Poverty." *UCLA Law Review* 14 (May, 1967): 1071.

Bernstein, Marver H. *Regulating Business by Independent Commission.* Princeton: Princeton University Press, 1955.

Bishop, James Jr. and Henry W. Hubbard. *Let the Seller Beware.* Washington, D.C.: The National Press, 1969.

Campbell, Persia. *Consumer Protection in the New Deal.* New York: Columbia University Press, 1940.

Caplovitz, David. *The Poor Pay More: Consumer Problems of Low Income Families.* New York: Free Press, 1963.

Congressional Digest. "The Question of a Federal Consumer Protection Agency: Pro and Con." 50 (February, 1971): 33–64.

Cox, Edward F., Robert C. Fellmeth, and John E. Schulz. *The "Nader Report" on the Federal Trade Commission.* New York: Baron, 1969.

Drew, Elizabeth Brenner. "The Politics of Auto Safety." *Atlantic Monthly,* October, 1966, pp. 95–102.

Edelman, Murray. *The Symbolic Uses of Politics.* Urbana: University of Illinois Press, 1964.

Fatt, A. C. "Let's Take The Politics Out of Consumerism." *Nation's Business,* January, 1969, p. 82.

Fellmeth, Robert C. *The Interstate Commerce Omission.* New York: Grossman, 1970.

Galbraith, John Kenneth. *The New Industrial State.* Boston: Houghton Mifflin Co., 1967.

Harris, Richard. *The Real Voice.* New York: Macmillan Co., 1964.

Hart, Philip A. "Can Federal Legislation Affecting Consumers' Economic Interests Be Enacted?" *Michigan Law Review* 64 (May, 1966): 1255–1268.

Kefauver, Estes. *In a Few Hands: Monopoly Power in America.* New York: Pantheon, 1965.

Kohlmeier, Louis M., Jr. *The Regulators: Watchdog Agencies and the Public Interest.* New York: Harper & Row, 1969.

Magnuson, Warren G., and Jean Carper. *The Dark Side of the Marketplace.* Englewood Cliffs, N.J.: Prentice-Hall, 1968.

Main, Jeremy. "Industry Still Has Something to Learn About Congress." *Fortune,* February, 1967, pp. 128–135.

Metcalf, Lee, and Vic Reinemer. *Overcharge.* New York: David McKay Co., 1967.

Mintz, Morton. *By Prescription Only.* Boston: Houghton Mifflin Co., 1967.

Mintz, Morton, and Jerry S. Cohen. *America, Inc.: Who Owns and Operates the United States.* New York: Dial Press, 1971.

Nader, Ralph. "The Great American Gyp." *The New York Review of Books,* November 21, 1968, pp. 27–34.

Nader, Ralph. "Protecting the Consumer: Toward a Just Economy." *Current,* December, 1968, pp. 15–24.

Nader, Ralph. *Unsafe At Any Speed.* New York: Grossman, 1965.

Newsweek. "Meet Ralph Nader." January 22, 1968, p. 65.

Sanford, David, ed. *Hot War on the Consumer.* New York: Pitman Publishing Co., 1969.

Schnapper, Eric. "Consumer Legislation and the Poor." *The Yale Law Journal* 76 (1967): 745–768.

Time. "U.S.'s Toughest Customer: Ralph Nader." December 12, 1969, p. 89.

Turner, James S. *The Chemical Feast.* New York: Grossman, 1970.

University of Pennsylvania Law Review. "Translating Sympathy for Deceived Consumers into Effective Programs for Protection." 114 (January, 1966): 395–450.

Weiss, E. B. *A Critique of Consumerism.* New York: Doyle, Dane, Bernbach, 1967.

Young, James Harvey. *The Medical Messiahs: A Social History of Quackery in Twentieth-Century America.* Princeton: Princeton University Press, 1967.

Zalaznick, Sheldon. "Bitter Pills for the Drugmakers." *Fortune,* July, 1968, p. 82.

Public Documents

U.S., Congress, House, Committee on Government Operations. *Creating a Department of Consumers: Hearings on H.R. 7179.* 89th Cong., 2nd sess., 1966.

U.S., Congress, House, Committee on Interstate and Foreign Commerce. *Class Action and Other Consumer Protection Measures: Hearings on H.R. 14931 [and other bills].* 91st Cong., 2nd sess., 1970.

U.S., Congress, Senate, Committee on Government Operations. *Establish a Department of Consumer Affairs: Hearings on S. 860 and S. 2045.* 91st Cong., 1st sess., 1969.

U.S., Congress, Senate, Committee on Government Operations. *Federal Role in Consumer Affairs: Hearings on S. 2045 [and other bills].* 91st Cong., 2nd sess., 1970.

U.S., Congress, Senate, Committee on the Judiciary. *Consumer Protection Act of 1970: Hearings on S. 3201.* 91st Cong., 2nd sess., 1970.

U.S., Executive Office of the President, Consumer Advisory Council. *First Report*. Washington, D.C.: Government Printing Office, 1966.

U.S., Executive Office of the President, Office of Consumer Affairs. "Consumer Legislative Monthly Report." Mimeographed, issued monthly.

U.S., Executive Office of the President, Office of Consumer Affairs. *Consumer News*. Washington, D.C.: Government Printing Office, issued periodically since April, 1971.

U.S., Executive Office of the President, President's Committee on Consumer Interests. *A Summary of Activities, 1964–1967*. Washington, D.C.: Government Printing Office, 1967.

Index

253